ERRATUM

The author regrets that on page 9 of this
volume* a statement made by Spiro Agnew and
cited in William Small's To Kill a Messenger
(New York: Hastings House, 1970) is incorrectly
attributed to Mr. Small, then CBS Washington
Bureau Chief, rather than to the former Vice
President.

_____

*Robert M. Batscha, Foreign Affairs News
and the Broadcast Journalist (New York: Praeger
Publishers, Inc., 1975).

Foreign Affairs News and the Broadcast Journalist

Robert M. Batscha

The Praeger Special Studies program—
utilizing the most modern and efficient book
production techniques and a selective
worldwide distribution network—makes
available to the academic, government, and
business communities significant, timely
research in U.S. and international economic, social, and political development.

Foreign Affairs News and the Broadcast Journalist

PRAEGER SPECIAL STUDIES IN U.S. ECONOMIC, SOCIAL, AND POLITICAL ISSUES

Praeger Publishers   New York   Washington   London

Library of Congress Cataloging in Publication Data

Batscha, Robert M
    Foreign affairs news and the broadcast journalist.

    (Praeger special studies in U. S. economic, social,
and political issues)
    Bibliography: p.
    1. Television broadcasting of news—United States.
2. Foreign news.   I. Title.
PN4888. T4B3   791. 45'5   75-56
ISBN 0-275-07350-5

PRAEGER PUBLISHERS
111 Fourth Avenue, New York, N.Y. 10003, U.S.A.

Published in the United States of America in 1975
by Praeger Publishers, Inc.

Printed in the United States of America

ACKNOWLEDGMENTS

This study was possible because so many network television correspondents and producers gave so much of their
time to interviews and informal discussions. While they
may not all agree with the conclusions I have reached, I
am indebted to them for sharing their experiences, ideas,
and insights with me.

This study would not have materialized had it not
been for the invaluable assistance and guidance of W.
Phillips Davison, Professor of Journalism and Sociology,
and Donald Puchala, Professor of Political Science, of
Columbia University. Their encouragement, criticism, and
recommendations from the first draft to the completed
manuscript were invaluable. My debt to them is immense.

I would also like to acknowledge a special indebted-
ness to the late Philip Mosely. His intellect, professionalism, and compassion distinguished Columbia University's Department of Political Science for many years and
it was an honor and privilege to have been one of his
students. His guidance has been invaluable and his dedi-
cation, an inspiration.

For all errors of fact and opinion, I bear the sole
responsibility.

CONTENTS

The poet Archibald Macleish, introducing Edward R. Murrow, the pioneer of American electronic journalism, described him as a man who had "accomplished one of the great miracles of the world," who had destroyed "the most obstinate of all the superstitions--the superstition against which poetry and all the arts have fought for centuries, the superstition of distance and time." (Kendrick, 1969, p. 269.) How has television redefined distance and time, and how does this affect our perception and understanding of the world around us?

The underlying political assumption of our democratic system postulates the need for a well-informed people. Today 60 percent of our people consider their primary source of information to be television news. The pictures in our minds of what is happening in the world, and our conceptual framework of events, are increasingly being constructed through the medium of television. Even our daily language is affected: what print-oriented individual has not at one time or another felt the embarrassment of exclusion when confronted with the question, "You mean you didn't see that on the news the other night?" The potential impact of television news is enormous. It also represents the most advanced method devised by humankind to disseminate its symbols.

Few will forget the four days in 1963 when this medium enabled the American people to witness and participate in the national trauma that accompanied the asassination of the 34th President, to be followed five years later by the assassinations of two more leaders, Martin Luther King and Robert F. Kennedy. The Watergate Hearings and the related Senate Judicial Committee proceedings captivated the populace and exposed a national scandal. Whether it be in an allusion to the war in Vietnam as "the living-room war," in an accolade of "star-reporter," or in the insistence that television has the most powerful influence over public opinion, it is recognized that the broadcasting press has come to serve an important communication function.

It is surprising to discover that in the academic literature this subject has been almost totally ignored. The journalistic function and the related principle of freedom of the press are indigenous to the American

political structure. For Thomas Jefferson the free pursuit of this journalistic role was essential to democratic
politics. The press, with guarantees enshrined in the
First Amendment of the Constitution, was conceived as an
independent institution outside the normal controls of
government, an exterior check on the government, and a
conveyor of information to the populace. In 1792 Thomas
Jefferson wrote to George Washington: "No government
ought to be without censors, and where the press is free,
none ever will."

The greater part of a citizen's knowledge about political affairs usually comes directly or indirectly from
the mass media. The newsman's role as gatherer, screener,
and composer of the information of the day's events as
transmitted through the mass media is therefore important
to the American political system. Douglass Cater was one
of the first to point to the political power of the newspaper press as a determiner of what is news:

> News is a fundamental force in the struggle
> to govern. Each day hundreds of thousands
> of words are spoken, tens of dozens of
> events occur. The press and other media
> perform the arduous task of sorting out
> and assigning priorities to these words
> and events. This capacity to choose with
> speed and brevity which stories command
> widespread attention and which go unnoticed
> constitutes a power far more formidable
> than the purely editorial preferences of
> the press. (1964, p. 4.)

Today two major studies dominate our understanding
of newsgathering and its political implications: in the
field of political science, Bernard Cohen's The Press
and Foreign Policy, and in sociology, Dan Nimmo's Newsgathering in Washington. Both studies analyze the political functioning of the newspaper press by examining how
the participants define and perform their job. These
studies have proved to be invaluable to the social scientist in understanding the communication function of the
written press.

There are, however, two arms of journalism, the
written press and the electronic press. The latter,
broadcast journalism, has been all but ignored by social
scientists, in spite of the fact that television's role
and function have increased enormously. This study,

therefore, following the precedent established by Cohen and others, proposes to examine the behavior of the individuals who control the composition of television news. These individuals are important political actors, if only because their product now reaches the largest percentage of the American public. It is important, therefore, that social science analysts understand their behavior so that they can more clearly distinguish the actions of other actors in the political system who are affected by this medium, and therefore by these actors, for gaining the public's attention.

HYPOTHESES AND METHODOLOGY

Because so many people receive their information from television, we can safely assume that the content of television news will affect the political behavior of people and that this content will be a function of the characteristics and attitudes of the people who assemble the news and of the mechanics and structure of the medium. This investigation, therefore, is intended to discover (1) the nature of the messages that are transmitted via television and the kind of "map of the world" that is being pictured and (2) the reasons, such as the behavior of the newsmen and the mechanics and structure of the medium, that cause the world to be pictured as it is.

Hypotheses. There are features of the electronic medium that are distinctive to it. Print exists in space, but broadcasting exists in time, and the audience during this time has less opportunity for selectivity than have newspaper readers. In television, journalism is only part of the media, not the essence of the media as in newspapers. Television is government-regulated and must concern itself with such rules as "equal time" and the Fairness Doctrine. For television the costs are higher and the equipment more bulky. On television the picture story is of greater importance. The television audience is a national one. Television coverage is often "live," and of course it is visual and not printed. Therefore the working hypothesis of this study is that in the area of foreign affairs coverage the television medium has both mechanical and structural characteristics that have caused members of the television press to define and perform their role in a manner that is distinctive to this medium.

Specifically, it is hypothesized that the mechanical characteristics of television news coverage--a concern with time, picture, cost, and audience attention span-- have a perceptible effect on the behavior of the electronic journalist in his determination of what news to cover, how to report that news, and how to transmit that news through the television channel. For example, it is hypothesized that the concern with time and picture affects what stories will be covered and reported, with certain advantages accruing to a particular kind of story or event, perhaps the action-oriented, easily photographed story, such as a plane crash or the pounding of a shoe on the table at the United Nations. Conversely, it is hypothesized that this excludes, or makes difficult, the coverage of other stories, perhaps economic problems, specific contents of a speech, or extended analysis of developmental problems.

It is hypothesized, furthermore, that certain structural characteristics--the corporate nature of television, its primary interest in entertainment with a secondary concern for journalism, its public accountability, its concern with mass audiences, and its "nonjournalistic" hierarchical structure--play an important role in the television journalist's behavior and role conception that affects the news that is broadcast. For example, it is hypothesized that television's orientation to entertainment values spills over into the journalism side of broadcasting and affects the values that determine news coverage and reportage; that the concern with a mass audience, in itself a distinctive characteristic of electronic journalism, has a generalizing and leveling effect on the news that is covered and the manner in which it is presented; that government regulation has, for the electronic journalist, the effect both of an external and internal censor; and that the enormous costs of news coverage and reporting give increased weight and influence to the commercial values within the medium.

Finally, it is hypothesized that these mechanical and structural constraints not only affect the behavior and role conceptions of the electronic journalist, but also that the underlying presuppositions of the profession also affect recruitment and the type of individual who would be attracted to the medium. These hypotheses represent the major gap that exists in our knowledge about the kind of political map of the world that is being transmitted through this newest information machinery; that is, about the kind of information that can be acted upon politically.

The literature about television and the news is sufficient to indicate the validity of the assumption that there is a discernible pattern of behavior in electronic journalism to distinguish the institutional character of that activity. Such book titles as <u>Electronic Journalism</u>, <u>Factual Television</u>, <u>Television and the News</u>, and <u>The News Twisters</u> support this assumption. Indeed, if an empirical study of the institutional character of electronic journalism fails to produce evidence of a consensus, then the institutional nature itself is problematic. In his parallel study, Dan Nimmo writes: "Questions of the responsibility of government in informing the citizen, of the press in representing the public's interest, must be based on a realistic understanding of the consensus of the actors regarding their functions, procedures, orientations, and responsibilities." (1964, p. 16.) This study seeks to clarify these areas as they relate to the characteristics of this broadcast medium.

The focus of the study is on foreign affairs news, and specifically on the foreign affairs correspondents and producers.* Television news as such is not the major subject of study here, but rather the people working for this medium who are responsible for gathering and interpreting, reporting and composing, foreign policy news in the United States. (1) Who is the electronic journalist, and what are his role concepts and group properties? (2) What are his perceptions of the mechanical and structural characteristics of this medium, and how do they affect his newsgathering activities? (3) How does the news gathered by the television correspondent come to be broadcast; what are the role concepts and group properties of the producers, and how do the mechanical and structural characteristics of this medium affect their activities?

<u>Procedure</u>. Most local stations, because of cost, depend on the three major networks as their sources of foreign affairs news. Therefore this study has limited itself to the foreign correspondents, producers, and executives working for the three major networks, CBS, NBC, and ABC. Given the small number of foreign policy specialists in the electronic press, there was no important sampling problem involved. Because of its form, special editing and newsgathering procedures are imposed, and there is more central control than on an average newspaper.

---

*The television producer is the equivalent of an editor on a newspaper.

The initial phase of this study involved a thorough
survey of the literature. The materials available include
television news--policy statements, reporters' memoirs,
speeches of policy and criticism, audience analyses, and
the like--but these materials are random, incomplete, and
though potentially suggestive, quite limited. From the
beginning of 1972, for a period of five months, I conducted a series of unstructured interviews with members
of the foreign affairs news departments of the three
major networks in New York, in Washington, and at the
foreign bureaus in Paris.

In each network the following categories were involved: president and vice-president in charge of news;
executive producer; Washington bureau chief; Paris bureau
chief; associate producer; news editor; correspondent;
commentator; reporter; and, variously, writer and copy
editor. There were, however, some exceptions. Usually
for reasons of illness or conflicts of schedule, some actors could not be formally interviewed. Nevertheless,
conversations on an ad hoc basis were held with most of
these people in the course of my research at the network
production centers during their regular workday schedule.
Only two responded negatively to the letter that requested
a half-hour interview. Both are nationally known commentators who have been interviewed regularly; there exists
an extensive body of literature about them or written by
them that is available either through published sources
or through the files at the respective networks, which
were made available to me. Correspondents located at the
various foreign bureaus were not interviewed, with the
exception of those in Paris. However, of the 65 correspondents interviewed, at least one and often two at each
network had had a tour of duty at each of the foreign
bureaus now in existence, and at some, like the Latin
American bureaus, that were no longer operative. In
other words, a minimum of three interviews with correspondents with experience at one of each of the foreign
bureaus are included in this sample.

Accounts of these interviews are presented in a manner designed to preserve the anonymity of the persons interviewed and the confidential nature of the interview.
The interviews were not mechanically recorded because I
found that this tended to make the respondents hesitant
and because of the length of most of the interviews. Extensive notes were taken during each interview, which I
immediately transcribed into long form or onto tape so as
to retain, as accurately as possible, the actual words

used by the respondent. Quoted material from the interviews has, when necessary, been edited to prevent identification. Although this procedure was not insisted upon by
any individual interviewed, it was adopted to promote free
discussion. Only published materials are directly attributed to the respective respondents. When quoted, these excerpts are not meant to represent evidence for proof but as
illustrations and enlargements on points under analysis.

Time Period of Study. The time period during which this
study was conducted requires brief but necessary discussion. In 1969, that is, three years before the beginning
of this study, the Vice President of the United States
launched a vigorous campaign of criticism against the
television press, adding to a chorus of critics that had
already raised their voices. Of the year 1970, the Survey
of Broadcast Journalism reported that "the discussion of
broadcast journalism and its responsibilities was not left
to practitioners and experts alone. It became everybody's
second favorite topic of conversation. Broadcasters were
watching themselves, and being watched, as never before."
(Barrett, 1969-70, p. 9.) I anticipated either defensiveness; caution; or perhaps on the other hand, aggressive-
ness, on the part of those to be interviewed, especially
after I read a statement written by the president of NBC
News, Reuven Frank, that "these social science types . . .
tend to be nice people . . . although not very interesting and . . . take more time to answer than it's worth"
(1971). Indeed, I assumed almost a bias against the academic.

> Have you ever had your work analyzed by
> people who used words like "information
> retrieval"? It may sound reactionary,
> but if I had known thirty years ago news
> was going to become "information retrieval,"
> I should have sought another business. . . .
> I have never known a self-proclaimed objec-
> tive student who sought to evaluate my per-
> formance because he thought I was doing
> great. (Ibid.)

In actual practice this was not the attitude that I found.
Only two people responded to my letter in the negative
(the writer of the above passage was not one of them).
Those with whom I could not arrange formal interviews
(eight in all) made every reasonable effort to meet with
me.

xv

This initial letter requested an interview no longer
than half an hour, but no interview lasted less than one
hour, most averaging about one and one-half hours and one
lasting as long as five hours. In addition to the interview time, there were occasions for accompanying a correspondent on his beat, attending governmental press conferences, attending the Paris peace talks press conference
on two occasions, spending two to three full days with
each of the New York producers of the network news programs, spending comparable periods of time in the Washington bureaus of each network, and discussing equipment and
filming techniques with cameramen and soundmen at the networks. I found the members of the electronic press to be
very cooperative.

Furthermore, whereas in a few instances it was felt
that the correspondent was somewhat defensive about the
attacks made against his profession, in general no significant behavioral characteristics were noted that could
reasonably be labeled defensive, cautious, or assertive.
If anything, the attacks seemed to have forced some reflection about role objectives on the part of the correspondents, which appeared to have enabled them to describe
their activities and articulate the justifications for
them more explicitly. It is my interpretation, based on
generalized reactions from those interviewed, that the
critical statements voiced against the medium during this
period did not affect the conclusions that could be de-
rived from the data I had accumulated.

One other concern for the time period in question
requires mentioning. One must keep in mind the fact that
historically television is a very new medium for transmitting human messages; it is only in its third decade of
development. There exist only a few books on the mechanics and methodology of the medium, and most practitioners
feel that these were out of date before they were published. In 1972, when these interviews were made, Vietnam
was the big story. With American disengagement in 1973
this problem area no longer consumed the same amount of
broadcast time. In 1974 Watergate became the big story,
and then Nixon's resignation and its aftermath captured
the broadcast hours. Yet, although there will always be
a new big story, a certain plateau in television news
seems to have been reached in terms of format, budget,
staff size, and equipment. Whether one dates the reaching of this plateau from the increase in time allotment
from 15 to 30 minutes and the doubling of staff and budget in 1963, from the changeover to color coverage a few

years later, or from television's first war and the development of highly portable equipment and satellite capabilities, a period of sufficient duration has elapsed to provide an institutionalization of newsgathering and editing processes that further enables us to discover what these processes are.

We have experienced television's first "real war"; if in the future a war of similar nature occurs, it is probable that television's coverage will follow the guidelines that were developed as a result of the lessons learned from the war in Vietnam. Again, coverage of the Watergate controversy did not differ significantly from television's previous handling of live Senate debates during the Vietnam crisis, of similar trial stories, or of Johnson's decision not to run for reelection in 1968 and of the concluding days of his administration. The pattern for coverage had previously been set from lessons learned when television broadcast similar events for the first time. The mechanics of response to these events have become institutionalized, and the observations to follow should clearly indicate what they are.

This study is exploratory in nature. Its concern is not so much to point out the advantages or inadequacies of the medium as contrasted to the printed press, but rather to illustrate and analyze the distinctiveness of the medium's message as it creates a "picture" of foreign affairs in the world, and its implications for the political process. Rather than being concerned with how that message is received, this study concerns itself with how that message is composed.

What is the television correspondent who specializes
in foreign affairs like? He or she ranks very high among
the hierarchy of television correspondents. The correspondent's name is familiar to audiences across the country. He or she has lived in at least three world capitals, has traveled widely, and is cosmopolitan in outlook.
The correspondent is familiar with the world leaders of
our time. After two decades of recruitment and development, television has a competent press corps with trends
indicating a further raising of standards. Wrote Sig
Mickelson, former vice-president of Time-Life Broadcasting, Inc., "You can put any of the network staffs against
the New York Times or the wire services or any other staff
and they come out pretty well, or they may even have generally better personnel." (International Broadcasting
Institute, 1970, p. 22.)

THE FOREIGN CORRESPONDENT

Statistics have been compiled from the interviews and
conducted and supplemented with network biographies in order
to develop a profile of the general characteristics of the
electronic correspondent. I interviewed 55 correspondents,
and the statistics presented in Table 1 represent the 78
foreign correspondents employed at the networks. These
statistics have been divided into three categories: total
figures and, for purposes of comparison, foreign correspondents hired before 1963 and after 1963.*

---

*The 1963 season seems to have been a benchmark
period for television news. At that time the networks
doubled the length of their evening newscasts and

TABLE 1

The Foreign Correspondent

	Total	Hired before 1963	Hired after 1963
Age at time of appointment	32	30	35
Education (in percentage)			
BA	89	80	98
MA	20	20	24
Training (in percentage)			
Newspapers	44	49	38
Television	41	38	48

Note: A total of 78 correspondents were analyzed. Divided into two groups, those hired before 1963 and those hired after 1963, there were 43 correspondents in the before-1963 group and 35 in the after-1963 group.

Education. The typical television foreign correspondent is college educated--about 89 percent in total figures, 80 percent before 1963, and 98 percent after 1963. These statistics indicate not only an increase of 18 percent over hirings before 1963, but it seems reasonable to conclude that, today, a college degree is a prerequisite for employment with a network. Before 1963 the sample indicated that 20 percent had a masters degree; after 1963 it was 24 percent. One correspondent (employed before 1963) had a doctorate, and two had honorary doctorates. Although only 22 percent had advanced degrees, interviews and biographies indicated that perhaps as many as an additional 20 percent had engaged in some graduate study, although no degree was received. Most of those interviewed had majored in political science, economics,

committed themselves to spending $70 million for news and public affairs programming. This was the year that the Roper surveys first showed television to be the public's major source of news. During that season the networks averaged about six times as much hard news as in 1950 and about 100 more hours of documentaries than in 1952 (Quaal and Martin, 1968, p. 97).

sociology, and history; 25 percent indicated that they had majored in journalism as undergraduates, but few recommended such a course of study at this level. The social sciences were unanimously recommended as areas of concentration.

Recruitment. About 86 percent, or almost all the television correspondents, had been drawn from newspapers or local radio and television news departments (the figure is probably larger but some of the supplemental biographies included no information indicating previous employment). Medium recruitment statistics show some interesting patterns. Before 1963 almost half of the correspondents, or 49 percent, had been recruited from newspapers, while 38 percent had been drawn from local radio and television stations. After 1963 it is almost the reverse: 38 percent had come from newspapers, while almost half, or 48 percent, had come from radio and television. In other words, there seems to be a trend toward hiring people with previous experience in television. This corresponds to the increased interest in news shown by local stations, the increased importance of television news on the local level, and the greater competence and maturity among those in the electronic journalism profession. This also corresponds to recruitment attitudes expressed during the interview sessions.

Age. Of the correspondents, 49 percent were in their late thirties and early forties; 20 percent were in their middle thirties, and 30 percent were in their late forties or over fifty. Before 1963 the correspondents were hired by the network at the average age of thirty; after 1963 the average age at hiring had increased to thirty-five. Therefore the average correspondent is about forty years old, and it seems that they are being hired by the networks at an older age.

Assignment Pattern. An analysis of first and last assignments of foreign affairs positions indicates a random distribution with no discernible pattern. That is, for instance, there is no assignment pattern of a foreign post as opposed to a New York or Washington post, or of Europe as opposed to Asia. In terms of overall assignments, one pattern is discernible, and that is that most, or almost 75 percent, of the correspondents hired after 1963 spent some time in Vietnam. Those hired before 1963 seemed to be more frequently assigned to Western Europe. However,

5

in both groups the average correspondent has served in
two or three different foreign bureaus (most of which are
located in Western Europe) for periods of from three to
five years.

GROUP PROPERTIES

The electronic press corps is a fairly distinct group,
identifiable as a professional entity and separable by
the three networks. Some discussion of the group properties,* therefore, is of value in order to discover some
discernible characteristics of this group.

Group Membership. The membership in the electronic journalist press corps is distinct and clearly defined. As
earlier described, the electronic correspondent is a
middle-aged person, fairly well educated with many years
of experience as a newsman. He or she has traveled widely. Most important for our purpose here, the correspondent has been specifically recruited to one of the three
national and most prestigious of the television network
news corps. The television correspondent is a respected,
easily recognized, and well-paid individual. For example,
an Oliver Quayle poll taken in May 1972, involving 8,780
interviews in 18 states, questioned the degree of trust in
several public figures. Of those registered, CBS commentator Walter Cronkite received the highest rating, 73 percent. Others registered included Vice President Agnew
with 50 percent, Mayor Lindsay with 54 percent, President
Nixon with 57 percent, the average senator with 67 percent, and the average governor with 59 percent (O'Connor,
25 May 1972, p. 91). That they are easily recognizable
is a conclusion that can be drawn from this survey. By
way of illustration, this recognizability is interesting-
ly described by Alexander Kendrick as he records an inci-

_____

*The frame of reference for the following discus-
sion is drawn from Merton's "Provisional List of Group-
Properties " (1949, pp. 310-26.) Following Merton's own
recommendation, this provisional list is taken as a point
of departure, with the intent to develop a conceptual understanding of this group, although some properties are
not significant for the group under study, while others
need not be handled independently.

dent related to him by a friend of Edward R. Murrow's who was with him the day after the "See It Now" McCarthy broadcast.*

> After lunch we walked up Fifth Avenue; it was a rash thing to have done. Of course he was instantly recognized. First our own pavement was jammed with people who were determined to give him the hero's treatment, and then Fifth Avenue traffic was brought practically to a standstill as the news of his presence spread, and men and women came rushing across the road in all directions. (1969, p. 68.)

The television correspondent is well paid. The salary of the average correspondent ranges from $20,000 to $47,000. (Newspapermen in New York are paid $15,000 to $20,000.) The following salaries were reported for the most well-known commentators and correspondents: David Brinkley, NBC news correspondent, $250,000; Walter Cronkite, anchorman, CBS News, $250,000; Harry Reasoner, anchorman, ABC Television News, $200,000; Howard K. Smith,

---

*The McCarthy broadcast was aired 9 March 1954. After a presentation of film clips of McCarthy's statements, followed with the recitation of the true facts, Murrow concluded the broadcast with the following summation:
> We will not be driven by fear into an age of unreason, if we dig deep into our own history and our doctrine and remember that we are not descended from fearful men, not from men who feared to write, to speak, to associate and to defend causes which were for the moment unpopular. This is no time for men who oppose Senator McCarthy's methods to keep silent. We can deny our heritage and our history, but we cannot escape responsibility for the result. There is no way for a citizen of a republic to abdicate his responsibilities. . . . He didn't create this situation of fear; he merely exploited it, and rather successfully. Cassius was right: "The fault, dear Brutus, is not in our stars but in ourselves." (Friendly, 1967, p. 41.)

ABC Television News, $200,000 (Powers and Oppenheim, 1972, p. 11).* Some television correspondents belong to the most exclusive country clubs in Chevy Chase or live in the 16th Arrondissement of Paris. One secretary in Washington has posted on her bulletin board the nightly rates for the Plaza Hotel in New York, with alternative possibilities for suites with such features as a park view or a working fireplace, for the commentator when he must spend some time at the New York office. While respectability, recognition, and financial reward are not the boundary markers for this group, they are the accouterments of perhaps 100 specially selected members of this highly recognizable, prestigious, and nationally significant press corps.

However, while these three trappings distinguish them from other press members at the local stations and at newspapers and magazines, the correspondents unanimously insist that "our motives and our principles of news integrity and objectivity are no different from those of other media." (Cronkite, 1969.) This is largely accurate. Most network correspondents have attended the same schools of journalism, have worked for newspapers and local television stations, and probably represent the same geographical, religious, and ethnic mix.

Geographic Representation. Geographically the correspondents represent a national distribution that ranges from Missouri to North Dakota, to Montana, to California, North Carolina, Vermont, and Texas. They do, however, live and spend a considerable amount of their career time either in New York or in Washington, D.C. As will be shown at a later point, it is at these two centers, especially New York, that the major "gatekeeping" decisions are made. For the moment it is descriptively sufficient to say that although they travel widely and are exposed periodically and intentionally to the circumstances and attitudes that prevail throughout the nation, their focus of attention is often on Washington and always on New York. They are exposed unanimously to similar publications, including the New York Times; Newsweek; Time; and, in Washington, the Washington Post. They are similarly tuned in to

---

*By comparison, James Reston, vice-president of the New York Times, received $96,395; and the publisher of the same paper, Arthur Ochs Sulzberger, received $150,000. Frank Stanton, vice-chairman of CBS News, earned $398,500.

their own nightly news broadcasts and almost always to at
least one of the competing broadcasts. The CBS Washington Bureau Chief wrote:

> These commentators and producers live and
> work in the geographical and intellectual
> confines of Washington, D.C. or New York
> City--the latter of which James Reston
> terms the "most unrepresentative community
> in the entire United States." Both communi-
> ties bask in their own provincialism, their
> own parochialism. We can deduce that these
> men thus read the same newspapers and draw
> their political and social views from the
> same sources. Worse, they talk constantly
> to one another, thereby providing artifi-
> cial reinforcement to their shared view-
> points. (Small, 1970, p. 280.)

The control of this mass medium is in New York, as a result of technological distribution mechanisms: television is a centralized electronic medium with national
dissemination. An increased awareness of this centralization was found within the networks, and most respondents were at somewhat of a loss about how to respond to
this descriptive phenomenon, which was launched as an
editorial criticism in the late 1960s. Reflects Theodore
H. White on his experiences with the network:

> People in New York have a social life. . . .
> To go against the dominant thinking of your
> friends, of most of the people you see every
> day, is perhaps the most difficult act of
> heroism you can have. . . . [New York] as-
> sembles talent in a particular kind of cul-
> tural contact. You have Chet Huntley, go-
> ing back soon to Montana. During his so-
> journ in New York he has been a part of
> this culture and community, just as I am.
> Perhaps we are more sensitive. Perhaps
> because we came here looking for novelty,
> we are confusing the future with the pres-
> ent. (1969-70, p. 9.)

What characteristics are discernible of New York and how
they specifically affect the newsmen remains the subject
of a study yet to be engaged. It suffices for our

purposes to note the phenomenon and the consciousness of its probable effect on television correspondents.*

Duration of Membership. Electronic journalism is now entering its third decade of existence and, with regard to assignments, its second posting of foreign correspondents. The first had been the "radio type," the Schonbrun and Burdette type who had come from the newspaper, entered the radio medium, and being overseas with radio during the second world war and its aftermath, made the linear transition, like Edward R. Murrow and others, into television. Today the second posting, television news, seldom recruits radio-experienced correspondents, but rather those with newspaper experience who went into local television or those with only television experience. As noted earlier, there appears to be a continued trend toward hiring more correspondents with television experience than with newspaper experience.

Television is a relatively new medium, and as a result some interesting comments can be made about membership duration within the group and reasons for entering the profession. The television correspondent is nationally known and recognized. He or she negotiates, on a regular basis, a professional contract with the network news management. Some of the better-known correspondents have managers who represent them in these negotiations, and some of the television commentators are members of AFTRA, the television artists' union, which also includes singers, actors, and comedians. No correspondent at any of the networks indicated concern about losing his job. Indeed, once one has been promoted from reporter to correspondent there is a degree of permanence perceived to be operating within the system. With regard to assignment, there is a unanimous attitude of professionalism but also one of permanence and choice. The correspondent, if one of the most nationally acclaimed, would have gone to Saigon to cover the Vietnam story "if asked" but generally felt that he had the right to request an assignment.

---

*More than 90 percent of the respondents mentioned the New York office as a major source of news perception. A comparable acknowledgment was made to a distinctive "New York perception" pervading the broadcast content, and some showed dismay (between 30 and 40 percent) with this fact, giving one or another "resolves" for why this was an inevitability; for example, "The center has to be somewhere," "That's inherent in any institution," "I don't know any other way," and "It's not really a harm."

This freedom varies according to his competence, the wishes of the executive department, and the national reputation of the correspondent.*

Many (75 percent) of those interviewed responded to the question about "permanence" and "personal involvement" in the designation of beats. At the time of this research there occurred an illustrative example. One veteran correspondent in Washington was informed on Monday that as of Tuesday he would no longer be the network's correspondent reporting from that department but would be placed on general assignment. The correspondent's qualifications and competence in covering this particular beat were repeatedly acknowledged by his colleagues; and the unilateral reassignment, decided on the executive level (as perceived by the correspondents), was universally resented and by many considered to be one of the major causes for an atmosphere of low morale that had come to pervade this network news department. There are reassignments and demotions, and some correspondents do leave the organization, but there are subtle ways for accomplishing this (to be discussed at a later point), and as a general practice the expected duration of membership in this group is perceived as "permanent" and "personally negotiable."

Job Selection. The reasons why correspondents enter the profession provide additional information about their group properties. These include the general "newsman" reasons: desire to be at the scenes of major events, to meet the world's leaders and the great men of our time, and to tell other people what they have seen and to interpret for them. Representative of this attitude (90 percent, without any negative responses) was the comment by one of the White House correspondents:

> It's the most fascinating vocation that
> there is. You are paid to be a spectator
> at all kinds of events. . . . To see
> events, to talk to the people who made

---

*National reputation is not a term limited to the major commentators but, more important, includes White House, State Department, and general correspondent roles. Very often it depends on variables that include how well the correspondent is known, how identifiable he is with the network, and how long he has been a television correspondent.

11

those events, and to spread it around to
others in the form of news. You can get
so much into a life span as a reporter.
It's to be where the events are . . . not
far away from the instincts of chasing a
fire engine, I guess.

There is also the desire for personal enrichment.
As one Paris correspondent said, "Look, I've just been to
Malta, the Azores, Strasbourg, Greece, Marseilles, Cal-
cutta and have spoken to leaders, artists, had good food,
etc. It's an interesting life."
Naturally, special reasons were mentioned for select-
ing television journalism instead of another journalistic
medium. More money was an often repeated reason (75 percent) but seldom offered as the primary one. Most often
it was the newness of the medium itself, the desire to
learn about a new technical development. One foreign
news editor said, "I felt newspapers had too much ivy
growing on its walls. Television offered the possibility
of a new way, a better way." Relatedly, the newsman's
need to tell people about what he has witnessed has been
translated into the mechanics of the medium. "It seemed
exciting to be able to present news in pictures," said a
foreign correspondent at the Paris peace talks. According to a veteran of the European bureau now based in New
York, "You can do it better and faster and you can convey
a shared experience using senses not available to the
newspapers. The tools of our trade are themselves exciting." With equal frequency, correspondents cited the
fact that a large number of people could be reached, that
it was a national audience, that the audience could be
communicated with in a direct way. "Direct way" meant
that the correspondent was visually identifiable to his
audience, that he was a more recognizable and personal
conveyor of the news, and that he was affecting a larger
national audience.

There remains one more indirect recruitment item
that should be given mention. There was a discernible
attitude that was more often shown by the older (veteran)
members of the television press corps (40 percent as opposed to 20 percent). That is, there was a certain pride
in the increased role that television had come to play in
American society, almost a satisfaction with the criticism
that had been voiced against television newsmen for having
so much power in the political system, and a contentment
in having become a recognized and legitimate news operation.

One Washington-based correspondent, famous for his early European correspondence, said:

> We're no longer a newsreel operation. We
> had an inferiority complex around here and
> it has taken us a long time to get out
> from under it. It's only in the last 14
> to 15 years that network broadcasting be-
> came truly legitimate. We made a concen-
> trated effort to make it into something.
> . . . Now we measure ourselves against our
> own colleagues in television.

There still remains a slight (20 percent) defensiveness when the subject of audience dependence is mentioned. The limitations of the medium itself are cited as a defense for the absence of depth and comprehensiveness in news coverage. "You can't depend on television alone if you want to be well informed" is the much-repeated cliché; but in the next breath they proudly say, "We play an important role, more than 50 percent of the population depends on us as their primary source of news." They then conclude, "This is a new medium. We are always trying to improve."

In summary, television journalists are attracted to their work for many of the same traditional reasons as print journalists; that is, to be at the scene of the event, to meet important people, and to convey the experience to others. In addition, there are reasons distinctive to the medium. These include the ability to convey the story in picture form, a larger audience, a more personal relationship to that audience, and greater financial rewards.

Finally, there is a perceptible (20 percent) feeling of inferiority to the traditional print journalist, denied and decried to the outsider though discussed and acknowledged among the correspondents themselves. This is less than it appears to have been in the past, but nonetheless lingers, if only as the tail end of an attitude that may soon pass. However, within the field of electronic journalism the network correspondents are undeniably the most respected among the television press corps. Of a possible 1,000 to 2,000 television correspondents throughout the country, this group of about 100 to 150 correspondents on the national network news staffs represents the most prestigious corps within the structure.

<u>Criteria for Competence</u>. This raises the question of
what are the criteria for membership in this group.
Edward R. Murrow was brought from radio into television
to establish what was virtually the first television press
corps in the United States. Upon accepting this responsibility he informed the various vice-presidents at CBS that
he was building a corps of reporters, not announcers.
This established a precedent that has remained operative
in theory and has generally been fulfilled in practice at
all three networks. For inclusion into this group, the
potential member must be a trained and recognized reporter.*

     What other criteria are judged important by the pres-
ent correspondents to establish the competence of a broadcast journalist? As already noted, experience is important before one is accepted into the news staff. Almost
all correspondents felt that a justification for citing
this criterion was that it helped develop news judgment.
Said one foreign correspondent, "Judgment is everything--
to know what's important and not, who's lying and not,
which events are important and which indicate events to
come, and how to get information from people."

     Credibility is consistently mentioned (90 percent)
as an important asset. For example, one of the initial
fears one correspondent had at the suggestion that he

_____

     *The exceptions illustrate the point. In April 1972
the local New York affiliate of NBC, WNBC, hired Carl
Stokes, former mayor of Cleveland, as one of its new
anchormen. Stokes had no correspondence experience.
Newsmen at all three networks were indignant that a be-
ginner should be placed in this top position, and it was
a factor repeatedly cited as a cause for low morale at
NBC. John Chancellor, anchorman for the NBC network
news, was reported to be "dead set" against Stokes's appointment, not on personal but on professional grounds.
It was reported that he regarded the appointment as an
impropriety: "After all, journalists are supposed to be
scrupulous about avoiding links with the government that
might compromise their ability or desire to be critical
of the government, and now NBC executives had gone and
hired a retired Mayor. Hiring out-of-work athletes to
comment on sports was one thing, but hiring an out-of-
office politician to cover real news, political news,
was quite another," wrote Gene Maeroff in <u>New York</u> magazine (May 1, 1972).

present a regular commentary on the nightly news program was that he would lose "objective credibility" with his audience. This concept of credibility has been codified into actual network policy that forbids public participation in controversial issues by its news staff. Richard Salant, president of CBS News, quotes a ten-year-old policy: "It is imperative that such attitudes not endanger either the fact or the appearance of objective handling of the news on CBS." (CBS Memo, October 9, 1970.) This includes political behavior, financial conflicts of interest, and payola.

Another ground rule is to maintain distance from the news source. Failure to maintain this distance between the reporter and his source is viewed (by more than 80 percent) as an inhibitor of proper and objective reporting of the news. No respondent held to the categorical statement that the correspondent is unbiased and totally objective, but all seemed to agree that there was a traditional approach to the reporting of a news story, similar to what Reuven Frank, president of NBC News, has termed an "artificial innocence." He explained this concept in a statement to his staff:

> As individuals, of course, we have ideas
> of what we prefer. More important and
> less often discussed, we have ideas of
> the effect what we will report will have.
> We think about impact. But we must pre-
> tend as well as we can that we have no
> such ideas about impact on the one hand,
> and the world we should individually like
> to see, on the other. (NBC Policy Book,
> p. 7.)

These are criteria that would apply to any newsman employed with a major and reputable newspaper, magazine, radio or television affiliate news organization. And this is exactly the point correspondents want to make. "We are direct descendents of print journalism," wrote Walter Cronkite, "and, like the children of the privileged, we have had a head start in life. We inherit a great deal--commitment to truth, integrity, objectivity most of all--and we are trying to build on this invaluable legacy." (1969, p. 2.)

But television, too, has established some distinctive criteria. First, a television correspondent must be "especially versatile" (more than 75 percent). This

criterion includes a thorough knowledge of the medium:
film, the camera, audio techniques--the mechanics of the
business. This also includes the ability to write for
film. A Paris correspondent said by way of illustration:

> A French reporter writes to display his
> literary skill. He does not care for un-
> derstanding but for style. That's not
> good by American television standards.
> He's got to communicate and communicate
> to a large audience, to remain faithful to
> the educated and at the same moment to
> those who know nothing about the subject.

Versatility implies something else as well. Covering
a story abroad often finds the correspondent off on his
own, and although a discernible change is developing, in
addition to being the correspondent he is the bureau chief
as well; that is, he must also be a reasonably good admin-
istrator. Here versatility means that he is able to work
by himself and to have good, strong, and confident editorial and production abilities, since he is often his
own copy editor, his own department head, his own lawyer.
"There are less filters," said a foreign correspondent in
Paris. Finally, versatility means that he can adapt to a
foreign environment.
How does a person train himself to become a television journalist? There were many varied responses. Many
had gone to journalism school, but few (10 percent) recommended majoring in journalism as an undergraduate. Political science and economics were the subjects most often (90
percent) recommended as essential. Some believe the best
training comes from newspaper experience (mostly the older
correspondents, who themselves came by this route), while
others recommend training at a local television station
(mostly the younger correspondents with training from this
source). Their responses varied as frequently as their
own experience.
The reporter must be bright, versatile, presentable,
and experienced and have good judgment. He is also, almost always, a generalist. Eric Sevareid wrote: "We are
jacks of all trades and masters of none save the trade of
being jack of all, a trade by no means easily mastered.
We must always know enough of what is old to recognize
what is new, enough of what has been good for man to
sense what is going to harm him." (1967, p. 5.) An interesting comment, often repeated, concerned how one

recognizes a good correspondent. The typical first response, before the interviewer pursued the details of that statement, was: "You recognize him immediately. You recognize him because of your years in the profession and professional experience." Or, as a woman correspondent put it: "I think it's a type: part vagabond, rebel, voyeur, a small part intellectual, part innocent."

Stratification within the Group. Statuses and roles within the correspondent group are distinguishable essentially by two formal groupings: the correspondent and the reporter. The reporter (here an institutional title) is an apprentice. He has usually been hired from a local news station or newspaper and is being taught the "ropes" of the network news operation. His salary is not very high, but there are financial incentives for getting his story broadcast on the nightly television news program, on radio, or used for syndication. (For one network the bonus is $55 for an evening news spot, $45 for radio, and $35 for syndication.)

The reporter has a desk in the central newsroom and generally is assigned to the stakeout; that is, the story that may be a story. For example, a reporter will wait outside a hotel where a foreign dignitary is speaking, hoping to catch him as he leaves, pose some questions, and record the response. This is a role outside the standard beat. There are occasions when the reporter covers an important story, but they are exceptional. For example, a young Chinese reporter was assigned to cover the Chinese ping pong players during their visit to the United States. Again, a young woman reporter is assigned to cover certain aspects of a big story because a department head is known to favor giving exclusive interviews to woman correspondents. These are practices that uniformly meet with opprobrium among the correspondents and are decisions made by executive and associate producers and bureau chiefs. Appointment as a reporter is understood to be an apprenticeship position, and promotion to correspondent is expected in two or three years. If the reporter fails to be promoted he is rarely fired, but it is understood that his work is not highly regarded among the executives in the news department.

In general, little distinction can be made between the foreign and the domestic correspondent. Most domestic correspondents have had foreign experience and vice versa. The title of correspondent is the highest of the reportorial positions. Generally, though with some exceptions, a correspondent has a designated assignment and is a specialist in one or two areas. For example, the State Department correspondent may have a specialty in Soviet affairs, based on academic training and experience at the Moscow Bureau; a correspondent working on a special series of feature stories on the American way of life might be the "house specialist" on Latin American and Spanish affairs.

In Washington correspondents generally have a specific beat, such as the White House, the State Department, or the Pentagon. Other correspondents cover Congress, the Supreme Court, and other parts of the government. Abroad, there is generally one or sometimes two correspondents assigned to each bureau. In addition, especially in New York, there are correspondents with general assignments, who cover periodically important stories as they emerge from time to time. For example, a correspondent might be working on a methadone story, although just a month before he had been in Ethiopia doing a story on starvation.

There does not seem to be a discernible pattern of stratification among these assignments. The White House is a good assignment, but some prefer the State Department or the Congress. London is a good beat, but Paris affords the correspondent an opportunity to travel more and cover a wider range of stories. A very high percentage of correspondents have been to Vietnam. It seems to depend on the particular interests of the individual correspondent whether he or she prefers to be in New York, Washington, or abroad, and very often a correspondent will spend five years in Washington, ten years abroad, and then be on general assignment in New York or covering a Presidential campaign. Some respondents (25 percent) intimated a sort of "pendular" or "cyclical" phenomenon in promotions and assignments. "It depends," said one Congressional correspondent; "sometimes you have an important beat and sometimes you are between assignments. It swings, has its highs and lows. You are never totally secure in any assignment you have. You can expect perhaps five years at one place."

There is, however, a subtle but important stratification among the correspondents. There is the recognition (55 percent response once detected) that there are two levels of correspondents, levels that do not correspond to a particular beat. The boundaries are drawn along lines of "national appeal." Certain correspondents are recognized to be widely liked by the view-

ing audience,* and for this reason they will get first
play on, for example, a White House story when there are
other correspondents also assigned to the White House.
Again, if there is a vacancy for a fill-in position as
anchorman for reasons of vacation, illness, travel, or a
particularly heavy news day emanating from two locations,
this correspondent will be chosen to fill that vacancy.
Indeed, one correspondent who fills in as anchorman in
New York is good-naturedly referred to as "the star" when
he arrives. Those not in this category seem to accept
this phenomenon, satisfied to be working as active correspondents in the medium, and to see their national appeal
as less broad but their journalistic functions nonetheless valuable.

This stratification develops early in the employment
period of the correspondent. It very shortly becomes obvious which correspondents have this national appeal and
will therefore contend for the anchorman/commentator role,
and which will be delegated to covering the beat wherever
it will take them. The subtlety of this phenomenon is
what impressed me. It seems to be an accepted and seldom
talked about characteristic of the trade and the medium,
and one that apparently does not interfere with the smooth
functioning or morale of the news operation. Said one
White House correspondent:

> He's star and first man here. If the Presi-
> dent makes a major statement he covers it.
> But when he's in New York or covering an-
> other big story, the beat is my responsibil-
> ity. I have no complaints. I get on the
> air very often and my audience has come to
> expect me to take a certain approach to a
> story. That's the way this business oper-
> ates.

The commentator is the top man among the correspondents. His appeal is national, and he is selected for,
among other things, his national projection of personality, credibility, and reassurance via the television

---

*The distinction being drawn here is not to be mis-
understood as one between the commentator, who is acknowledged by all as the "star" of the broadcast, and the
correspondent; it is drawn between the correspondents
themselves, for example, between the State Department
correspondent and the Congressional correspondent.

camera. He does not, however, engage actively in the newsgathering process once he is elevated to this position.

The delineation of hierarchies beyond this point is not especially clear. Some correspondents draw more money than others, seemingly on the basis of ability, experience, years of service, and national acceptability. For the correspondent, it is the exception who still receives a special bonus for the stories he covers; those special bonus arrangements that still exist in individually negotiated contracts tend to be eliminated when they come up for renewal.

Whether the delineation of hierarchies is between reporter and correspondent, domestic beat and foreign assignment, "star" correspondent and general correspondent, or commentator and correspondent with a newsgathering assignment, the group property is one of "cooperation." "In cooperative groups," writes Newcomb, "mutually high attraction was the rule; status differences were slight, in spite of the fact that tasks were divided up; and members had ready communication access to one another." (1965, p. 351.)*

Group Interaction. Interaction within the group is intense. During the day the correspondents are at their beats covering their stories. By 5 p.m. the stories are taped, and the correspondents return to the bureau in New York, Washington, or elsewhere. From 5:30 to 7:30 they talk about politics or their stories and view their own broadcast and then the broadcast of at least one of the other two networks. The telephone is the constant link between them and the bureau, the producer, the news desk and the executive producer. Most of them have lived many a story together, whether it be a national election, an international crisis, a Presidential trip abroad, or the yearly story roundup. As Newcomb points out, this is important to the group's functioning, for

---

*Another group division is the person hired as a "stringer," a nonstaff news worker in the field, in the domestic or foreign area, who is paid by the news department either by retainer or on time rates. He is usually called upon when there is a shortage or an emergency. Because he is not a regular member of the news staff, his interaction is intermittent, and the stringer is therefore not included in this study.

as interacting persons exchange more and
more information, they tend increasingly
to share the same attitudes, to subscribe
to the same norms, and to have higher
levels of attraction toward one another.
. . . The less the distance, in terms of
communication access, among group members
as compared with their distance to other
persons, the greater the probability that
they will develop role relationships char-
acterized both by shared interests and
interpersonal attraction. (1965, pp. 344-45.)

Interaction among the networks varies according to
individuals, but generally it is superficial, though attentive. Competition is a prime motive force, and it
pervades their every move. They see each other regularly
when covering a story and sometimes chat; but competition
is ever present as they watch each other's reports broadcast on the competitors' newscasts and carefully evaluate
and compare their own handling of each story to that of
the other networks. NBC and CBS have very little knowledge of the operation of each other's news department.
They know who their competitor's correspondents are and
are acquainted with some, although few, of the competitor's producers, editors, and writers. This is not the
case between CBS and ABC, because ABC entered the evening
news competition fairly late and hired many people away
from CBS. But ABC and NBC do not have these ties and are
not knowledgeable about the internal functionings of each
other's news operation. It seems reasonable to infer
that in time the ties of familiarity between CBS and ABC
will begin to fade and disappear, if previous examples
are indicative.

The internal interaction and familiarity with the
outcome of one another's product and the constant and
continuous monitoring of their competitors' broadcast
products promotes a pattern of expected conformity. This
can be observed on two levels: individual training, and
product production. There are differences of opinion and
variations in political partisanship, but if there is a
discernible bias or ideology, it is one of "objectivity"
(80 percent response) and "centrism" (60 percent response),
with various reasons given to explain this perception.
The most frequent explanations given are professional,
objective news criteria (about 80 percent), experience in
the field (80 percent), education (70 percent), American

21

pragmatism (40 percent), and the journalistic tradition
(65 percent). For example, John Chancellor, veteran foreign correspondent and NBC "Nightly News" anchorman, said
in response to an interviewer's question:

> You find few extremists in national journal-
> ism. That is because we've all gone through
> the process of remembering what politicians
> have said and promised and then seeing what
> they have delivered. We've seen the poor
> first hand. We've seen war close up.
> We've seen a lot of varied and unpleasant
> things and people. Most journalists after
> a couple of decades become at least prag-
> matic, certainly skeptical, and maybe cyni-
> cal. That chases you right into the center.
> No, I didn't choose the center. The center
> chose me. (Penthouse, 1972, p. 40.)

Recruitment tends to promote this centrist attitude.
Said one former foreign correspondent, now vice-president
in charge of news: "We don't recruit a particular point
of view." However, political ideologists or outspoken
partisans are looked at with disdain. The networks recruit and the correspondents look for a "type." The
training is long and the process is basically the same
for all, whether it is from a school of journalism, newspapers, or radio or television experience. The national
character of the medium promotes this homogenization.
The correspondent is trained to temper his regional accent. Standards of dress, though not prescribed, are understood. National acceptability and accountability are
perceived to suit the demands of some vaguely distinguishable national audience. Michael Novak described this,
critically, as a world "in which the professional outlook
rises to the top: a new, universalistic culture all its
own." (Barrett, 1971, p. 129.) Walter Cronkite, discussing the open-mindedness, uncommittedness, and political independence of the correspondent, wrote, "We are not
affiliated with any special interest and we are not addressing a 'like-minded group' but people in the mass.
In taking the middle road, we are subject to sniping from
the sides." (1969, p. 12.)
Conformity results from the competitive nature
of the medium as perceived by those in the electronic news
operation. The competitive nature of the television
broadcast news process, which so dominates the environment,

will be discussed at a later point; it suffices to say
now that each network news staff is in full competition
with the others and that the criteria employed are, to a
major degree, the same. Briefly, these criteria include
a good picture, speed, inclusion of the same important
stories, clarity, and a scoop (each given by over 75 percent as a criterion for judging a good story). The competing news staffs monitor one another and evaluate each
other's product, each network press corps judging accom-
plishment by the same journalistic and medium criteria.
In short, the networks employ the same criteria of evaluation for judging one another's product, and the intense-
ness of their competition promotes a conformity both in
the coverage of a certain story and in its inclusion in
the broadcast.

Deviation, when it does occur, is usually a "scoop,"
a particularly good film piece, or a format (or story)
that corresponds to a minor selection nuance of a particular network. These are usually feature stories, or
mini-documentaries, and might cover such a subject as
Soviet taxi drivers, show the first photographs of the
gas explosion in an internal combustion engine, or be an
exclusive film story on church attendance in Castro's
Cuba. This type of feature story will be discussed in
greater detail in the section on newsgathering.

CHAPTER
2
ROLE CONCEPTIONS

Exiting from the taxi on Avenue Kleber in front of the Hotel Majestic at 10 a.m. on a typical Thursday morning in Paris, press card in hand, you are directed by the gendarme to a side door of the eighteenth-century palace, and as you pass through the entrance door the familiar sounds of the teletype and banging typewriter keys greet you. The room is a large conference hall with long aisles of desks one behind the other. Before these aisles stands an elevated platform with a desk and microphone. Behind, there are the teletype machines. On the right side there is a security guard, who is also the distributor of mimeographed statements of the opening remarks made by the members of the delegations that are parties to the Paris peace talks on Vietnam, for the moment in session in another section of the building. You secure a seat among the correspondents from different countries in Europe, Japan, the United States, and elsewhere. Some are reading newspapers, others typing, a few perusing the mimeographed statements. A two-man crew has begun assembling cameras, lights, and sound equipment. They finish; it is now 12:30 p.m. People drift in and out; conversations begin and end; and the "drill" is on again.* At 3:30 p.m. a bell rings, signifying that the delegates have concluded their discussions. At 4 the American representative appears first, makes a brief statement, and answers questions. The cameras record his answers. He concludes,

---

*"Drill" is the term used by American television correspondents in Paris to describe the weekly peace conference assignment.

leaves, the representative of the NLF appears, and so on. By 5 the press conference is concluded, the cameras packed away, and the room deserted. That evening from New York, a 45-second story of the session is broadcast across the nation. Next week, as in the weeks prior, there will be another "drill."

The viewers of the 45-second story give little thought to the six hours involved in collecting that story, to the editor in Paris who put the film together, to the satellite transmission from London, or to the inclusion process in New York. It's one story in a 30-minute broadcast. The correspondents in Paris, New York, Washington, or perhaps in Beirut, Saigon, Tokyo--what do they believe the function of the electronic press is, and what do they see as the larger purposes of their work? Is it to dissent, persuade, chronicle, or reflect? The right to choose is there, as Reuven Frank, the president of NBC News remarked:

> This system of journalism being impelled
> by internal needs and supervised by internal
> controls is what we call free journalism.
> It exists in very few countries. It exists
> as the structure of journalism by television
> in even fewer countries. It is the system
> under which the reporter demands access to
> facts and events for no other reason than
> that he is who he is, and his argument is
> always accepted. (1969, p. 94.)

But to what end and for what purpose? What is it that the television correspondent tries to do in his daily reporting of the news? This is the subject for exploration in this section.

Bernard Cohen, setting forth his own discussion of the newspaper journalist's role, uses the political and constitutional model discussed by Weisberger in his study, The American Newspaperman. Writes Cohen:

> He [the reporter] holds two sets of concep-
> tions of the role that the press plays, or
> should play, in the foreign policy-making
> process--one set involving him only as a
> neutral reporter, providing information
> that enables others to play a part in the
> fashioning of policy; and the other set
> that defines his active participation in

25

the policy-making process. The first set of
role conceptions relates the reporter chief-
ly toward the public participants in the
process; while the second set relates him
toward the official policy-making level.
(1963, pp. 19-20.)

While this is not a study comparing newspaper correspondents with television correspondents, structurally it
is of value to analyze the role conceptions of the broadcast journalist historically from a political and constitutional vantage point, both as a check of the assumption
that the television journalist engages in traditional
journalistic functions and also for the political scientist, who might be interested in making, himself, a comparison of Cohen's findings with those presented here.

In varying degrees, the television correspondent
does envision himself serving (1) neutral and (2) participant purposes, as outlined by Cohen. In addition, it was
discovered that the television correspondent envisions
additional purposes, or roles, especially distinctive to
the television medium. These were (3) as a visualizer of
events; (4) as a catalyst for newspapers; and (5) at crucial moments of intense national concern, as a national
role responsibility as instant and continuous chronicler
of transpiring events.

THE NEUTRAL REPORTER

Reuven Frank wrote:

As for the news we put out, we put it out
because we think it ought to be put out.
We are the current stage in the centuries
of evolution of our kind of free journalism, governed by tastes and ethics passed
on through what is essentially oral tradition reacting to conditioned criteria of
importance and public interest, hemmed in
by some law but not much, consciously or
subconsciously always responding to the
need to be current, relevant and involving.
Relevant to what? To the public and what
it cares about. (1969, p. 93.)

The television correspondent sees himself as exercising
the traditional journalistic function of a neutral link

between policy participants and the public. Conceived in the traditional philosophy of the national heritage, this function is understood to be a vehicle whereby different segments of the society are provided with some of the fundamentals for an improved capacity to participate constructively in their assigned roles. This role conception corresponds very closely to the journalistic tradition and seems to be reflective of the basic training patterns common to most journalists. Said Edward R. Morrow:

> The communication system . . . is totally neutral. It has no conscience, no principle, no morality. It has only a history. It will broadcast filth or inspiration with equal facility. It will speak the truth as loudly as it will speak a falsehood. It is, in sum, no more or no less than the men and women who use it. (Fang, 1968, p. 218.)

The conceptual framework of this role is inherent in any journalistic function, irrespective of the medium. To fulfill this role, the perception demands that the journalist be neutral, objective, and without interest in his own personal gain. The television correspondents repeatedly pointed to the need for impartiality, to the need to represent no special interests and to work conscientiously toward dispensing only truthful information.

The Reporter as Informant

In order to fulfill this journalistic function, the television journalists (unanimously as a group) understand their "primary role," their "fundamental responsibility," their "essential task" to be to provide their audience with factual information about developments in foreign affairs, to tell it the way it really is. Writes Fred Friendly:

> Every day there is more for the people of the world to know, and every day, what we don't know can kill us. We . . . believe that our job is to try to cast a little light, create a little more understanding of what bothers people, what helps people, what can kill and what can save. (Swallow, 1966, p. 78.)

27

Their aim is to keep the issues of the day before the people.

This function is perceived, not as a self-serving one, but as essential to the operating of the democratic process. This unanimously accepted role conception of the television correspondents is most adequately illustrated in a speech given by Reuven Frank, responding to governmental criticism of television news for broadcasting "negative" combat information about American actions in Vietnam that was contradictory to the official accounts:

> The subject is not personal danger or personal heroism. The threat is not to American reporters and editors. We are not faced with prison, torture or even loss of income. It is more dangerous to cover the Vietnam war freely than to rewrite the handouts and lead the cheers. . . . The threat is to those receiving the information, the public. After all, the First Amendment was written to protect them, not us. If the public is led to believe that the news it gets is shaped to please those in power, whether voluntarily or through control, they will in time feel separated from their government and totally distrustful. (1971.)

It follows from this that the better informed the population is and the truer the picture of reality it possesses, the better able it will be to fulfill its democratic role. This does not imply that the correspondent sees the populace as making foreign policy decisions. Rather, the journalists' information-dispensing role is seen as essential to an informed public, which is a requirement for the effective operation of the democratic process.

The country has gone through difficult times, and television has found itself to be a major chronicler of the issues, personalities, victories, defeats, and frustrations of them. Many voices have been critical of the medium for disseminating this information, lamenting that the medium's role has become that of conveyor of information about events that disturb the viewers' "contentment" with things as they are. For example, in 1967, during the riots in Detroit, television station WXYZ received many calls from its viewers demanding that it "stop the riot right now." It was not that the viewers were accusing the station of manufacturing the riot, but rather

that they felt that if the pictures were not being broadcast, the events would not be happening. The television
correspondent is very conscious of this criticism, both
from viewers and those in the political arena: conscious
that with the increase in influence of the medium as an
information dispenser has come an increase in criticism
of how it fulfills this role. This dilemma is generalized
into a paradox: the people are "sensitized by television
to specific issues in our world, criticizing television
for not enough exposure of these issues--issues they would
not have known about or at least would have known less
about without the medium." (Frank, Winter 1970, p. 18.)
This is accepted, however, as part of the inevitability of
the correspondent's neutral, informant responsibility,
unanimously accepted to be inherent in the function of
every journalistic medium.

Television correspondents do not hesitate to defend
this responsibility or its potential consequences. Examples are plentiful. Said the veteran correspondent,
Walter Cronkite, "Without any intent to foster revolution,
by simply doing our job as journalists with ordinary dili-
gence and an extraordinary new medium, we have awakened a
sleeping giant. No wonder we have simultaneously aroused
the ire of those who are comfortable with the status quo."
(December 1970, p. 54.) There were the reports of American war crimes, violence in the streets, and corruption in
government, but, continues Cronkite, "as professional
journalists we have no more discretion in whether to report or not to report when confronted with the facts than
does a doctor in deciding to remove a gangrenous limb."
(Ibid.) Along the same lines, Reuven Frank said: "I
gather Americans are tired of television forcing them to
look at the world they live in. I refuse to consider
that we can do anything else." (Small, 1970, p. 10.)

Correspondents are not ignorant of the inability of
the viewer to be selective in the same manner as the newspaper reader, who can choose which stories to read and
which to ignore; nor are they unconscious of the potential impact of filming a soldier cutting the ears off a
captured prisoner or the dead bodies piled high in mass
graves, the result of a war crime.' A former war correspondent said, "Film is symbolic. . . . It has an impact.
But we don't consciously seek that impact. We are seeking
it in this 'dumb way'." "Dumb way" was understood to mean
the reportage and filming of what has happened, not for a
specific impact, but because it happened and it was important and it was there to be recorded. Pervading this

entire role conception is the people's right to know, and
the press as the major source of information. Repeatedly
I heard, "People are entitled to know what happened. Limitations cannot be placed on that rule without placing a
barrier of censorship between the people and the truth."

Increasingly the television journalist sees himself
in a new role as "informer." That is, he feels he is now
playing a more important role as a dispenser of information to the decision-making elite. He is conscious, for
example, that the President often listens to his broadcast, that department secretaries and Washington officials
tune in to the 6:30 p.m. broadcast in ever-increasing numbers. The foreign correspondent often hears from foreign
ambassadors assigned to Washington that television news is
considered a more potent force than the New York Times or
the Washington Post. He may hear, for example, that dis-
patches sent by the ambassador from Mexico contain an increased percentage of information drawn from television.
In other words, increasingly correspondents see their
linkage role to include the providing of information for
use among different sections within the government as
well as between the government and the populace. Walter
Cronkite attests to this fact:

> If there is safety in an informed electorate,
> there is added security in an informed of-
> ficialdom. A good news service can provide
> information to government officials that it
> would take them far too long to get . . .
> if indeed they ever got . . . through secret
> communications. (1967, p. 18.)

While this has been traditionally a function of the newspaper, it is increasingly becoming a conscious role perception among television journalists.

The Reporter as Interpreter

The right to interpret, that is, to posit judgments
about the significance of events, is basic to the role of
the press. This role has been transferred to television
and recognized on the network level in an almost matter-
of-fact manner, as represented in an NBC Press Circular:

> The correspondent or reporter does have
> the right to put news into perspective,

to interpret and to analyze. It is more
than a right; it is an obligation to the
extent that the bare statement of a development may confuse and mislead when it is
divorced from essential background and
context. (Press Circular Release, 1971,
"How NBC News Does Its Job," p. 12.)

Interpretation is regarded as an essential component of
the news:

I maintain that a raw fact, unexplained,
is not really news and that turning broadcast circuits into conduits for unanalyzed
information is not only bad journalism but
even slightly dishonest. . . . I argued
that I did not want our correspondents to
make up our viewers' and listeners' minds
on a course of action but that for Sevareid
not to add perspective on the Santo Domingo
situation, or for Collingwood not to accent
contradictions in Vietnam, or for Marvin
Kalb to ignore what he knew to be the facts
in favor of a State Department handout
would be more of a news slant than the
hard facts alone. (Friendly, 1967, p. 199.)

A sharp distinction is drawn between an interpretive
judgment and an editorial opinion. Interpretation of the
meaningfulness of a news item is a justifiable addition
to the presentation of information on that item, but the
correspondent is not permitted, for instance, to express
his own personal judgment about the worth, good or bad,
of a news item, or to declare whether an event should or
should not have happened. Said one Pentagon correspondent, "We should be able to say that when the Department
of Defense says it is cutting its budget, that they are
only transferring costs to other departments. Correspondents must get hold of the system and go behind the ob-
scuration of the political debate."

Although television correspondents recognize the in-
herence of this role, they lament that in reality television does not do enough interpretive reporting. In
February 1972 a high-level panel criticized television
for increasing the flow of information without providing
the background within which this increased flow might be
interpreted. Correspondents acknowledge this fact and

31

give various explanations: "We have inherent limits of time"; "we are supposed to be a headline service"; "that's the job of newspapers"; "we just don't do it; I don't know why, but we don't do enough of it." At the same time, they acknowledge the fact that foreign affairs is particularly complex; that the viewing audience does not command the background information necessary to untangle all the information it receives; and that television can and should provide it with this background information to a greater degree. Many of those interviewed pointed to the improvement of background information through the minidocumentary when network news increased its time allotment to 30 minutes. An increase in time to 60 minutes was the most frequently suggested way of presenting more interpretive information (about 60 percent suggested this alternative). In short, there appears to be a dual recognition: (1) that there is unquestionably an interpretive role inherent to the profession, and (2) that to this date television falls short in fulfilling that objective.

The Reporter as Instrument of Government

Bernard Cohen, discussing this role, hypothesized that the more "neutral" the press was, the more it limited itself to the simple recording of events without interpretative data, the easier it was for public officials to use the press. The television correspondent has been accused of being especially susceptible to being "used" by news sources because of the inherent mechanical need to have a picture.

Very often it is true that the television press corps is easy to manipulate, especially because of the mechanical demands of the medium. The President commands attention, and all reporters, newspapermen and television correspondents alike, respond because the President is always news. "Take China for example," said one Washington bureau chief. "That's the kind of story you can't resist. It's important historically, but it's especially good as a television story. When the President invites cameras to follow him, the likelihood is that we'll be there."

Like all newsmen, the television journalist is dependent on sources to get his story and especially dependent on getting public officials to respond to recorded interviews. It is readily acknowledged that it is more difficult to get an official to consent to record his response than to get him to comment to a pad-and-pencil journalist.

The official's willingness often depends on his good will
toward the electronic journalist, and often there is the
possible behavioral tendency for the correspondent to
"keep out of trouble," what the French call "autocensure."
But the television correspondent, at least verbally, does
not see his role as being a conscious instrument for social control. Words such as "complicity," and "abhorrent,"
are used to describe the situation when government succeeds in "using" the electronic press. At the same time
that correspondents almost uniformly respond that they
"hate to be used," they also recognize the desire of government officials to manage the news and propagandize
their policies and the frequency with which they succeed.
Television, they concur, because it tends to cover more
stories with fewer words than a newspaper, is often more
subject to "use" by officials. Every correspondent has
an example of how the press was "manipulated"; this kind
of manipulation is discussed openly and freely and recognized as an inherent danger that correspondents must protect themselves against to maintain the neutral role responsibility of the press.

During the Nixon administration the television press
came under sharp governmental criticism. The form this
criticism took and the correspondents' response to it requires, if only briefly, some discussion. Two categories
of criticism could be distinguished: (1) criticism of
the integrity of the press in pursuing its acknowledged
goals and (2) some rejection of these goals themselves.
The latter criticism stems from the governmental notion
that the press should be "part of the team" in garnering
support for government policies. Walter Cronkite, a
correspondent with many years of experience and himself
one of the pioneers in television journalism, spoke representatively on this subject:

> A newsman of my generation has been able
> to watch, year after year, the spreading
> of a tendency among political leaders,
> to forget what they once knew intellec-
> tually, and to react to criticism in-
> stead, emotionally. Instead of accept-
> ing the newsman and the dissenter as
> seekers of truth, they more and more have
> come to believe that the only responsible
> newsmen are those clearly commited to
> their cause. (February 1967, p. 18.)

This is considered a threat to the neutral role responsibilities of the journalist.

Television is specifically singled out, apparently for two reasons: (1) television is perceived to have great nationwide emotional impact, and (2) it receives less protection under the First Amendment.* Said one Pentagon correspondent,

> I approach my job with the same attitude as the newspaper reporter, but the Pentagon has an entirely different attitude toward me. This administration is convinced that television has had an enormous impact. They are worried about what I do and how I do it. They are extremely cautious, and it's very difficult to find a source around here.

The policy of television news executives has been uniformly adamant, at least in the published materials, in resisting any governmental attempt to censor or inhibit their news rights and obligations. Responding to criticism by the Vice President, the president of CBS News wrote the following in an in-house memo to his staff:

> I am confident that none of us will psychologically or subliminally so react to these attacks that we will trim our sails, or engage in self-censorship or suppression or softening. . . . All of us recognize our own fallibility. And we recognize that honest journalism makes it impossible to please all of the people all of the time or, indeed, some of the time. So be it: We are journalists. We cannot, we must not, consistent with any definition of

---

*The constitutional question will be discussed in Chapter 4. At this point, general note should be taken that the television press, by and large, does not accept any diminution of its constitutional freedom-of-press rights, although it accepts its charter requisite to act in the public interest. Whether this has been true in actual practice will be discussed in that later chapter, but a precise measurement of effect remains the topic for another study.

sound and responsible journalism permit
ourselves to be mere transmission belts
and amplifiers for the Government or for
any group or individual. (Richard Salant,
Memo, November 18, 1969.)

This attitude is consistent with the "neutral reporter" role concept and the press's democratic trust as
dispenser of information to the general public. Another
president of news operations said:

If the public is taught to consider reporting these mistakes as malicious and self-
serving on the part of reporters, it will
be inclined to think the mistakes were not
made. American public officials fear the
public as no other officialdom does. If
the whole news system is undermined, this
fear need no longer exist, since we have
no other system through which the public
can learn what officials do not want it to
know. (Frank, 1969, p. 3.)

Finally, there was acknowledged an advantage that
the press corps has in meeting the criticism and regula-
tory threats periodically posed by governmental officials.
That is, "they challenge the media and that challenge is
fought out on the media, and we are the media."*
The whole question of government threat and criticism
of television is a very complicated one, and its effect is
difficult to measure. For our purposes here it is sufficient to note that the correspondents were aware of this
criticism; that news department policy, at least at face
value, supported and defended the free and neutral role
of the correspondent; and that if there was a "chilling
effect" resulting from governmental criticism, it was not
readily perceptible. In every instance the neutral, informant role was considered primary to the responsibility
of the press. A necessary ingredient for the fulfillment
of that role was free access to and free transmission of
information.

_____

*This does not deny the legal constraints that tele-
vision is subject to but rather only affirms an advantage
available to the medium.

PARTICIPANT ROLE OF THE PRESS

The active participant role of the press in the policy-making process most closely corresponds to Douglass Cater's description of its extraconstitutional role as the "fourth branch of government." As put into historical perspective by Walter Cronkite,

> It was the free press that in large measure exposed the failings of older systems, that brought about reform, that became the people's surrogate in observing the performance of those servants in government—a vital service without which democracy would have been a hollow word. (May 1971, p. 8.)

There are attitudes supportive of this role reflected in controversy and espoused by the television journalist. Edward R. Murrow worked in this tradition, and it was inherent to his conception of the role television journalists should have. Alexander Kendrick wrote:

> Murrow was the one who defined the purpose of controversy and believed its function was not only to provoke but to illuminate. The focusing searchlight affixed to the mirror made his kind of television truly a window of the world he felt it was designed to be, and took it out of the shadow realm of parlor games, soap opera, idle chatter, synthetic personalities and old movies. (1969, p. 36.)

There are four distinguishable participatory roles. Only the first, the role of representative of the people, received significant acknowledgment (50 percent) as a major role conception from the television press corps. The other three were intimated, but by less than 50 percent of the respondents, and some categories were forthrightly denied as actual participatory roles engaged in by television journalists. These findings are distinctly different from those reported by Bernard Cohen (1963, p. 32) of the print journalist.

Representative of the People

This role is conceived as one in which the press represents the interests of the people: at the press

36

conference the correspondents pose questions on behalf of
the general public, to hold officials accountable and to
protect the democratic system. It carries a sense of responsibility that involves access to information and the
public right to be informed. The press is seen as the
hurdler of barriers placed before the free flow of information. It carries the idea of holding government accountable, of pursuing issues. It is this interaction of
the reporter with his sources that distinguishes this
role from the "neutral" role conception.

   This role is perceived to conform to the responsibility of the press to provide information to the public, to
search unswervingly for the truth, and to guard the public
interest. Television newsmen share with those of the
printed press a common dilemma between their obligation to
report the truth and their obligation to protect their
country (Reston, 1966, p. ix.). They know that they often
embarrass officials by reporting the facts and even interfere with public policy occasionally, but they go on doing
it because somehow the tradition of reporting the facts,
no matter how much they hurt, is stronger than any other
(Ibid.). Those who responded affirmatively to this role
conception felt that in order to protect their responsibilities they, and not the government, have to be the
judges of the public interest when it becomes a question
of determining whether a discovered story should be broadcast. Otherwise, they said, they could be subjected to
unbearable government management.

   There was no acceptance of censorship. Walter
Cronkite wrote:

> Just as there is no such thing as good
> censorship, there is no such thing as a
> little censorship. And, by the same
> token, while the "big lie" in the rarest
> of cases might be justified to save us
> from imminent disaster, there can be no
> little lies in the relations of govern-
> ment to the press, through it, to its
> people. (1971, p. 19.)

The press operates in the public interest, fulfilling its
role as the custodian of a free press and free speech.
Supporting this perception the veteran correspondent,
John Chancellor, said:

> We newsmen, I think, liked to believe that
> we were loved in the sense that the public

had a real regard for our profession. We
hoped that they viewed us not as heroes,
maybe, but certainly as their champion.
. . . I was forcibly reminded that a
journalist should not seek to be loved and
adored. He must give love. He must love
his work. He must love the service to
which he has dedicated himself. And he
must at least try to love the people, col-
lectively, even when they're throwing
rocks at him, individually. (Penthouse,
1972, p. 122.)

This participant role of representative of the people was
the one most often mentioned (50 percent) as being crucial to the television correspondent's professional responsibilities.

There were important examples cited of occasions
when the television press has exposed secret information
that it considered important for the public to know. For
example, Eric Sevareid reported U Thant's disclosure that
there had been peace feelers on Vietnam from Hanoi, which
had been repeatedly denied by the U.S. government. Yet
even the advocates of this role acknowledge that the television press was "lax" in fulfilling these responsibilities. The NBC Policy Book formally recognizes that the
Freedom of Information Act is "too little used by the
media, although it is designed to enlarge their access to
information on behalf of the public." (p. 36.)

Although this role conception received the highest
percentage among the participant role categories, it did
not compare to the almost unanimous acknowledgment of responsibility for the various neutral role concepts. Furthermore there was noticeable dismay among those who
cited the importance of this representative aim, that the
television press has not been so diligent in fulfilling
this traditional role as it might have been, and to their
perspective should have been.

Critic of Government

"No government ought to be without censors; and
where the press is free, none ever will." (Thomas Jefferson, September 9, 1792.) This critical role has a long
tradition in the United States, as a means, indeed as an
obligation, of keeping the government responsible. One

particularly strong advocate of this view commented that the only way to protect the responsibility of the press was through competition among the different press groups and that this competition was good "but not enough." Government, he said, "who has the potential power to subvert all freedoms, has no competition": the press is required, therefore, to put itself into a competitive relationship with the government. This idea is not only supported by the founders of the Republic, but as George Reedy, former Press Secretary for President Lyndon Johnson wrote:

> Of the few social institutions which tend to keep a President in touch with reality, the most effective--and the most resented by the chief beneficiary--is the press. It is the only force to enter the White House from the outside world with a direct impact upon the man in the Oval Office which cannot be softened by intermediary interpreters or deflected by sympathetic attendants. (Small, 1970, p. 230.)

However, interviews with television correspondents found them divided, fifty-fifty. That is, 50 percent of those interviewed felt that it was television journalism's responsibility to act as a critic of government, while the other 50 percent either were hesitant to accept the role designation or categorically denied that it was a journalist's responsibility.*

Those who support the role of the television press as critic make a distinction between criticism and editorializing. Editorializing is the expression of a personal view toward a policy, while criticism is more related to the correspondent's behavior or the manner in which he handles government information. In this latter case, the key expressions used were "skepticism," "distrust of power," and "to put before the people the unfinished business of our times."

---

*Cohen, in his study of the newspaper press, had found the role of critic "described and evaluated in positive terms by virtually all of the foreign affairs writers and analysts. There was about as much unanimity with respect to this role as there is conceiving the informative role." (1963, p. 34.)

Skepticism was cited to be important to enable the
correspondent to weigh the truth and validity of information received from his news source. Said one correspondent, "I'm not an adversary to government policy. But my
job is to ask, what's your evidence? Why are you doing
it?" Another, a Pentagon correspondent, said in reference to Vietnam,

> I see myself as an adversary--but not al-
> ways in the negative. When they don't
> talk, for example about the air war over
> the North, I want to find out why. Or if
> they use euphemisms like "the battlefield
> above the DMZ" to cloud the picture, I
> have to set the facts straight. We don't
> use these euphemisms on television.

In August 1971 the Committee on Interstate and Foreign Commerce of the House of Representatives, instigated
by its chairman, Harley Staggers of West Virginia, insti-
tuted contempt of the House proceedings against Frank
Stanton, president of CBS, for failure to provide the committee with certain materials from a documentary program.
The House of Representatives failed to concur with the
recommendations of the committee. After the vote Stanton
wrote in a memo to his news department:

> That skepticism and animosity exist between
> government and journalism comes as no sur-
> prise. This is inevitable if the journal-
> ist is diligent in his job of reporting
> government activities. And we must never
> allow the ire of officials, elected or ap-
> pointed, to compromise our dedication to
> the people's right to know and to question.
> (August 18, 1971.)

Another explanation for this critical role finds its
roots in the foundation of our political philosophy, a
distrust for power. Said a young correspondent, "You
can't go overboard in mistrusting power. Like Jefferson
put in, you must distrust power at all times." A correspondent on general assignment in New York said,

> Power tends to congeal. Government is
> often drawn from an establishment that is
> too often very limited. The press should

watch power and make it accountable--not
just government power, but corporate power,
university power, etc. He must somehow
present himself as a counterweight to the
clash and the crises of the momentary
events, to inform not just the public but
provide a counterweight of information for
the policy-makers themselves, and, to make
power more visible.

Underlying all of these statements is the acknowledgment
of a belief, reflected in Lord Acton's words: "Power
tends to corrupt, absolute power corrupts absolutely."
     Finally, some correspondents saw themselves as a
permanent critical opposition to a government that still
has unfinished business. Wrote Theodore H. White:

The national media . . . believe that their
chief duty is to put before the public the
unfinished business of our time, and therefore no government will satisfy them . . .
because the unfinished business of our time
is enormous. There is pollution, . . .
discrimination, . . . violence, there is
traffic, there are all sorts of problems.
No matter what any Administration does,
national media say why not more, why not
quicker? It is where Agnew was wrong. He
thinks they're just against Richard Nixon.
(1969-70, pp. 11-12.)

This "unfinished business" includes broadcasts of the
Pentagon Papers, the Anderson Papers, the White House
tapes, and the like. Indeed, said one foreign correspondent with many years of experience who was called the
"house intellectual": "If we had been doing our job all
along there would have been no need for the Pentagon
Papers. We could have had the job done sooner."
     But these correspondents do not concur with the
criticism that they have too much power and that this
power is placed in too few hands. They do not deny that
some 150,000 newspapermen and only some 300 network newsmen decide the news that some 200 million Americans will
receive, but they question what alternatives are available. Should the White House decide, or the national
committees, or who? On the contrary, they feel that
their power to criticize the government is very limited;

that television could do more; and that it is its obligation to do more. "The television press is a cap pistol,"
said one correspondent, "a cap pistol without a bullet.
Sure, with a cap pistol if you make a loud enough noise
you will get someone to take notice. But it is different
from government power."

For this group the model is Edward R. Murrow. His
name was most often spoken and his programs frequently
quoted. In this role capacity, Alexander Kendrick wrote
of Murrow:

> Murrow always regarded himself as a reporter
> rather than an analyst, but he was more. He
> was a disturber of the peace and a collector
> of injustices. Radio and television are by
> their very nature ephemeral. He endowed
> them with a sense of permanent substance by
> giving them a purpose. (1969, p. 12.)

These role conceptions reflect the perceptions of
about 50 percent of the respondents. The other half
varied in degree of opposition to this role, from hesitant disagreement to total denial. Said one bureau chief,

> We have gone too far when we consider our-
> selves as the chosen arm to embarrass the
> government. . . . I much prefer the corre-
> spondent who asks questions to get his
> story, and if he has his own ideas on for-
> eign policy, keeps it for coffee discus-
> sions with his colleagues.

Said a New-York-based correspondent,

> We are not the "fourth branch of govern-
> ment." The New York _Times_ has a differ-
> ent reaction, but they see their newspaper
> as read by high officials. This is not
> the intent of television--we are the neu-
> tral reporter. We try to be as objective
> as possible. . . . Government is an
> elected organization--they represent the
> people. We are not the government.

Of the work of Edward R. Murrow, little mention was vol-
untarily given by this group. When pursued, the typical
answer was, "He was unique and functioned in a unique

time [McCarthy], and because it was early in our development, his impact was unique."
    The role as critic of government is strongly held
among its advocates. They represent, however, only half
the television press corps. The other half, with varying
degrees of intensity, disagrees. Of this latter group
the explanation for denying this role varies, including
references to television's "national responsibility"; to
support of its neutral and informative role; to the non-
elective nature of the press corps; and to the distinctive quality of the picture reflecting the event, which
they say supplants the traditional critical role.

                     Advocate of Policy

    In the newspaper tradition, criticism and advocacy
are clearly distinguishable by the manner in which they
independently proceed toward different ends. To advocate,
to editorialize, is an accepted role of the newspaper
press and is separated and assigned to the editorial page.
In television there is no editorial page. An NBC News
press circular had the following to say about editorializing on television:

        One fundamental rule is that NBC News does
        not editorialize. It takes no editorial
        position on any issues or candidacy. Nei-
        ther may NBC News broadcasters editorialize
        on their own behalf--that is, take a position
        for or against an issue or candidate, or go
        beyond reports on what they believe exists,
        to state what they think ought to be.
        (1971, p. 11.)

Most network executives explain this policy by saying
that to editorialize on the network level would be to
harm the interests of the local affiliates throughout the
country, which are subject to different local and community pressures that do not readily conform to a single,
national point of view. It is also felt that an editorial
judgment given by the news anchorman could jeopardize his
credibility among the viewers as an objective chronicler
of the news.*
_____

    *However, there were editorials aired over radio dur-
ing the 1930s, when the commentators dominated the medium

                            43

Very few correspondents (15 percent) exhibited an interest in editorializing, with notable exceptions. For example, former television executive Fred Friendly has said:

> At a time when many Americans get most of their news from broadcast sources, it is essential to fill the void between a "just stick to the facts, boys" attitude and recommending a definite course of action. Abdication of this opportunity because of technicalities or fear of overstepping the line is to "throw the reader into a sea of facts and leave him on his own whether he can swim or not," as Lester Markel, former Sunday Editor of the New York Times, once put it. (1967, p. 204.)

A well-known commentator and one of the first to comment on television news editorially said: "If the facts call for a position to be taken by a journalist, he should present that position to the audience." But these two comments are the exception rather than the rule. Most correspondents do not believe that there should be an editorial judgment expressed on the evening news. Their reasons were many: television is a national medium and directed to the masses; its role is to inform, not to persuade; in its role as informant the objectivity of the correspondent is crucial, and expressed editorial judgments would compromise that objectivity; the television press is subject to regulation by the FCC and is inhibited from presenting editorial judgment not so much because of the attitudes that might be expressed but by the legal requirements of free and equal time to reply, which would consume too much of the news air time;* television is too powerful a medium to permit any one group to advocate opinion on policy regularly to a national audience. For whatever reason, editorializing, the conscious advocacy of policy, was not considered an important role for the television journalist.

---

news programs. The commentators represented all points of view, and their commentary was not identified directly with the broadcast management through whose facilities it was heard.

*The FCC regulation does not require exactly the same number of minutes or the same air time, but rather requires a balance.

Policy Maker

This role sees the correspondent as an actor in the
foreign-policy-making process, trying to influence opinions and behavior both in the governmental and public
sectors. This is not a role engaged in by the television
journalist. Even the simplest and least effective policy
making, the use of the medium for trial balloons or the
leaks of government secrets, is more commonly done by way
of the newspapers. For advice, consultation, and the
like, most television correspondents acknowledge that
policy makers prefer to talk to someone from a newspaper.
One well-known and nationally respected correspondent
lamented, "I thought that when Sadat came to power, since
I knew him very well, that I would be called in for my
impressions. But no, we are not called in for advice on
policy." Another well-known commentator and one of the
first television journalists said: "That's not a role
most want to play. Muskie sent a copy of his speech for
my comment and there was an uproar around here when they
found out."
The absence, almost total, of this role conception
can be accounted for in two ways. First, television correspondents are simply not approached by policy makers
for their opinions; and second, the most involved of the
participatory roles is the least acknowledged in a medium
in which the correspondents show little interest in participant aims.
There is an additional participatory role in television, the result of the mechanical nature of the medium,
which is that the presence or absence of a camera at a
news event can alter the character of that event. For
example, the Kerner Commission, investigating the 1967
race riots in our cities, found that television, by its
very presence and its broadcasting of the events, had had
a perceptible effect on those events. This role conception is discussed in greater detail in a later section.

THE TELEVISION CORRESPONDENT AS A
VISUALIZER OF EVENTS

There are role conceptions distinctive to the television correspondent. The first and most often encountered (88 percent of the correspondents made reference to
this role) is the result of television's capacity to
transmit experience. In addition to seeking the who,
what, where, when, and why of the news story, the

45

television journalist searches for the sound and look of
the story. The viewer becomes an eyewitness to the event.
"There is an immediacy and a vicarious association with
the picture," said one foreign correspondent.

The limitations of television's time, detail, and
depth are readily acknowledged, but television has an inherent attribute that is described as "particularly personal" and "graphic" in its impact on viewers and brings
the audience closer to being physically present at the
scene of an event. It is what Reuven Frank calls "transmitting experience":

> I do not mean that we transmit to the
> viewer one participant's impression of
> what it was like to undergo the experi-
> ence, but that we ourselves transmit to
> him the essence of the experience itself.
> Ideally we should make him smile and sweat,
> fear and exult. We want him to feel that
> he is crossing the Vietnamese march under
> fire, that it is he who faces the problem
> of learning a new trade and moving his
> family to a new city. (1969, p. 89.)

Reuven Frank graphically describes a moment at the Democratic Convention in Chicago (1968) illustrating the
mechanical potentialities of recorded sound for the television news story:

> How does one evaluate an event that had no
> lasting value? Like the dissident delega-
> tions, New York, California, Wisconsin,
> some others, singing the refrain from The
> Battle Hymn of the Republic after the film
> memorializing Senator Robert F. Kennedy.
> At first it was a strange and apparently
> spontaneous act of reverence. Then it re-
> fused to die; it became an act of defiance.
> The band was playing, I seem to remember,
> God Bless America. The gavel pounded in
> vain. If it had not been for the radio
> microphones of our floor reporters--not
> their reports, only their microphones--no
> one would have heard Glory, Glory, Hallelu-
> jah. The podium microphones, the official
> microphones, carried only God Bless America
> and the pounding of the gavel. No newspaper

reporter lives who could have captured
what television captured of that moment.
For better or for worse. (Ibid.)

Correspondents regard television as an important
"acquainting" medium. One correspondent who interviewed
India's President Indira Gandhi was asked what the purpose of the interview was: "She was new in office and we
wanted to introduce her to American audiences. She was
the symbol of a movement and we wanted to show her personality." As correspondent Don Hewitt put it, "The
fellow listening in his car radio hears the name 'Willy
Brandt' and, because of television, he visualizes somebody." (Bluem and Manvell, 1967, p. 121.)
Television captures the sights and sounds of political events and dispenses these audible pictures to rich
and poor, literate and illiterate, alike. In the 1960s,
when there was an important event, television was there.
Civil rights was the first crucial issue of the decade,
and the correspondents are very conscious of the role the
medium played. One of them put it this way: "TV can
show a bigot on the screen. Agnew reflects the trauma of
this country. Television visualizes the bitter division
in the nation today."
In foreign affairs, television is considered especially important, since it brings the unfamiliar into the
viewers' homes. Starvation in India, a ride on the Orient
Express, slaughter in Bangladesh, wine in Bordeaux, a
primitive tribe in Australia, and the war in Vietnam, have
all been seen on television. Besides civil rights, Vietnam was the other major issue of the 1960s captured on
television; it has been called America's first television
war. Michael Arlen entitled his book the Living-Room War
and chose the title

because during the period I was writing
. . . [Vietnam] seemed to be the central
fact in American life. . . . It was a
changing shape beneath everything else in
American life in that period, in a way
that no other war we'd experienced had
been, and most of us knew about it, felt
about it, from television. . . . It was
there in presence, in all those almost
hopelessly routinizing film clips of combat on the evening news shows, those young
TV correspondents standing beside some

47

hillside outside Pleiku describing gun-
fire while we drank beer, played with our
children, thought, felt God knows what.
(1969, p. xi.)

The correspondents were particularly conscious of the possible impact the television picture had on the war in
Vietnam, probably because they had been criticized for
their coverage by government officials. However, their
sense of impact reflected more their concept of the reporter as a neutral, not a participant or advocate of
policy. Said one veteran of three separate assignments
in Vietnam,

> I am convinced that television had much
> more influence in shaping American atti-
> tudes toward the war than newspapers--not
> in terms of intent, but because the pic-
> tures that were being seen were an insis-
> tent graphic reminder. Seeing devastation,
> wounding, death; seeing the effects in
> this country. All this had a profound ef-
> fect--not just by showing what was happen-
> ing--but as a constant reminder that the
> war was going on and on and on.

Broadcasting confers a sense of reality and inhibits
the individual fantasies of the viewers. Said Frank
McGee: "Television has conveyed--or is in the process of
conveying--what it's like out there. . . . There was a
time when people were spared the knowledge of war almost
altogether. That time is almost gone." (Zeidenberg,
1968, p. 288.) Hans Morgenthau, an early opponent of the
Vietnam War and a leading participant in the early nationally televised debates between proponents and opponents
of the war, wrote to the CBS Washington bureau chief:

> [Television] demonstrated for all to see
> and hear that the opponents to the war
> were not wide-eyed idealists, irrespon-
> sible radicals, or eccentrics in general
> but well-informed, serious and responsible
> people who presented rational arguments.
> For instance, many people who were favor-
> able to the Administration's position have
> told me that they became dubious when they
> witnessed Bundy's attempts to discredit

me personally rather than to meet my arguments. (Small, 1970, p. 112.)

Planners of events cannot afford to ignore the demands of television in their overall plans. Television
is there; the pictures and the sounds are inherent in its
reportage; and its absence from an event would probably
be more obvious than its presence. Television correspondents are very conscious of this, and it is this aspect
of their role that has accounted for a large part of the·
criticism that has been voiced against their activities.
While the correspondents perceive television as an en-
larger of the viewer's reality, they recognize that at
the same moment, although they are not thought of as having been unfair, for example, in the presentation of violence at the 1968 Chicago Democratic Convention, they are
somehow mystically held responsible for the violence they
reported. Their general reaction to this idea was uniform:

> They (the critics) experienced the prob-
> lems, . . . they did not learn about them.
> And . . . this was not because of what
> television reporters do and did, but be-
> cause television exists. This more recent
> criticism blames the messenger for the
> message. (Frank, Winter 1970, pp. 19-20.)

TELEVISION AS A CATALYST FOR NEWSPAPERS

The development of the electronic press virtually
eliminated the newspaper "extra" because it is a faster
and a more pervasive disseminator of news across the country. Television's priority has been the reproduction of
the front page news of the day, which it does quicker and
more efficiently than a newspaper could ever hope to do.
Today there are fewer newspapers than before, and while
there were at one time several wire services in the United
States, there remain only two. The majority of the television correspondents (75 percent) see fostering a diversity of news sources as part of their role.
With dwindling numbers of newspapers and magazines,
television provides still another outlet for information.
Many communities have only one newspaper or a single ownership of newspapers, and the television correspondent
feels a responsibility to provide these communities with
an alternative to those sources. Television is perceived

to have a monitoring role over single-newspaper communities, to "assure that they do not plot or inadvertently
miss an important story." For example, William Small observes:

> Newspapers which had treated stories light-
> ly (some did so even when it was in their
> own city) began to give the civil rights
> movement more attention. Local radio and
> television, in some places as protective
> of the Establishment as the local news-
> paper, were shamed into coverage because
> it was there, on the network newscasts.
> (1970, p. 45.)

Specifically with regard to foreign affairs news,
correspondents are very much aware of the fact that most
people receive the bulk of their international news from
the network news broadcasts. "We actually cover more
foreign news and news of national importance than the
local paper does," said Walter Cronkite (1972, p. 18).
"Local papers in this area are so poor," observed a State
Department correspondent, "that we have had to assume
this function that others have abrogated."

Finally, some correspondents who explain the nightly
news as a "headline service" perceive that part of their
role is to provide the viewer with an outline of the
day's events, from which he can pick and choose, to follow his interests for more information in the newspaper.

Whether it be because of the speed and immediacy of
the television report, because of the one-newspaper communities, or because of the daily outline, television
correspondents see themselves acting a role either more
efficiently than the newspaper, or which the newspaper
has abrogated, or complementing the needs of the audience
for information.

PARTICIPANT IN A NATIONAL MEDIUM WITH
A NATIONAL RESPONSIBILITY

Television is distinct from the newspaper in that it
is a national medium. This is recognized in its legal
charter and among the correspondents in each news department. With this national capability there is a recognized
national responsibility. When the President of the United
States requests time to address the nation about a national

emergency, it is unquestioned that he has a right of access to this medium. When the first American is on the moon, when the President is in China, when there is a political convention, or when a national leader is felled by an assassin's bullet, it is automatic that television is there. Correspondents are very conscious that they played an important national role during the aftermath of President Kennedy's assassination and that they helped hold the nation together. "We were not aware of it at the time," says one commentator. "We were just doing our jobs in a period of crisis. But when you think how many millions of people were dependent upon us to know what was happening and to be reassured that everything was holding together, you can't help but feel that you played an important role." In short, the correspondents are well aware that their reports are major sources of information for the national population and that their medium, during periods of crisis, is an important channel linking the events with the people.

THE CORRESPONDENT'S DEFINITIONS OF NEWS AND OBJECTIVITY

News

Before discussing the mechanical and structural characteristics of television and the actual newsgathering behavior of the electronic journalist, I felt it was important to ask the correspondent how he defines the product he reports, the news. In general, the response to this question reflected the finding of the earlier studies by Cohen and Warner that there are no precise definitions and understandings among the participants of what constitutes news. The imprecise definitions are discussed, nonetheless, in order to provide a more complete picture of the newsgathering activities in television. Indeed, a consciousness of the unarticulated nature of "news" definitions provides an understanding of the background circumstances in which the mechanical and structural variables have come to play so important a role in the work of the electronic journalist.

Correspondents exhibited some difficulty in describing in words what they thought was news: "News is a sense: you have a 'nose for news'"; "A story is a story when it's a story." Said a veteran European correspondent, "I used to know. I don't know anymore." Most often newsworthiness is a matter of both personal and professional judgment. John Chancellor, a correspondent with long experience in newspapers and in television, responded to an interviewer:

> It may be arrogant to say it. But, look, news is selected by human beings who work by various criteria. David [Brinkley] does choose the news he reports and it is, indeed, what he says it is because somebody has to say what it is. . . . Critics seem to believe that there is some totally authoritative, almost divine, source of judgment about news, as if the untrammeled word of God were available to us and we were just ignoring it. Let me tell you that we're looking for it all the time. If I could have access to it I would go to it every day! But I don't have it. Nor does anyone else. (Penthouse, 1972, p. 40.)

By and large, that personal and professional judgment is found somewhere in the middle of the political and/or ideological spectrum. Reuven Frank commented:

> The country is full of small groups at odds with the rest of us. . . . Television is a medium through which most of us can be reached. When a professional news judgment is made that this group is saying something which is news, and that one is not, then the ignored group proclaims damage to its right to speak. (1971, p. 3.)

John Chancellor includes television with other news services as in the pursuit of "objective" selection and judgment:

> The TV network coverage, the AP, the UPI, the major newspapers, all tend to cover the broad, middle part of opinion in the United States because that's where the action is. The extreme left isn't shaping events or saying much that makes sense to people any more than is the extreme right. So when we make judgments about news we make them in terms of the stories that

52

will affect a lot of people. That's why we
carry stories on the draft, on tax, and on
large movements within society which affect
a lot of people. . . . That woman [Edith
Efron], and a lot of people whose thinking
she represents, believe in using journalism
creatively for the society they perceive,
to help their point of view. Well, that's
propaganda. And we're not in that business. (Penthouse, 1972, p. 90.)

The television correspondent, through professional
training and long experience, develops a "sense" for the
news, which he or she reconfirms by contrasting and comparing the news broadcast with those of the other networks and with the front pages of the leading newspapers.
However, there are no hard and fast rules for the selection of news. Many words are employed to define the news
but they are ambiguous and nondiscriminating.

There are discernible classifications for news. For
example, the television correspondent, like the newspaper
correspondent, believes personalities make news. Wrote
Edward R. Murrow, critically:

The bias I refer to is in the direction of
authority, and in this case Authority
means anything which is organized, which
has a name, and which gives speeches.
This bias is by now so natural and so much
a characteristic of the press that it is
rarely even mentioned. . . . In covering
the news in all these fields the press
tends . . . to take its cues from established Authority . . . [and] are dominated
by articulated opinion. (Lyons, 1965,
p. 154.)

The President, members of his administration, and world
leaders are always news. However, their role in the news
is often, if not always, dependent on the event, which
they have either created or in which they are involved.
This criterion, too, is not as explicit or discriminating
as it appears. At what point the event determines the
significance of an official's role or, conversely, at
what point the individual is significant irrespective of
the event, is never clearly delineated. This distinction
is especially inarticulate with people (names) who are

well known but who do not hold official positions. These
can include the son of an important official; an unknown
person caught in a dramatic scene, such as a scorched
child running from a bombed village in a war-torn country;
or a national celebrity, defined by Boorstin with more
than a semblance of truth as one who is known for being
well known (1961). In each case respondents varied widely
in their reactions about what was news and who was important.

"Change," "something new," that which is "out of the
ordinary" or "immediate and interesting" were criteria
offered with some degree of frequency. News should not
be the ordinary occurrence of every day. It is unusual,
extraordinary, often bad rather than good, although "bad"
need not be an absolute criterion, so long as it is unusual. Often it is the interruption of the norm that is
news. An entirely different point of view advocates the
need to focus on the normal and the usual in order to provide balance.

If we look at the criteria of "new" and "immediate,"
we find many contradictions, representative of which is a
statement written by the sociologist Tamotsu Shibutani:

> Since news has immediate relevance to ac-
> tion that is already under way, it is per-
> ishable. This suggests that news is not
> merely something new; it is information
> that is timely. Even if it is about events
> long past, the information is necessary for
> current adjustment; it relieves tension in
> the immediate situation. . . . This tran-
> sient quality is the very essence of news,
> for an event ceases to be newsworthy as
> soon as the tension it has aroused has been
> dissipated. Once a decision has been
> reached, the quickening sense of urgency
> and importance disappears, and public at-
> tention turns elsewhere. (1966, p. 41.)

But this immediate and new quality of the news is readily
contradicted: correspondents complain that television
does not adequately report foreign affairs stories that
are composed of underlying and long-term trends or contained in the minds of men as ideas rather than events.

That a story, for example, a land reform in Latin
America, must become political before it will find broadcast space is often mentioned. With equal frequency the

correspondents refer to economic and social stories that "burst onto the scene with such force" that they cannot readily be ignored, as might an international monetary crisis or the latest findings on minority reading scores.

Human interest was frequently mentioned by the television correspondents.* Said one, "Because we look for the picture we focus on the humanity of the story and we tend to try to humanize the story for an American audience." As Howard K. Smith commented, "Television news is pictures, plus words, plus personality."

The television correspondent is trained in the traditions of American journalism and therefore reflects many of the attitudes expressed in earlier studies of the definition of news. One classification that commonly receives a most explicit response is "conflict, controversy, and crisis." These three terms were mentioned with great frequency among television journalists. A Paris correspondent said, "We're interested in the fast breaking event. War, tragedy, disaster are all generally strong television news stories." According to another correspondent, just returned from the Middle East, "Riots are good stories. Wars better: there are good moving pictures, drama, conflict." The common ingredient is conflict. Television is often described as being well-equipped for this type of story:

> By its nature television is best suited to the coverage of the kind of story that the viewer can take in at a glance. This sort of story usually falls in the "event" category, more emotional than mental, more the sharing of an experience rather than the understanding of vital information.
> (Pennybacker, 1969, p. 53.)

These criteria seem to be especially important for television because of the perception that television news is dramatic, that it can visualize the event, that it can get people to react on camera, and that it can capture the movement of the event.

---

*Bernard Cohen found just the opposite among newspaper reporters: "Human interest as a classification . . . does not show up very often in the news typologies of foreign affairs correspondents." (1963, p. 56.)

These different perceptions of news are presented
with varying degrees of frequency. Common to all these
definitions, classifications, or categorizations is an
absence of explicitness, a failure to discriminate between
differences or overcome its tautological nature. What is
interesting about this term "news," whereby the profession
gains its name and distinguishes its activities, is that
it is by and large an unarticulated and ill-defined concept among its actors. The term is accepted as a given,
sensed through training, and confirmed in practice. In
short, whether news was described as a sense, as a judgment, as an authoritative name, as change, as the uncom-
mon, as the immediate and interesting, as crisis, as conflict, or as controversy, the responses from the television journalists corresponded to those elicited from newspaper journalists, and our findings confirm Bernard
Cohen's conclusion that "these definitions are not useful;
they do not make reliable distinctions between what is indisputably news, and what is equally indisputably not
news." (1963, p. 57.)

Objectivity

Objectivity of news reportage, over a period of perhaps 100 years, has become almost a communication "ethic"
(Almond, 1960, p. 45) in the American journalism tradition. Whether viewed from the perspective of the journalist or from that of the audience, objectivity is something
that has become to be expected by all; yet to this day it
remains a concept that has resisted definitive formulation.
Is it lack of "slant"? is it presentation of only the
"truth"? To be objective, does the journalist seek without interest, expunge his or her own biases, provide balance, or what? Each actor will offer a different combination and conclude that it cannot be defined; the television journalist is not an exception.
Objectivity was undeniably a goal sought by almost
all of the respondents. It is something they had been
trained to strive for; it is an objective that has continuously been reinforced in the news departments; and
it is inherent in their professional credo. Walter
Cronkite is representative:

> I assure you that I never heard nor guessed
> nor felt that in making a news judgment
> that any one of those decisions was based

on a political or ideological consideration. . . . Since I am not entirely naive
I do know that, like an insidious, taste-
less, odorless gas, prejudice and bias can
sneak in and poison the decision-making
process. But like a fireman in a smoke-
filled room, a deep-sea diver with the
first symptoms of narcosis, a surgeon
with a second sense that the patient is
failing under his hands, we _feel_ the creep-
ing danger and most of the time . . . we
react and we bend over backwards to regain
balance in the report. (Walter Cronkite,
Testimony Before the Subcommittee on Constitutional Rights, United States Senate,
September 1971.)

Balance is one criterion for objectivity, but others describe this criterion as often potentially unobjective:
A spokesman is sought in order to balance one opinion
with another even though the second opinion is balanced
only insofar as it is given equal time (Frank, 1971).
Murrow went so far as to say that it was not "humanly
possible for any reporter to be completely objective,
for we are all to some degree prisoners of our education,
travel, rearing--the sum total of our experience."
(Kendrick, 1969, p. 344.)

Judgment has always been an essential ingredient in
news reporting. The reporter always sees more and knows
more than he reports. Selectivity is at the essence of
this procedure: the journalist must choose which stories
to report and what to report about those stories. There
is no escape from this procedure. In television there is
the additional selection of what pictures to record. However, the attitude among correspondents is one of trying
to "cleanse oneself of bias"; to "make the bias explicit";
and not to mix prejudice, which is regarded as opinion,
with judgment, which is a journalistic tradition. Reuven
Frank succinctly describes the goal in terms of what the
"objective" expectations of the audience should be of the
news it receives:

To me, the First Amendment means that the
American at home is guaranteed that whoever
gathers his news do so freely, and whoever
presents it does so for no conscious purpose other than to present it. He must

57

know that his news is neither gathered nor
given by men or women seeking office or advantage by what they do with the news, or
by those who think the news is the means
to some better tomorrow only they discern.
(1973.)

Objectivity, like news, seems to resist verbal definition. It seems reasonable to suggest that other factors are more capable of affecting the correspondents'
behavior than they would be if these professional criteria
were more clearly prescribed. In the television medium
there are two discernible characteristics that were found
to have a perceptible influence on the correspondents'
behavior: these are the mechanical and structural components distinctive to the medium. It is important to
look more closely at each of these features and analyze
the way they affect the correspondent's daily pursuit of
a news story.

Role Conception Findings and
the Political Process

The personal capabilities and role conceptions of
the television journalist provide both advantages and disadvantages for the political process. The network journalist is a highly educated, experienced individual, as
good as, if not sometimes even better than, his or her
colleagues in the other media. What distinguishes television journalists from the others are their reasons for
entering electronic journalism, which, in addition to the
professional journalistic reasons shared by their print
colleagues, include the mechanical and structural characteristics of the medium. Television is more personal,
immediate, new, visual, and competitive, with a wider and
more dispersed audience. Like their counterparts in the
print media, television journalists are excited by their
presence at the scenes of events that will shape future
history and by their opportunity to interpret the significance of what they see for an audience. Because television journalists are attracted by the very electronic
characteristics of that medium, they want to visualize
that event for their audience. Death in Vietnam was not
something the television correspondents wanted to describe,
but it was something they could show. For them, no words
could so easily recreate the juxtaposition of a solitary

Czechoslovakian citizen with the armor and steel of a
Soviet tank as a moving picture.

Through the traditional informant role of the correspondent, coupled with the electronic journalist's visualizing role perception, television news can enlarge the
awareness, if not the comprehension, of the American public of the world around them. It can accomplish this,
not simply because it reaches a nonreading audience, but
also because this is a time in which the newspaper's influence as a "map maker" for foreign affairs has declined.
If it is not the sole source of foreign affairs news for
large segments of its audience, television very often is
the catalyst, or trigger, that causes its viewers to seek
out additional information on a particular subject in the
print media. This, too, is an important new role conception for the electronic journalist, and it enhances the
significance of television's "map-making" function to an
audience of more than those whose sole source of information about the world is from the electronic medium.

Whether as a result of its character; from an un-
warranted faith in the "truth of pictures"; from the newness of the medium; or because of its public responsibility, the television correspondent does not conform strong-
ly to the traditional participatory role conception of the
press. Whereas earlier studies (Cohen, 1963, pp. 31-47;
Dunn, 1969, pp. 7-18; Nimmo, 1964, pp. 18-93) attest to
the unanimous appreciation among press reporters of their
roles as representatives of the people, critics of government, advocates of policy, and secondarily as policy
makers, television journalists were very much divided
about these roles. Fewer than 50 percent supported any
one of these activities, and very strong opposition to
them was expressed among significant proportions of the
electronic press corps.

Television journalists favor full disclosure of information, free access to information, and an informed
public. They perceive this, however, as a neutral role
conception and are hesitant to accept a more participatory
role as inherent to their activities. They are much more
concerned and explicit about their ability to transfer
experience than they are about being a check on the government. As a result one must conclude that electronic
journalists are more susceptible to control or use by the
government.

Television correspondents are often caught in the
situation of being the mere transmitters of government
and political propaganda. Their role perceptions tend

to promote the medium's use simply as the disseminator of conflicting views on issues or events, with little participatory action on the part of the correspondents other than as the recording intermediaries of that event or controversy. This neutral and "objective" transmission of the news event potentially, if not really, cedes the policy initiative to the policy maker, both as disseminator of policy information and as a news source for comment on that information. The selection of which events to transmit and the accompanying descriptions may be important controls that the television correspondents have, but the alternatives to be presented and the initiative remain most often in the hands of the policy maker.

The professional criteria of objectivity and neutral reporting discipline the correspondents to look to the political center. This is reinforced by their concept of television's national and heterogeneous audience; by the complementary attitudes of their colleagues, employers, and competitors; and by their perceptions of audience expectations. Centrism reinforces the status quo or at the most accepts modifications of that status quo. In seeking to occupy the middle ground, the correspondents again have a propensity to balance opposing viewpoints, intimating that truth is to be found somewhere in between. Too often bias is perceived to occur automatically when the correspondent veers away from the center; as a result, the center itself becomes a journalistic bias.

An academic who engages in research about journalism is immediately struck by the difference in approach toward explaining phenomena between the journalists and himself. The academic must not permit his frame of reference to obliterate that of the journalists or the journalist's approach to eliminate his. The television journalist, like most other journalists, tends to eschew the discipline of social science methodology and place in its stead a more action-oriented exploration of phenomena. For the television correspondent, truth, or perhaps only an approach to understanding, is to be found by going out in the field to "talk with sources" and to assay the event. Carried out on a day-to-day basis, however, such factors as the limitations of available resources for background preparation and the need to record the event on film result in a fragmented, often superficial, and not always reflective view of the event. As a result the correspondent is too often the victim or unwillful transmitter of the policy makers' propaganda.

The closest the electronic journalist comes to playing an active participant role is in his role concept of visualizer of events, showing the malignancy of our cities, the human heartbreak of war, the inequities of class, and the like. Again, however, this is more of a role of recorder of injustice than of check on power; of citizens' representative against injustice, of advocate of change, or of searcher and discloser of truth. Television correspondents intend to reflect what they find rather than evaluate it or suggest what to do about it. That is, they provide the conduit whereby advocates of the various sides present their views, and they present the visual evidence, but they restrict themselves to the "objectivity" of the event, with the idea that they are enabling the viewers to decide by themselves between opposing viewpoints. Once again, the potential participatory role is mitigated by the withdrawal of the correspondent from the story and by dependence on the visual to represent the story's content.

In attempting to put into perspective the findings of the two previous chapters, one is quickly reminded that the central consideration always returns to the issue of the role the American press should play in our political system. It is certainly not a new issue in the debate among political actors, journalists, and academics. Whether the press is conceived as the critic of government, the upholder of the status quo, the fourth branch of government, or the representative of the people is as much, if not more, the result of the actual role conceptions of the participants in the press corps as it is of our philosophical and political traditions that attempt to prescribe what its role should be. This debate has never been settled. Even Thomas Jefferson, who in the early years of the Republic so articulately and forthrightly defended the crucial role of the press to uphold the integrity of the government and the information function for an informed public, lamented the press's power once he himself ascended to the most powerful governmental position in the land. The debate and the contradictions still abound, perhaps with even greater passions. An investigation of the mechanical and structural characteristics of the television medium should provide additional information, which when coupled to what has been learned about the electronic journalists' role conceptions, will show how this debate has carried over in actual practice into this new medium.

PART

II

GATHERING
THE NEWS

3

THE CORRESPONDENT'S
VIEW OF THE
MECHANICAL CONSTRAINTS
OF TELEVISION

At different periods in history, certain societal and technological changes have combined to form new patterns of communication flow and information distribution. One such period in American history occurred in the 1830s. Societally, the role of the average American citizen was changing as the growth of commercialism brought about the emergence of the middle class. Technologically, the steam engine was harnessed to the rotary press; cheap wood-pulp newsprint was abundant; and the hoe cylinder press was in operation. What this latter innovation meant for information dissemination was that people previously not reached by the limited circulation, subscription newspapers were now being appealed to. With this new technological capability came a redefinition of "news."

In the United States various approaches were tried, but it remained for Benjamin H. Day, with his New York Sun, to inaugurate this era of the mass-circulation newspaper. Day abandoned subscriptions and sold his paper in the streets for only a penny. To maintain the price, he had to appeal to a large number of people, which had to include those who had not previously been newspaper readers.

One of the most important features of Day's penny paper, and of those which followed it, was the redefinition of "news" to fit the tastes, interests, and reading skills of this less educated level of society. Up to that time, "news" generally meant reports of social or political events of genuine importance, or of other happenings that were of wide-spread significance. Benjamin Day,

however, filled his paper with news of another sort--accounts of crimes, stories of
sin, catastrophe, and disaster--news the man
in the street found exciting, entertaining,
or amusing. . . . It was aimed directly at
the newly literate working masses who were
beginning to participate in the spreading
industrial revolution. There was some serious material in the paper to be sure, but
its editorials and reports of political and
economic complexities were much more superficial than in the earlier partisan papers
written for more politically sophisticated
readers. By 1837, the Sun was distributing
30,000 copies daily, more than the combined
total of all New York papers when the penny
paper was first brought out. (DeFleur,
1970, p. 13.)

Day's formula was quickly imitated; new technology was employed; and a redefinition of the news was the result.

A century later radio came onto the scene with three
clear advantages over the newspapers: (1) it could report
fast-breaking news, hours before the newspapers could put
their copy on the street; (2) it could reach a greater
audience not exposed to foreign affairs news by their local newspapers; and (3) its correspondents could communicate more directly with their listening audience.

In the 1950s the electronic medium coupled the sound
with a picture, and the television era began. The inherent mechanical characteristics of television include
audiovisual techniques, sequential presentation, and a
fixed time. We have observed how the new technology for
newspapers brought about a redefinition of the news. It
is proper to ask now what redefinitions have been made to
correspond to the new electronic technology that has been
coupled to the traditional journalistic activities.

A VISUAL MEDIUM AND THE DISCIPLINE OF PICTURES

"I think in television terms" commented a foreign
correspondent covering a story on French prison reform.
"As I go around taking pictures I write the script."
Television is pictures. The visual dominates. It is accepted that for moments at a time no words will be spoken,
no music or sounds will be broadcast. There can be silence,

but there must always be pictures. For example, the correspondent in Paris always made a film of the weekly peace conference and sent it off to New York, even though there usually appeared to be no story. He did this as insurance. Should a story on the war break elsewhere with a direct bearing on the Paris talks, there would be fresh film on hand to illustrate the story. "Finally," he said, "our medium is pictures and an American correspondent must understand that from the start."

A CBS News publication, Television News Reporting, says:

> Television news properly emphasizes the frankly pictorial aspects of the news, thus respecting the nature of its own resources. By doing so, it can perform a unique service in making the viewer an eye-witness to much of the news as it happens. The largest and the smallest events are recorded by the camera in a fashion which makes seeing understanding. (1958, p. 84.)

Correspondents uniformly acknowledge these demands and respond that the shape of the news on television results from the discipline of pictures. But it is not just any picture that television demands; it requires interesting, active pictures. Explained David Brinkley: "Television is a pictorial medium essentially, and if there is no picture, if there is no movement, and if there is nothing happening, nobody is going to listen." (Hohenberg, 1971, p. 487.)

Pictures, contrary to initial reactions of "seeing is believing" or "I saw it on television, it must be true," do not tell the whole story. Their field of vision is limited to a tunneled point captured by the camera lens. Generally the lens is pointed toward moments of impact, and it may not be representative of the whole. Eric Sevareid illustrated this point:

> I was extremely conscious of this last Spring in Vietnam. Buddhists staged some riots in Saigon and Da Nang. The TV cameras wheeled up. They focus, of course, on whatever is most dramatically in motion. They act like a flashlight beam in the darkness. Everything else around, however vital to the full story, is lost in the darkness

and ceases to exist. The pictures could not
show you that a block away from the Saigon
riots the populace was shopping, chatting,
sitting in restaurants in total normalcy.
The riots involved a tiny proportion in
either city; yet the effect of the pictures
in this country, including the Congress,
was explosive. People thought Vietnam was
tearing itself apart, that civil war was
raging. Nothing of the sort was happening.
(1967, p. 14.)

Words, too, are important, but the relative importance
of their role is more controversial. Although most correspondents describe television news as the combination of
words and pictures, they acknowledge that progressively
fewer words are being used in television, that there are
greater gaps between the words, sentences, and paragraphs.
One correspondent rarely uses a story of more than 175
words for a spoken, on-camera report. A film report seldom runs over 350 words. In comparison, a front-page
story in the New York Times runs to about 1,000 words or
more.

It is not that words are unimportant, but that they
have a special limitation on television. They cannot be
called back: A person reading a newspaper article on
defense-spending proposals for nuclear weapons who for-
gets the conflicting figures involved can stop, go back
to the beginning of the column, and check them out. This
is not possible (yet) with television. The viewer cannot
stop the news report and replay an earlier section. Awareness of this limitation causes the correspondent to make
the text of his story simple and readily comprehensible,
since if the viewer misses a detail he does not have a
second chance to recall the correspondent's words.

There is, therefore, a problem for the television
journalist caused by the medium's two dimensions: the
audio and the visual. That is, the visual cannot always
be interesting and is capable of capturing only part of
the story, while the audio is numerically limited and
evanescent.

Among the correspondents the emphasis that these two
dimensions should receive in a news story varies on a
visual-audio continuum from "the best television story is
one in which the picture tells the story without the need
of words," through the most traditional "the product is
words and pictures and each should have its time," to

"we should be like the French and ignore the picture and talk the news. It's the information not the picture that the citizen needs." These are important differences and require some elaboration.

In a rough division of this continuum into categories of (1) primacy of the picture, (2) equal importance given to audio and visual, and (3) primacy of the audio, the responses were 10 percent, 75 percent, and 15 percent respectively. However, in the 75 percent group there was such great variance or ambiguity, and the distribution was so wide, that no meaningful statistical conclusions could be drawn.

A quantification of responses does not adequately explain the difference, but some generalizations can be made, although with notable exceptions depending upon the prestige of the individual within the press corps and the basis of his national reputation. Correspondents favoring the picture more than the words tended to be younger (hired after 1963), trained in television, and most interested and involved in overseas assignments. Only one correspondent over 45 years old and hired before 1963 felt pictures were more important than words. Three of the Washington correspondents leaned toward the picture over the word: all three were on general assignment in Washington with foreign experience and awaiting reassignment abroad. Very few correspondents hired before 1963 with training in newspapers favored the visual over the audio; they tended to place themselves in that group giving equal importance to both. Correspondents holding masters degrees also placed in the center of this category. In general, however, the Washington-assigned correspondents stressed the importance of words and the limitations of pictures. Why this last group put its emphasis on words relates directly to the nature of the story available in Washington, which will be discussed in detail in a later section of this chapter.

Why the television correspondent should be interested in visualizing the story and should stress the importance of the picture is obvious by the very nature of the medium, and it is likewise understandable that he or she should offer this capability as a reason for entering this branch of journalism. However, the reasons why correspondents stress the importance of using words give us insight into some of their perceptions of the limitations of this visual medium. Henry Fairlie, testifying before a Congressional committee in 1967, represented most of these correspondents' views when he said:

However paradoxical it may seem, the only
immediate answer to most of the problems of
television news lies not in pictures but in
words. Given the powerful impact of the
pictures, the words covering them must supply the corrective. Most television reporting just describes the pictures, and by
doing so reinforces them. But the object
of words in television should be to distract
from pictures, to say: "It was not quite
so. This was not the whole story." (Rivers
and Schramm, 1969, 143.)

For Edward R. Murrow, words also were to distract from
the visual, to provide qualification and make more complicated; the reporter through this dimension should

make watching as difficult as reading [be-
cause] street riots and battle scenes may
be real enough, but they carry no meaning
unless it is supplied by something besides
the camera eye. (Kendrick, 1969, p. 32.)
. . . .
[Cameras] could produce distortion rather
than the true reflection of "a mirror behind." The commanding need in television
news was to "sift and sort it through the
mind," . . . to insure human instead of
merely mechanical discernment. (Ibid.,
p. 360.)

The correspondents perceive that New York producers,
the men who put together the television broadcast, demand
a picture. "What didn't move wasn't news." This they say
is changing slightly, that the producers "are learning
that a few thoughtful words can often be more revealing
than a thousand pictures." Part IV will discuss the role
and perceptions of the producer and will confirm the
validity of the correspondents' perception that the producer is intent on pictures and considers words to be
only an accompaniment to the picture.
The television news story as understood by television
journalists has major limitations, but the journalists are
quick to point out that other media do as well. For example, the newspaper is not instantaneous, while radio is
not visual. Some of these pictorial limitations are mechanically inherent, while others are perceptually imposed.

Part IV will show how the producers' conception of a good television broadcast imposes pictorial constraints not inherent in the medium on the types of stories that are gathered by the correspondent.

Television has certain advantages in covering a news story that are inherent in the correspondents' role conception as visualizers of the news. (See Chapter 2.) There are, however, constraints. One has already been mentioned: the viewers' inability to call back a story and the resulting need for the correspondent to prepare his story in simple and readily comprehensible terms. The pictorial constraints fall into six categories: (1) ideas are difficult to photograph; (2) "talking heads" are nonpictorial; (3) certain things should not be photographed for reasons of taste; (4) picture images favor certain personalities; (5) the very nature of many events prohibits their being photographed; and (6) the equipment needed to record the picture and sound reduces the mobility of the electronic journalist.

Edward R. Murrow gave constant acknowledgment to the problem of reporting news through pictures. How you photograph the ideas in a man's mind is the dilemma. Paul White, correspondent and former head of CBS News, has written, "Television's chief flaw in news coverage today is inherent in the news itself. News so often nowadays is ideas. Ideas are hard to photograph." (1953, p. 84.) There are some news stories that just cannot be told in photographs; each and every news beat has its own example. Washington correspondents attest to the fact that the nation's capital is not a picture story; foreign correspondents ask how they can be expected to photograph a Common Market story that takes place behind closed doors where cameras are barred; while Supreme Court correspondents have had to present such complicated and involved decisions as those on reapportionment and the balance of payments. Stories using figures cause a problem. A Pentagon correspondent said, "I've got this story about bombing in Vietnam. How do you illustrate one million tons of TNT? I have to translate it for television. I could translate it into box car lengths and truck loads but that's not the story." As James Reston wrote, "It's hard to psychoanalyze a President with a television camera or to take a film of what hasn't yet happened." (1966, p. 93.) Said one State Department correspondent: "It's my agony. New York wants to visualize as much as possible. How do you visualize policy in the making, secret negotiations, policy in transition? You have to reduce it to a 'stand up' talk piece."

The "standupper" or "talking head" are terms that describe a story in which the reporter simply stands in front of a camera attempting to put an event in the news into perspective only in words. All correspondents attested to the fact that there is a definite bias against "talking heads" as a general principal. Why? They are not visual. However, if the news is of overwhelming importance it will be broadcast, and it will not matter if the standupper is the only report, although sometimes it is as long as four to five minutes. Its nonvisual quality, nevertheless, is an important constraint. Said a well-known correspondent, "You know that the network is not interested in a talking-head piece so you don't press for it and it's not broadcast."

There was a discernible degree of discontent about the producers' dislike of the standupper as not visual, especially in Washington, where few, if any, of the stories are naturally pictorial. Most correspondents prefer to cover a visual subject, but there is a wide-spread undercurrent of dissatisfaction among them that more time is not given to standuppers that give the correspondents greater time to interpret the events they are trying to photograph. That is, in their professional judgment the pictorial valuation is constraining them from fulfilling their complete journalistic responsibilities.

Obviously certain pictures are withheld for reasons of taste. Said a former Saigon correspondent, "Television exercises a kind of self-censorship. We are careful about what we show in hospitals and how some people got burned by the bombs." There are many examples, including such items as pornography, personal tragedy, and live murder. Often they are described verbally by the correspondent, but the complementing picture is absented.

Television favors some personalities and not others. "Joseph McCarthy was great television: he was active and he knew how to react on camera," said a veteran correspondent who had reported during that period. Murrow hesitated after his televised program with McCarthy and offered a reflective thought:

> Is it not possible . . . that an infectious
> smile, eyes that seem remarkable for the
> depth of their sincerity, a cultivated air
> of authority, may attract a huge television
> audience, regardless of the violence that may
> be done to truth or objectivity? (Kendrick,
> 1969, p. 67.)

A Washington correspondent said:

> Look at George Meany. He is colorful and
> his language is evocative. He always makes
> a good film story. Elliott Richardson, on
> the other hand, with his Harvard accent and
> his Brahman ways, is very colorless, and we
> usually give it to Walter in New York to
> talk the news about him.

Both of these factors, censorship for taste and the photogenic quality of some personalities, although not crucial,
are mechanical constraints more predominant in this medium.
    There does not exist a television camera on every
street corner, in every public and private abode, or tuned
into the thought patterns of potential news makers. While
this probably would not be a desirable circumstance, it
does create a logistical problem for television. Six
bombs go off in a dance hall in Algiers. How do you
photograph it? In Paris the correspondent is sitting in
an outdoor cafe and sees a U.S. government official, sup-
posedly in Washington, pass his table. How do you photograph the story when the camera crew is back at the bureau? Most international events do not wait for the camera crews to arrive and set up their equipment. While
the newspaper reporter can pick up the details and phone
or cable in the story to New York in much the same manner
as he would for most events, the television correspondent
finds himself with all his modern equipment at the scene
after the fact. He needs to find someone or something to
report. He cannot provide the visual evidence of the
event and must try to show the aftermath evidence. "The
need for picture and sound, and to translate a past event
into television terms," says a Paris correspondent, "makes
television news harder to do." A good many television
broadcasts are visual accounts of the scene of an event
after the fact, descriptive recreations of that event,
limited by the mechanics of the medium.
    Finally, the equipment needed to record sound and
picture is cumbersome. Observed Theodore H. White: "Television is a medium where you are carrying a twelve ton
pen and you have a hundred people helping you carry it."
(1969-70, p. 10.) There are technical and logistical considerations in covering a news story that are relevant
only to television. For example, what locations are suit-
able for deployment of cameras and equipment? "The coverage is influenced by ideas about how the equipment can be
put to best use. (Cameras are obviously less mobile than

the roving eyes of reporters and so many decisions need to be made in advance.)" (Lee, 1970, p. 112.) How extensive will that coverage be?

> The extent to which news content is, or should be, guided by available visual material and commentary is restricted to what is shown on the screen. Whatever the decision, it affects the image the viewer perceives, particularly when events shown are ambiguous. (Ibid.)

Moving the film presents such problems as having trucks at an airport to move equipment to the scene of the event once it arrives; getting satellite time for transmission from Hong Kong to New York; or transporting the film from Kennedy Airport to Midtown. The networks have special motorcycle couriers to carry the film reels through city traffic, to avoid what might be crucial delays during rush-hour traffic, which occurs at exactly the time most film is being sent in for the evening broadcast.

The mechanical and technical capabilities of this medium have increased enormously since its initial inception, and the news staffs are able to cover more news faster and with greater depth. The 1960s were the beginning of the satellite age in television news. Satellites have enabled the exchange of audio-visual information beyond the limits of line-of-sight transmission between sending and receiving points. Technically, the satellite enables transmission from any one point on the globe to any other point, from Asia to Africa, Australia to New York, Los Angeles to Washington. Satellite transmission is still very expensive, about $2,300 per minute, and its use is relatively slight although increasing; 40 hours of material were transmitted in 1965, while 660 were sent in 1968. The use of satellite transmission is determined by the importance of the story and the availability of circuits and is a management-approved decision.

Other technical improvements include full-time leased cable lines to Europe and Asia (the networks are no longer dependent upon commercial lines) and teleprinter and printout circuitry. Telex equipment has improved to such a degree that it takes only ten seconds for a message sent from Tel Aviv to be received in New York. Finally, television news is now broadcast in color.

Mobility of equipment has increased with new techniques and miniaturization. Logistically it is now

74

possible to transmit, via coaxial cable, the audio-visual story instantaneously (or prerecorded) to the Washington or New York bureaus without nonmechanical intermediary transmitters. However, the equipment problem still exists. According to Walter Cronkite:

> Our tools still are somewhat gross. . . .
> Miniaturization and other developments
> eventually will solve our problem, but for
> the moment our camera and our lights and
> our tape trucks and even our microphones
> are obtrusive. It is probably true that
> their presence can alter an event, and it
> probably also is true that they alter it
> even more than the presence of reporters
> with pad and pencil, although we try to
> minimize our visibility. (December 1970,
> p. 54.)

The bulk of the electronic equipment, the limited range of the camera eye, and the need to have a sufficient quantity of light cause important mechanical constraints. Thomas Whiteside illustrates the problems involved in covering a story burdened with electronic cameras and the constraints imposed by the cameras' lenses as they affected television coverage at the Democratic Convention in 1968:

> I believe part of the answer is that indi-
> vidual reporters and photographers possess
> much greater mobility in such scenes . . .
> of disorder than do television crews, bur-
> dened by cameras, lights, and sound equip-
> ment (and when the television crews are
> working with electronic rather than film
> cameras, their equipment usually is tied by
> coaxial umbilical cord to a parent truck
> carrying recording and relaying equipment).
> Television people usually need room in which
> to operate; they work only with difficulty
> in groups. The electronic cameras on top of
> a mobile television unit have an elevated
> view and are equipped with lenses that can
> zoom in or out of scenes in a telescopic
> manner, and this is a great advantage in
> certain situations, but again not necessar-
> ily in crowds, since an overhead telescopic
> show of part of a dense crowd usually gives

75

such a foreshortened effect that action
taking place within the crowd is hard to
distinguish--especially during a scuffle,
when some of the people involved may be on
the ground and out of sight (a still pho-
tographer, using a miniature camera and a
wide-angle lens, can work very close to his
subject, and encompass a great deal of action in his field of view). Further, a
press reporter is in a better position to
isolate and record the relationship between
a particular action and reaction in a crowd
or confrontation; when he sees, for example,
a provocation such as a taunt that is followed by some reaction on the part of the
police, he connects the two in his account;
the television cameraman, unless he trains
his lens continuously on one spot, is hard
put to record the instant when provocation
draws police action. He may record the
police reaction, but his camera has no mem-
ory of what happened before he pressed the
camera trigger; it has no capacity for generalization, and the cameraman himself is
no writer; he usually hands his film on to
a courier with a hasty note about the subject matter. (1968-69, p. 49.)

At present scientists are working on a camera that
can record pictures in any light that is sufficient for
the human eye. This still remains to be employed for
widespread commercial television use. Until then the need
for artificial light remains an important constraining
factor for the television journalist:

It comes up when news develops in darkness
out of doors: a military maneuver, an ac-
cident, a demonstration. The battery-
powered handlights which cameramen call
sun-guns illuminate a foreground; but instead of a middle distance there is black-
ness. The extent of the scene, the size of
the crowd, is hidden. This is why there was
a slightly disproportionate emphasis on
fires in the television coverage of such
disturbances as the one at Cleveland in July

1968. Besides being a powerful symbol of
pillage and ruin, a fire is its own source
of light. (Whale, 1969, p. 30.)

These constraints are readily discussed by the television correspondents, and a sampling of their responses
is illustrative of their awareness of them. Said a State
Department correspondent, "Everywhere you go the equipment hampers you. No one likes to be on camera. It makes
things less informal. It's a very different atmosphere
talking to someone at State on camera than it is at a pad
and pencil conference." A foreign correspondent just returned from Israel gave this example:

With the camera it is very difficult to get
some places and you're not always welcome.
The Israelis captured some important Russian
secret equipment at the Bar Lev line. The
pad and pencil correspondent was permitted
to go, but it was weeks before the television correspondents were flown in.

"You're never incognito," lamented a woman correspondent
with experience in Vietnam.

Television equipment is bulky and obtrusive, and its
presence is obvious when it arrives on the scene. Because
the television news story involves not only the reportage
of the story but a visual account that requires electronic
equipment to record and transmit it, production is not the
product of one person but of a team. Indeed, what particularly distinguishes television news reporting is that
it is a cooperative effort between the correspondent, the
cameraman, the soundman, and most recently the field producer. "Television is a cumbersome medium," says Walter
Cronkite. "It takes about four TV people to every one
reporter to cover such a story." (Newsweek, February 21,
1972, "Made for Television," p. 100.) Television is group
journalism; it takes a lot of people to carry its paper and
pencil. Team production requires a congenial relationship among all concerned, and the personality interplay
is important. The commitment of the crew and the reporter
to one another and to the story are crucial to the team's
smooth functioning and the success of the filmed report.
Theodore H. White wrote about one pervasive difficulty
involved in shooting his television version of The Making
of the President 1968:

We had two crews on the road all the time.
. . . I was busy writing my book and reporting and I couldn't direct the film
crews, so about nine months later when I
finally got to Hollywood to put the film
together, I found that these young people
absolutely adored Eugene McCarthy and
Robert Kennedy and there was not a bad shot
of either Gene McCarthy or Bobby Kennedy
in the thousands and thousands of feet that
we took. The images were glowing. On the
other hand, these people who worked with me
did not bring back one human shot of Hubert
Humphrey. . . . I had to work with film
that showed Hubert Humphrey only as a sinis-
ter character. Such problems are even more
pointed when you come to the daily TV shows.
You're in the hands of the hundreds of people who are feeding material to you. No
single person controls television. (1969-70,
p. 10.)

The cumbersomeness of these tools has prompted many
critics to conclude that the function of the television
correspondent has changed. That is, they say, he finds
himself preoccupied with the logistical problems of pho-
tographing the story, of "getting the picture"; and the
reporting aspect, including the search for news and the
surfacing of important stories, becomes secondary.
The validity of this criticism will be discussed
later in this chapter. However, it is important to indicate that network news departments were, and still are,
concerned that the equipment might overwhelm the newsgathering responsibilities of the correspondent. It was
this fear that prompted the network evening news programs
to introduce the role of field producer, as employed by
the documentary program. The need for a field producer
developed as television began to devote more time to the
evening news and to produce longer film stories, and as
the cost of producing these mini-documentaries soared.
The field producer is the new member on the team and is
ostensibly there to relieve the correspondent of logistical problems, freeing him to pursue his story with
greater care. This is how one director of operations
explained it:

A man who is a competent newspaper reporter
needs to know very little about the home

office. For example, how linotype works.
In broadcasting we want our correspondents
to be knowledgeable about the technical aspects so that he can translate the story
into film. But ordinarily, in addition to
these considerations he has had to worry not
only about directing and explaining the
story to the cameraman and soundman but to
concern himself with equipment availability,
satellite feeds and so on. The field producer relieves the correspondent of many of
these technical problems. He's essentially
another hand on the scene. While the correspondent is gathering the story the field
producer can move in the equipment and prepare for the finished product's return to
New York.

Correspondents have mixed feelings about field producers, however, and the division often occurs between
older and younger correspondents, the latter more accepting of the new addition. Said one young foreign correspondent formerly assigned to Latin America:

I think it's one of the most valuable additions. I'd spend 30 to 40 percent of my
time when alone working on logistical problems. The field producer does that now.
Also, two heads are better than one and in
an informal way, over drinks, in the car,
etc., we have brainstorming sessions.

Another said: "The producers went out in advance and laid
out the story. I was responsible for the attitude of the
story and the writing followed it."
The addition of a field producer contains some potential difficulties, the most prominent being the question
of who has final say and responsibility. Everyone in the
management sector will insist that it is the correspondent,
but most correspondents can provide examples of important
exceptions to this rule. A Paris correspondent found that
there were both positive and negative values in having a
field producer:

In Paris it's good to have the producer
(he's usually in London) to bounce ideas
back and forth. It's better to have him
in London than New York, where they are

79

surrounded by American problems. The man
in London reads the London _Times_ as well as
the New York _Times_ and is in Europe. He is
physically and emotionally closer and his
job is to listen to me and to get my story.
He can sell the story to New York and is
also more likely to do the kind of story
New York is interested in. On the other
hand, they often come over here with preconceived notions and do not always fit into
the reality of the scene. For example, when
I was in Israel I had six pieces I wanted
to do on the war of attrition. I was going
to focus on the military and the field producer came with the idea that there was a
youth revolt. But there just wasn't a
youth revolt--a gap but basically no revolt.
It took me a long time to get this notion
out of his head. We got a compromise: we
talked about youth but didn't say much.

The danger of having a field producer is that the
correspondent may end up doing only the writing and talking of the story.

In the old days [the 1950s] you went from
Suez to Kenya just gathering background
materials for a story. Today, before the
team goes out on the scene, they have a
clearer idea of what they want. The role
of the correspondent has been diminished.
There is more help whether he wants it or
not.

Two clear types of field producers were described.
The first is the "team man." In this relationship the
correspondent is the head and it is his or her view of
the story that prevails. The other is the "arrogant"
type, who comes on the scene unfamiliar with the story
and with a preconceived notion of what is wanted; and the
correspondent ends up writing the story the way the field
producer prescribes it. Said one Congressional correspondent about this type:

He's inexperienced in Congressional affairs
and comes with a "visual" concept of the
story. He comes here, is overwhelmed with

his first impression, can't put it into perspective, and tends to overdramatize. He should be well versed in the area so that he can recognize the news that will have impact. The problem is who has the last word.

The incorporation of the field producer into the "team" journalism of television is an important factor to keep in mind for our understanding of the newsgathering process. On average the field producer has about 50 percent less journalistic experience in either newspapers or television than has the correspondent. He is more likely to have been trained in television and is recruited to this position not for his journalistic qualifications but rather for his understanding of, and ability to deal with, the technical capabilities of the medium, especially the ability to produce visually interesting news reports. Very often, particularly out in the field, the field producer is the intermediary, if not the direct link, between the correspondent and the New York producer. More often than not, having the same training, and with career aims geared toward the position of executive producer of the evening news program, the field producer reflects the same tastes, opinions about the news, and compositional ideas as the producers who compose the broadcast in New York.*

A sampling of their attitudes toward the news indicates a disproportionate interest in the visual over the audio (25 percent visual and 75 percent audio-visual, respectively), more of a desire to humanize the stories, and a greater propensity to stress the difficulty of covering stories on economics and ideas and correspondingly less interest in covering such stories. He is not often assigned to a regular beat and is likely to be less well-informed and less able to "grasp the pulse of the news" than the correspondent, who in addition has more experience in gathering news.

Very often the producer does have sway over the direction of the story. For instance, the correspondent may think the producer understands the desires of New York better. The correspondent may also be insecure about his own comprehension of the mechanics of the medium, or the

---

*The same director of operations quoted above, later described the field producer as "usually the one who came up with the ideas on how to better package the product."

producer may be able to convince New York that the story
is as he sees it and get New York to send a directive to
the correspondent.

Correspondents are quite conscious of the presence
of the field producer. A new addition to the group, his
influence is potentially more threatening to the correspondent's primacy than the simpler mechanical inputs of
the cameraman and the soundman. The field producer provides a more important and closer link with New York and
increases the likelihood that the final story will reflect the values of the broadcast center.

THE HIGH COST OF TELEVISION NEWS

Television is a very expensive medium for producing
news stories. A major expense for every news operation
is salaries, and television correspondents' wages are
double those of their newspaper colleagues. Production
costs are higher as well. In 1970, according to the FCC,
the three networks spent an estimated $115,538,000 on
news and public affairs, exclusive of sports. Divided
among the networks, the estimates are that ABC spent about
$30 million, NBC about $36 million, and CBS about $49
million (Powers and Oppenheim, 1972, p. 12).* An expensive year for television was 1968, which included the
assassinations of Martin Luther King and Senator Robert F.
Kennedy, two political conventions, and a Presidential
election. Estimated costs for that year exceed $150 mil-
lion, with an estimated cost for the coverage of the
Presidential campaign set at $30 million. In 1970 the
costs for production of NBC's Nightly News were estimated
at $9 million. The following is a list of estimated ex-
penses by all three networks for major news coverage of
important events:

- Pope Paul's visit to the United States (one day):
  $10 million
- a space flight: $1 million
- a moon shot: $2.5 million
- coverage of the Middle East conflict (1967): $3
  million per network

---

*NBC estimated in 1966 that its local cost for net-
work news, radio news programming, and owned television
stations to be $60 million (Robert Kintner, Letter to the
Chairman of the Board of NBC, February 25, 1966).

- a national convention: $10 million
- one year of Vietnam coverage: $5 million
- Nixon's trip to China: at least $3 million per
  network for the period the President was there.
- 1974 election-night coverage: $8.5 million

In 1965 NBC Nightly News broadcast a five-minute
story on the royalists in Yemen. That story cost $20,000
to produce.

There is cross-utilization of staff and equipment,
and while the news sector is a non-profit-making division
as a whole, the evening news telecast does not lose money.
Sometimes the daily half-hour broadcast brings in as much
as $34 million a year.

Satellite transmission is very expensive, and transporting equipment, retrieving film, and leasing cable
lines also contribute to the high cost of producing television news stories. A decision to satellite in a story
is based on the worth of the story compared to its cost
of transmission. Less than 25 percent of the budget for
film stories is allotted for enterprise, or nonroutine,
stories, since cost limits the number of news teams a
network can afford to assign to a particular story, or
indeed to the events they have funds to cover. Theodore
H. White explained:

> To cover technologically in pictures a
> thing like the Arab-Israeli war, the Viet-
> nam war, a great assassination, a national
> convention requires millions of dollars.
> You can't have a hundred TV stations in the
> country each giving its own point of view
> nationally and each reporting a national
> election. The coverage is so expensive.
> (1969-70, p. 10.)

The exorbitant cost, which has caused most local stations to depend on the three networks to cover these
stories, also limits the amount of personnel the networks
can provide. Said a State Department correspondent: "The
New York Times has at least three correspondents covering
this place. I'm the only one from my network. If I'm
out sick or covering a special story we have no one here."
That is, television does not have the number of newsmen
available to cover stories that major newspapers and wire
services have. While the New York Times has four correspondents at State, two or three at the Pentagon, four at
Capitol Hill, and so forth, each network has only one

correspondent covering each of these beats. There are
fewer film crews available. Often the same crew that recorded the story at State is filming at the Pentagon,
while the White House correspondent anxiously awaits their
arrival at 5 p.m. In short, the cost of production is
very high for television news, and the networks are con-
strained in their ability to mechanically cover all events
of major concern with the depth and variety available to
newspapers.

STORIES IN TIME NOT SPACE

One of the most serious differences between television and newspapers is that television's concern is not
with space, but with time. A television correspondent
writes his story in terms of minutes and seconds and not
in column inches or hundreds of words. Within a one- or
two-minute time slot he must fit the necessary words and
pictures to tell his story. Time affects the product in
a number of ways: the broadcast is nonselective; the
format is prescribed; and the reports must be brief and
capsulated.

A television news broadcast does not permit the
viewer to select the stories he is interested in or to
ignore others. A newspaper reader can look at the front-
page headline, find a story on the Middle East that interests him, and read as much of that story as he chooses.
The reader may then pass over a story on police corruption
and turn to the editorial page to read his favorite colum-
nist. A special story on Albert Einstein may be too long
to read on the train from Westchester to New York, so the
reader saves it for after dinner. This is not possible
with television: the television viewer must accept the
newscaster's choice. The broadcast is one half-hour long
and shown at one specific time each day. The viewer's eye
cannot skip over the inflation story he has seen so much
of; he may be tired of Watergate, but there it is again,
and he can't avoid it by turning to another section. The
correspondents are well aware of this constraint.

> If we could by some magic show the front
> page that we put out, as a totality, let-
> ting people pick and choose what they want,
> they'd be more comfortable. But we can't.
> So we must hit them with the unemployment
> figures and then pile on the war news and

then the natural disasters and so on. It's
a restriction built into the medium. (Penthouse, 1972, p. 40.)

Television, too, cannot be selective of its audience.
It aims for the broad spectrum of the national audience
and cannot appeal to the special interests of limited
audience groups. Therefore there are no horoscopes, rec-
ipes, or chess articles on network news. Limited-interest
audiences cannot select these stories, and the wider audience, which is not interested in the subject, could not
select it out. This also seems to be what prevents the
presentation of opinion in controversy on the network
broadcasts: in a newspaper it can be selected out by the
reader.
The correspondent and producer must also consider the
audience attention span. The viewer cannot choose to read
only the first three paragraphs and ignore the story's
continuation on page two: in television there are no back
pages; there is only a page one. The telecast must also
sustain the viewer's attention throughout the thirty-
minute broadcast. Finally, a newspaper can vary the presentation of "what is news" and map out a hierarchy of
emphasis through placement and the size and boldness of
the printed headline. Television has only placement to
work with to indicate hierarchy, since the presentation
of the story usually tends to receive equal emphasis.*
The network newscast is broadcast in the early evening, from 6 to 6:30, from 6:30 to 7, or from 7 to 7:30
depending on the network and the local affiliate. This
time slot is a hangover from radio. Ostensibly the broadcast is 30 minutes, but after commercials, announcements,
and credits, the average broadcast ranges from 23 to 25
minutes. A half-hour of broadcast time is roughly 2,500
to 3,000 words, less than one-half the amount of words
contained on the first page of the New York Times.† There
is validity, however, in William Small's comment: "The
power of television is hardly measured by the number of
words or pictures it offers. The power is on 'how' it
does this and how it is received." (1970, p. 13.) In
support of the "how" of television, Walter Cronkite stated:

---

*Consideration of these latter characteristics is
primarily the responsibility of the producers and will be
discussed at length in Part IV.
†Probably more, however, than the average newspaper
reader finds in his local paper.

A major problem is that imposed by the
clock. . . . Clearly the structure demands
tightness of writing and editing, and selection unknown to any other form of journalism. But look what we do with that time.
Twenty items in an average newscast--some
but a paragraph long, but all with the essential information to provide at least a
guide to our world that day. Film clips
that, in a way available to no other medium
introduce our viewers to the people and the
places that make the news. Investigative
reporting--pocket documentaries--that expose
weaknesses in our democratic fabric. . . .
Feature film reports that explore the by-
ways of America and assure us that the whole
world hasn't turned topsy-turvy. Graphics
that in a few seconds communicate a great
deal of information. Clearly labeled analysis, or commentary, on the news. (1969.)

The specifics of this statement, however, need exploration. That twenty different news items are presented
within a twenty-five-minute newscast is the result of two
factors: (1) many items of importance that need to be
covered within a limited allotment of time and (2) a conception of the limited attention span of the television
viewing audience. As a result the electronic journalist
can present only a capsule of the total news story. Explained David Brinkley, "It is impossible--physically and
otherwise--to cover news in complete and voluminous detail
on television. It just cannot be done." (Hohenberg,
1971, p. 189.) In September 1963, when the networks increased their time allotments to one-half hour, the mini-
documentaries, or "pocket documentaries," were incorporated
into the news programs and television news moved away from
being simply a headline service. However, almost all the
correspondents pointed to the problem of telling the story
in one minute and twenty seconds, or even in three or four
minutes.* "We can't tell the whole story in a half-hour
news program. We can't go into things in depth the way

---

*Most nonpicture stories read by the commentator are
no longer than 20 or 30 seconds. The "talking head"
story, considered nonvisual, is encouraged not to run
beyond one minute, and the producer accepts a two-minute
report only after great hesitation.

newspapers can. We give people the framework of what they
need to know." William Small, in a discussion of this
problem of capsulation, offered the following hypothetical
situation to illustrate this point:

> If Moses came down from Mount Sinai with
> the Ten Commandments in an era of television,
> he would certainly be greeted by camera
> crews.
> "What do you have?", they would ask.
> "I have the Ten Commandments," replies
> Moses.
> "Tell us about them but keep it to a
> minute and a half," they would say.
> Moses complies and that night on the
> news in still more abbreviated form, the
> story is told. The newscaster begins,
> "Today at Mount Sinai, Moses came down with
> Ten Commandments, the most important three
> of which are. . . ." (1970, p. 15.)

Correspondents agree that the need to capsulize often
leads to distortion, to being able to give only a headline
to one story and 20 seconds to another. It is felt that
if there were time to give a second paragraph or explain
the first paragraph and make it clearer, then the reports
could be more objective.

International affairs stories are among the most difficult to cover. They are acknowledged to be complex, and
the viewer is perceived to lack the background for full
comprehension. During a 30-minute broadcast, the political debates cannot be adequately covered. In November
1971 NBC received a secret copy of the Pentagon Papers,
soon after the New York _Times_ received its copy. Three
television correspondents were put to work on it. Their
report was never made. "The complexities and nuances were
too hard to handle on television. You couldn't read it
all and it wasn't visual and all we could do, at best, was
to skim the highlights. The best thing to do is an hour
documentary on the subject. We necessarily have to be
brief and simple."*

---

*The more complicated news stories, the longer re-
ports, and those items that might find a spot on page two
of a newspaper are very often broadcast on the morning
news program or given to syndication, where the broadcast
is longer and there is less of a demand for speed and
currency.

Television tries to cope with complex or ongoing stories by telling them in parts. For example, in April 1970 correspondent John Laurence did a six-segment story on the activities of Company C of the 2nd Battalion of the 7th Cavalry, 1st Airborne Cavalry Division, U.S. Army, in Vietnam. Separate segments dealt with mail delivery, a departing captain, the soldiers' hopes and fears, a soldier who collapsed from overwork and the heat, and a near mutiny. However, this tends to promote fragmentation and an incomplete picture, particularly if the viewer misses important parts of the series. Michael Arlen wrote representatively of correspondent dissatisfaction with the fragmented reporting from Vietnam:

> I think it is indeed true that, as in the
> case of Vietnam, a highly complex political
> situation was treated for many years by
> televising news as a largely military opera-
> tion--the dramatic battle for Hill 937, and
> so forth. Not only that, but the whole war
> was presented to us in isolated, disconnected
> bits of detail--a 30-second bombing raid
> here, a two-minute film clip of Khe Sanh
> there, another minute of President Johnson
> at the Manila Conference, 30 seconds of a
> helicopter assault--with the result that,
> even if we had been given the real informa-
> tion we needed to come to terms with the war,
> the way we were given it made it doubly dif-
> ficult. (1972, p. 240.)

Correspondents are well aware of these handicaps and try to balance the need to present a comprehensive analysis of the news event with the limitations of time and the viewer's attention span. They feel restricted, however. Many complained that the format of the program puts them on "the edge of strangulation"; they want to break out of the format. They very often complained that correspondents are inadequately used at the networks.

> We are so preoccupied with the daily news
> developments and putting it on film in the
> shortest period of time that we have little
> opportunity to give perspective or an over-
> view of what happened today, this week or
> during the month. The morning news does it
> but who watches?

Or, "We have to break the format. The correspondents should talk and debate the news instead of preparing, rehearsing, and filming it. We would get more criticism but we would have more integrity and the viewer would get more candor."

There was general dissatisfaction among the correspondents, and many pointed to a 60-minute evening newscast as an alternative. But even this perception supports the contention of television's inadequacy of format for dealing efficaciously with the daily news. CBS News president Salant acknowledged the need for more time.

> We need an hour news show every night and an extra hour of prime time for news every week. We can't give stories enough length or depth. Things are always left out. There is a backlog of mini-documentaries, in-depth looks at problems, that don't get on the air because we just don't have the time. (Barrett, 1969, p. 16.)

Eric Sevareid envisions a different format:

> In that hour, we could do what we should always be doing, in my long-sustained opinion: we could provide room for rebuttals . . . from ordinary listeners, letters to the editor, if you wish. For years the situation has cried out for this and had we been doing it for years, perhaps much of the accumulating gas of resentment would have escaped from the boiler in a normal fashion. (Barrett, 1970, p. 72.)

The likelihood of this kind of new format seems to be very slight. No one interviewed thought it would come about soon, although all pointed to its need. The loss of an additional half-hour of commercial entertainment time was most often mentioned and also the FCC ruling requiring an additional half-hour of prime time that must be produced locally and therefore lost to total available network prime time. Local stations also pose a problem. In December 1968 NBC News extended its nightly report by one-half hour to show the Apollo VIII moon flight and the release of the Pueblo crew in Korea. Other examples included a half-hour, five-day extension for coverage of Nixon's trip to Europe and the highlights of the Senate debate on the ABM. Commercial considerations (discussed in the next section) brought loud complaints from the local affiliates in each instance, however.

Speed of transmission is still another time factor that should receive brief mention. Most correspondents cited the importance of getting the fast-breaking story into New York in time for broadcast. Television journalists sometimes are guilty of the same tendency toward speed as the newspaperman; that is, overanxiousness to scoop the competition on a fast-breaking event, with facts that are inadequately confirmed and sometimes misinformation. This does not occur frequently, however, and certainly is not distinctive of the electronic medium.

The technical capabilities of electronics have enabled the television press to telescope time and report its story in a matter of hours instead of days or weeks. Here is how one correspondent is affected by the time difference in television:

> When I worked for the Herald Tribune, I'd see what everybody had said in the afternoon papers, what AP and UP and the Washington Post were going to say the next morning, and then I'd get started writing at 6 o'clock; I had all the time in the world. And editors would read it before it got into print. In television, there is little or no time to edit a fast-breaking story. You rely on the ability and judgement of the man on the scene, whose "copy" goes direct to the viewers at home. (Kintner, 1965, p. 52.)

Although television correspondents and producers also have the benefit of the guidance of the AP and UPI stories and the newspapers printed earlier that day, their deadline is different, and the correspondent's story has less opportunity to be edited.

THE CAMERA-CREATED EVENT

In covering certain stories, the mechanical characteristics of the medium sometimes have a tendency to prompt events that would not have occurred had not their bulky equipment happened on the scene; that is, there are medium-created events. How the medium affects the outcome of events and how participants use the medium to their own ends would make an interesting follow-up study to this one but cannot be definitively analyzed here, only described. What is important to note is the awareness among the television news actors of this phenomenon and the safeguards taken to prevent media distortion. There are many instances in which the medium has been accused of causing an event. These range from the simple interview question, the response to which "makes news"; to the more serious situation in which the camera is victim to an event controlled by participants whose sole purpose is to gain widespread dissemination of their story; or to the actual staging of an event by the correspondent, such as a CBS documentary about a Chicago marijuana party. This is what Daniel Boorstin (1961) has labeled a "pseudo-event."

"Television has been burned and we learn from our mistakes," commented a former Vietnam correspondent. Indeed, the correspondents were all too well aware of this ability of the medium to cause events, whether they cited the findings of the Kerner Commission Report;* their experience with staged Buddhist protests in Vietnam, which were ostensibly against the ruling South Vietnamese regime, but protesters carried placards that were written in English and apparently aimed toward the television cameras for transmission to an American viewing audience; or the circumstance of a correspondent arriving early at a protest scene, to discover the demonstrators lounging about awaiting arrival of the cameras before commencing their "spontaneous violent indignation against the offender." Correspondents acknowledge these mistakes of the past, and while anxious not to let them occur again ("If the story is affected by our presence we cap our cameras and move away from it"), none totally discount the possibility of their reoccurrence in some new form of activity for which they will be unprepared to take adequate safeguards. The Langs illustrate the subtlety of this phenomenon:

> There are TV-created events, even though
> they can never be manufactured out of whole
> cloth. In some instances, the event hap-
> pens only because of television--as when we

---

*The Kerner Commission, established by President Johnson to investigate the 1967 riots in major American cities, concluded that television's reportage of the events in one city had a tendency to promote similar reactions in other cities.

are dealing with an interview show, televised debates, or the fast count and projection of early election returns, when the
major news services pool their resources.
In other instances, television itself becomes the "event." Thus, it is quite clear
by hindsight that the furor in 1952 over
whether TV should cover the platform and
credentials hearings provided the Eisenhower
forces with an issue that helped assure his
victory over Taft. They clearly exploited
the presence of television to transform a
simple procedural issue into an issue of
"fair play"--moral issue. (1968, p. 155.)

Television correspondents are very self-conscious about
the mechanical nature of the medium and the fact that it
can change, alter, or create events. They recognize that
in some cases this does potentially constrain their activities. As television has become an older medium, however,
and correspondents have made mistakes and gotten "burned"
covering such events as the Chicago Convention, the Vietnam War, and antiwar protests, they have become ever more
conscious of their mechanical effect, more experienced in
the handling of their medium. As a result the long-term
prognosis is that they will be better able to report the
news and less likely to make the news inadvertently.
    Management policy is explicit in its directives ac-
knowledging this potential danger and insists that the
correspondent be ever alert not to fall victim to this
phenomenon. CBS policy stipulates that there

        shall be no recreation, no staging, no pro-
        motion technique which would give the viewer
        an impression of any fact other than the
        actual fact, no matter how minor or seemingly
        inconsequential. The only way there can be
        certainty is not to let the bars down at all.
        Anything which gives the viewer an impression
        of time, place, event, or person other than
        the actual fact as it is being recorded and
        broadcast cannot be tolerated. I recognize
        that strict application of this policy will
        result in higher costs and in a less techni-
        cally perfect or interesting "story" in cer-
        tain instances. But our field is journalism,
        not show business. (CBS policy notes from the
        president, unpublished memo, June 28, 1971.)

4

THE CORRESPONDENT'S VIEW OF THE STRUCTURAL CHARACTERISTICS OF TELEVISION

There are four distinguishable structural characteristics of television that potentially affect the correspondent's newsgathering activities. First, television
reaches a large national audience. Second, in the field
of news the networks are highly competitive, predominantly
for the same audience. Nevertheless, they operate within
a medium that has chosen as its primary communication function not journalism but entertainment. Third, in its
journalistic function television is subject to legal and
"public accountability" criteria not prescribed for the
other journalistic media. Finally, the decision-making
hierarchies at the networks are nonjournalistic in nature
and subject to structural demands that are nonexistent or
potentially less constraining in other media. Each of
these structural characteristics requires elaboration and
analysis for understanding the structural constraints imposed upon the electronic journalist.

A NATIONAL AUDIENCE

All three networks broadcast their newscasts to more
than 24 million households, daily and simultaneously, in
New York, Key West, New Orleans, Los Angeles, Seattle,
Chicago, Andover, and all points in between. It is a mass
audience, and it is a national audience; its composition
is nonselective and evanescent. The newscast is usually
transmitted directly into the home without any advance
warning of its content and without being able to select
its audience.

The viewing audience is comprised of two different
groups. (1) The print-oriented viewers watch the tele-

vision newscast as a supplement to their regular reading
of newspapers and magazines. They are interested in "seeing" the events and actors in the news and are concerned
with the "content" of the news. (2) The electronic-
oriented audience relies almost exclusively on television
for its news and in general includes the most constant and
heavy users of television for entertainment. (Lang and
Lang, 1968, p. 159). Television's problem is twofold:
not to talk down to the print-oriented group, and at the
same instant not to lose the larger electronic-oriented
group, which it must provide with the necessary information for the proper functioning of the democratic system.
Ithiel de Sola Pool describes the mechanical fact and
structural difficulty distinctive to this medium:

> One of the disadvantages of TV as against
> any print medium is that it has no easy way
> of satisfying many minorities at once. You
> can't run small, modest stories on this and
> that, expecting that people will pick and
> choose among them. In a newspaper the reader
> will pick the ones he wants and leave 75% of
> the paper unread. TV must go for the audience
> as a whole. (de Sola Pool, 1970, p. 20.)

Somehow that mass, national audience has to be reached,
attracted and maintained. The maintenance of that audience and the selection of content actually broadcast is
the responsibility of the executive producer and will be
discussed in the next chapter. However, it is important
to ask the electronic journalist how the national and
mass character of this audience affects the writing of
the television news story.

The correspondents' response to this query ranged
from that of a veteran foreign correspondent, now an executive in the News Department, who commented that "we
are trying to attract a mass audience--the fellow in the
T-shirt, beer can in hand, in Podunkville," to the description by Alexander Kendrick of Edward R. Murrow's
approach:

> He never addressed himself to some imag-
> ined or personalized figure or group in
> the audience as others did, but only to
> the subject at hand, and to the microphone.
> He was always more concerned with what he
> had to say than to whom. (1969, p. 347.)

Television correspondents have been criticized for
writing news with an image of their audience geared to the
lowest common denominator. This criticism finds some support among the answers received from correspondents, particularly at one network (the same network as that of the
executive quoted above). It would be unfair and incorrect
to say that this is the prevailing attitude among electronic journalists, however. Most of them have two criteria by which they judge their audience. First, since
they realize that they are writing for a national audience,
their images tend to reflect those of the wire services:
they tend to aim at the middle, to the viewers who require
their information simply and clearly stated. Said a Vietnam correspondent,

> I have no real concept of the audience. It's
> somewhere in the middle. Maybe the guy in
> Kansas. I tell it so that the people can
> understand it. My audience needs the ideas
> expressed simply and clearly, and accurately
> summarized, in plain and simple English.
> The New York _Times_ sees itself as a paper of
> record. We're not. We know that we are
> writers for a mass audience.

The second most prevalent criterion is professional;
that is, the correspondents write for themselves and their
colleagues. They have a professional conception of how
they should write the story. "Most of us have certain
standards when we write our stories. I have my own. In
that case you are not really thinking about an audience,
only the story and the camera." They seem most concerned
about the approval they receive from their colleagues as
they view their broadcasts and those of the competitors.*
Some correspondents feel that they have a specific audience to whom they especially appeal. This is most

---

*Each evening the correspondents stand before the
consoles at their bureaus and comment on the worth of
their colleagues' reports or provide excuses why their
pieces did not match the professionalism of their competitors'. They cheer the reports by their colleagues on
special assignment away from the bureau or remain silent
if they are poor, seemingly because their absence prohibits them from explaining the causes of obvious shortcomings.

prevalent among the "non-star" correspondents, who perceive their more limited audience to be "a little more
sophisticated," with a response large enough to justify
their staying on at the network.

As for the question of ratings, there is a certain
obvious pride in being employed by the network that is
first in the ratings or moving up, and conversely, defensiveness about being employed by the one that is slipping;
yet the general reaction among the correspondents was:
"If you showed me a ratings sheet I probably would not be
able to read it. Speak to the executives, it's their
problem."

The time of broadcast has an effect, although seemingly not crucial, on the correspondent's image of the
audience. A broadcast that is telecast in the early evening comes at a busy time in the home: children are doing homework; families are sitting down to dinner; people
are just returning home from work. Many have read much
of the daily news in the morning papers and want a wrap-
up of the day's events. At this hour the correspondent
perceives a fairly serious, mature individual viewing the
broadcast who is rather loyal to the news, "You either
watch the news or you don't, and if you do, you watch it
all the time."

Audience perceptions do, however, play an important
part in reporting the story from abroad. The American
correspondent always points to the importance of remember-
ing that while abroad he is writing for an American mass
audience. Said one Paris correspondent: "When I approach the story I have to bear in mind that it must have
some meaning for Americans. The audience is not very interested in things that are uniquely French. They are
interested if it has meaning for them." The monetary
crisis was described as important, but the Common Market,
usually not. Among Latin American correspondents, so
long "as America's ox was being gored" it was news; "But
Uruguay with 3 million people--how important is that to
the average American?" Most acknowledged that Western
Europe was most important to Americans because "that is
where most people have their roots." Said one of the
pioneer television journalists, "This is where we have
our ethnic ties, fought our wars, etc. Pearl Harbor made
us become oriented to the Far East. The Middle East appeals to the large Jewish population. Ireland is news
because of the many Irish in this country."

As the cold war declined, the daily report from Europe disappeared. The same was true of the news from

Japan. As Castro ceased to be news and anti-Americanism
ceased to flare out into the open, Latin American news
declined. Foreign news must be something that has "meaning" to Americans.

COMPETITION WITHIN AN ENTERTAINMENT MEDIUM

"Competition," wrote William Wood, "which had always
been keen among the networks has an intensity that has
not been seen among American journalists since the days
of Hearst and Pulitzer." (1967, p. 3.) That competition
among the networks is keen is obvious after only a half-
hour's conversation with a television correspondent or ten
minutes' presence at the production center. There is little exchange among correspondents working at different
networks.* There are gentlemen's agreements and there is
courteous talk, but the general relationship or objective
is "to beat the hell out of them." "I'll stop at nothing
to beat them," said a woman correspondent on her way to
the Far East. All actors attest to the importance of competition, whether it is because newspapers no longer have
this competition or because it challenges the television
correspondent to achieve his highest potential.

Competition among the networks is evaluated regularly
by three distinguishable criteria: (1) the speed and exclusiveness of the story, (2) editorial content, and (3)
technical quality.

"Being first" to broadcast a story is an important
indicator to gauge success or failure in the competitive
battle. NBC proudly displays its five "firsts" on China:
its correspondent was (1) the first to be permitted to
enter mainland China in 22 years; (2) the first U.S. television correspondent to report from Communist China;
(3) the first American correspondent to file a direct
report via telephone line from China to the United States
in 22 years. Its camera crew was (4) the first American
crew to shoot news film in Communist China and (5) the
first to send live television pictures from Hong Kong to
the United States that were taken in China.

---

*Correspondents at NBC tend to have a traditional
friendly relationship with AP and CBS with UPI. "It's
helpful and not competitive," said one correspondent. But
there are few friendships between CBS and NBC.

However, reacting faster than the competition, getting the exclusive story, is not a daily occurrence in
television. Occasionally one network will have film from
inside China or inside Cuba or pictures of a primitive
tribe in Australia, but the "scoop"--the report of a fast-
breaking event before the competition--is not very frequent. Said a foreign news editor: "Most of the reporters in an area have the same sources and access to the
same information--there is even the tendency to react to
the story with the same editorial judgment." Therefore
the correspondents compare the editorial content of a
story. Is there more than the wire services had? How
skillful was the network in picking out the essence of the
story and telling it in the shortest possible time? Was
it exciting? Was the interpretation right? These are
professional journalistic criteria.
Competition is also judged by pictorial criteria, the
visual quality of the story. Was it exciting? Was the
film editing better? Was there better technical quality
control? In sum, was it interesting visually? As the
news is broadcast the correspondents at each network gather
around the news desk and television set and exchange their
evaluations of the competitive race: "We got'm on that
one!" "Why didn't we have something on that?" "Theirs
was better visually but I'm glad we did ours that way."
Robert Kintner as early as 1965 could say,

> Competition between newspapers and broad-
> casters no longer exists in a true sense.
> The day of the extra is gone--a broadcaster
> can put the same news on the air, in starker
> detail, hours faster than a newspaper can
> set a banner headline and a one-paragraph
> bulletin, print the paper, and get it out
> onto the newsstands. (p. 50.)

But Murrow was right when he said: "It is an ancient and
sad fact that most people in network television and radio
have an exaggerated regard for what appears in print."
(Small, 1970, p. 21.) Although television does not compete with newspapers in speed or picture terms, the correspondent checks the New York Times, the Washington Post,
Time, and Newsweek regularly to compare how they handled
the same stories and to see if, perhaps, television had
the "scoop" on the newspaper and if television was given
credit. In actual practice, however, it very seldom occurs that the regular evening news reports scoop the
newspapers.

98

Competition among the networks is sharp, but so is the competition to get on the air, among correspondents within the network--I would be hard-pressed to determine which was more important to the individual correspondent. One State Department correspondent was particularly upset with the diminished role played by the State Department in foreign policy (from 1968 to 1972) and the centralization of policy decisions in the basement of the White House. This was less a theoretical conception of how government policy should be formed than a concern that the Vietnam story, Chinese-American relations, or East-West relations, normally stories for the State Department correspondent, now were under the purview of the White House correspondent. One needs only to witness a discussion among the head of the assignment desk in Washington and the White House and Pentagon correspondents as they argue about who does the story when the Secretary of Defense gives a policy statement on the lawn at the White House.

The executive producer in New York selects the stories that are finally broadcast. What criteria does he use? What kinds of stories does he seem to prefer? Each correspondent can, when he is willing, answer these questions rapidly and explicitly; he has thought about them often in the past. When a new executive producer is appointed, the correspondent spends much of his time evaluating this new man's behavior and selection criteria. When the correspondents congregate at lunch or in the newsroom, the most prevalent topic of discussion is the new producer's selection prejudices. Said one correspondent, "This is how I would do the story. But if I want to be sure it will get on the air I know that . . . [the executive producer] will want it to be a little more spicy." A Paris correspondent said, "This new guy, he wants fast-moving pictures. If I don't have them I think twice about pressing for the story." The examples are endless. The competition to get on the air is constant. This competition generally prevents a correspondent from specializing in a subject such as medicine or science, which would preclude him from frequent broadcast exposure.

As discussed earlier, one of the reasons the correspondent enters this branch of journalism is the ability to appeal to the audience more directly and personally. This requires that the correspondent find a time slot on the evening news, a decision made by the executive producer. The apprenticeship period, when his title is Reporter, promotes the competition within the network and also the need to direct attention to the selection criteria of the executive producer. The reporter is not paid a salary in any degree comparable to that received by the correspondents, but the reporters are given the opportunity to supplement this through a fee system that pays them for every news story they do that is broadcast on the evening news. Not only does the fee system supplement the reporter's income, but it is the fundamental avenue whereby the executives, the producers, and the reporter's colleagues can judge the worth of his or her journalistic skill and is an important indicator upon which future promotion will be evaluated. That this system, at this level, supports Marvin Barrett's assertion that "this can clearly tempt the newsman to concentrate on the sensational" (1970, p. 93) is doubtful and found no substance in this research. It does, however, indirectly increase the influence of the ideas and news judgment of the executive producer in New York and probably conditions the reporter, upon promotion, to continue to look to the producer for some cues about which reports will receive broadcast time.

Throughout its 30-year history, television news has been an adjunct within a medium of which the primary concern is entertainment. By and large, it is the opposite with newspapers. However, critics like Skornia (1968, p. 12) who assert that because the news operation is embedded in, and subsidiary to, the entertainment sector and is, therefore, "indisputably" affected by these predominant "entertainment values" (assumed to be evil) do television correspondents an injustice. That television is predominantly an entertainment medium; that is, that its prime perceived function is to afford the viewer diversion or amusement, is readily acknowledged by all concerned. Critics fail to do more than merely assert that because of this predominant role there is necessarily a direct linkage with the news operations and that this affects the television correspondent adversely.

It was my observation that it is incorrect to say that the television correspondent perceives his role as one of entertainment or that his behavior is in any way affected by "entertainment" values (understanding that term to mean simply amusement and diversion). Critics fail to distinguish between the correspondent's perceived need to visualize and make interesting a news story for a mass, national audience with the critics' own nondiscriminating and oversimplified pejorative attitude toward entertainment criteria. The fact that a television correspondent is directed toward visualizing his story does not mean that his primary concern is to "entertain," but rather that he must effectively employ the tools of his trade. Would these same critics pejoratively label a newspaperman as an entertainer who writes in a literary and vivid style instead of a dry and dull manner? The fact that the television correspondent must be "presentable on camera" is superficially described as a "show business" value, but is a newspaper likewise to be criticized for "show business" values when it does not hire a certain writer because his writing style does not correspond to the tastes of its readers or for when it tries to present a print layout with pictures that are "presentable" to its readers and facilitate their interest and comprehension?

Correspondents uniformly deny that they are in the entertainment business, and there do not seem to be any perceptible entertainment criteria employed. Their objective is to provide news by way of the television medium. This is not to deny that occasionally there are lighter feature stories on wine from Bordeaux or the taxi drivers in the Soviet Union, but they too are considered as part of the news format and as a perceived necessity that is demanded by the nonselective nature of the medium, not as an imposed or self-perceived need to entertain.

Where there might appear to be the employment of "show business" values is in the actual presentation makeup of the evening news. The news executives are the most concerned with ratings. It is illustrative of their attitude (to be discussed in a later section) that when the ratings of their news shows go down they do not see it as a concern that requires the hiring of more or better correspondents, but rather as the need for hiring a new anchorman, building a new set, employing a new producer, or finding another program advertising man. For example, on a local New York station that had substantially slipped in the ratings, a former black mayor and a well-received West Coast anchorman were recruited; the set designer of the Broadway musical "Jesus Christ Superstar" was commissioned to design a new set; and the producer of the number-one news program in the New York area was lured to that station to produce the show, as was that station's advertising man.

There is a high degree of personalization of the news, and this is most obvious with the medium's adoption of the "star" anchorman. One network researched audience preferences in a television news broadcast: there were 16 things that attracted audiences, and the first five dealt with the anchorman, with a wide gap in responses

between the fifth and sixth one. It is hard to say which
came first, the audiences' preferences or the networks'
identifying their news presentation with a name, dispos-
ing the audience to be attracted by personable stars, such
as "The Evening News With Walter Cronkite." That the networks realize this audience preference and appeal to it is
easily substantiated. (1) High salaries are paid to the
anchormen. (2) Anchormen have had to engage themselves
in a celebrity role. David Brinkley reported that he was
required to do the following things while anchorman: ride
a horse in a parade; appear for two days at an outdoor
fishing and hunting show; judge a beauty contest; cut a
ribbon opening a bridge; contribute a recipe to a celeb-
rities' cookbook; donate 27 neckties or other personal
items to 27 so-called auctions; make a speech on the foot-
steps of a new post office; make a speech on a flatbed
truck at the opening of a shopping center; cut the ribbon
at the opening of an all-night laundromat (Tobin, 1966,
p. 59). (3) An anchorman has been required to moderate
special events and documentaries in which he played no
reportorial role and was given a prepared script, in order
to make his name familiar to the audience and to associate
him with knowledge in multifarious activities. (4) The
promotional spots tell his biography and list his credentials as an advertisement for the program. Elmo Roper
has described these commentators as the "great dissemina-
tors," which indeed they have become by the very nature
of their association with the news program and the increased importance television news has come to play as an
information dispenser.

The commentator's primary role is to disseminate information. He is the principal source of facts and figures related to the events of the day transmitted to the
viewing audience. However, to say that the commentator
is the "star" or a "celebrity" or that the "star system"
came to television news from Hollywood in no way proves
that this role in any manner mitigates the information-
disseminating function.

There seems to be some truth in the criticism that
the commentator is engaged in a form of parasitic journalism, but this appears to be less the product of a star
system or of entertainment values than of the fact that
there are nonvisual news stories that need "talking."
Today, with only one exception, the national commentators
are experienced journalists, two of whom have experience
that goes back to the very beginnings of television journalism. Each has been a foreign correspondent, whether

as a newspaperman covering World War II or in television reporting from Europe, Asia, and Latin America. All the commentators are good writers and have published extensively in the print medium. Some commentators write all of their own stories, although these are the nonvisual reports of the day's news, which are not individually gathered but are taken from the wire-service reports or major newspapers and magazines. Only one commentator is simply a "reader" and does not write any of his own copy, but he is also the only commentator without extensive reportorial experience. Others vary in how much of their own reports they write, usually dependent upon the heaviness of their schedule; that is, whether it is a busy month for news, which might require that they prepare for convention coverage or a Presidential trip in addition to moderating the evening news.

Although they are conscious of their "stardom," the commentators are somewhat embarrassed by it. One present commentator earlier in his career quit a financially lucrative and prestigious anchor position on a morning news show because he considered it demeaning and nonprofessional for a newsman to do advertising commercials.

These observations are based on the commentators of the moment. Earlier there was a propensity to hire commentators who simply had the ability to read the daily news story well and hold their audience. This is still true of the local stations. In network news there is only one "reader." This may change, but the general criterion mentioned as often as the "charisma" of the commentator was his journalistic credentials. However, if and when the commentator does not write his own material, it will still be prepared for him by professional news writers who themselves have years of experience in journalism.

The argument here is that critics confuse the superficial form of entertainment with its content. The image may be found in the entertainment sector of television, but its intent and the result in its product is not behaviorally entertainment; it is not intended to amuse or to divert.

THE "PUBLIC INTEREST, CONVENIENCE, AND NECESSITY"

Regulation of the broadcasting industry stems from a technological premise, as stated by Chief Justice Berger when he was a member of the bench of the District of Columbia Circuit Court of Appeals, in the case Office of

<u>Communication of the United Church of Christ</u> v. <u>the Federal Communications Commission</u>:

> A broadcaster seeks and is granted the free
> and exclusive use of a limited and valuable
> part of the public domain; when he accepts
> that franchise, it is burdened by enforce-
> able public obligations. A newspaper can be
> operated at the whim or caprice of its own-
> ers; a broadcast station cannot. . . . A
> broadcast license is a public trust subject
> to termination for breach of duty.

The television spectrum is limited and cannot provide
enough frequencies to accommodate everyone who might want
to broadcast. The airwaves belong to the public with
their use franchised, and renewable every three years, to
different organizations, provided that they operate in
the "public interest, convenience and necessity." Legislation has established two legal considerations, the equal
time rule and the Fairness Doctrine.
The equal time rule states that

> If any licensee shall permit any person who
> is a legally qualified candidate for any
> public office to use a broadcast station,
> he shall afford equal opportunity to all
> other such candidates for that office in
> the use of such broadcast station. (Com-
> munications Act of 1934, 47 U.S.C. §315.)

Equal time considerations are network scheduling concerns
and do not apply to the regularly scheduled evening news
programs. The evening programs are, however, potentially
subject to the Fairness Doctrine, the major concept of
which is that if a station presents one side of a controversy it must provide an opportunity for the other side
or sides of that controversy to respond on the air. Related to the Fairness Doctrine is the personal-attack
ruling, which requires that within one week of broadcast
of the attack the named person or group be notified of the
date, time, and identification of the broadcast and be
provided with a script of its contents.
Network policy is explicit in its directives that
these two rulings should not be given major consideration
in the gathering of news and should not interfere with
its being reported. The <u>NBC Policy Book</u> for correspondents

104

states: "Generally speaking, your own journalistic stand-
ings and NBC's news policy would assure coverage of all
significant views on controversial issues of public importance." (p. 35.) CBS is even more adamant when it
states that the personal attack rules will not be taken
into account during any phase of the preparation of any
broadcast:

> In order to avoid that self-censorship which
> we believe is the most serious risk pre-
> sented by these rules, we are adopting the
> policy of not allowing the rules to affect
> news decisions. Normal news judgments will
> apply. . . . We shall make no judgments for
> the purpose of avoiding the consequences
> which the FCC rules may bring into play.
> Such judgments could only result in abdica-
> tion of our responsibility to the public and
> to the American tradition of a free press.
> (Richard Salant, Memo, September 11, 1969.)

These rulings, however, specifically exempt "bona fide
newscasts, bona fide news interviews, and on-the-spot
coverage of a bona fide news event."
    How do television correspondents view these legal re-
strictions, and do the restrictions, in actual practice,
constrain their newsgathering activities? The legal rules
themselves do not seem to affect the correspondents' actual reportorial activities. Responded one foreign correspondent interviewed in the newsroom, "The Fairness
Doctrine? That's probably the first time that these words
have been mentioned in this room. We don't think about
it. If the Fairness Doctrine has any handicap it is during the election period." David Brinkley responded to
criticism of intimidation by the FCC, that he was a newsman "not a lawyer and a corporation executive. . . . I've
had nothing to do with the FCC, and, to be honest about
it, care nothing about the FCC. They've never bothered
me. I've never bothered them."
    While their perceptions of the rulings are vague and
while with few exceptions they deny that these have a
"chilling effect," the same number of correspondents (85
percent) insist that they have and should have all the
rights and privileges of the First Amendment and that the
FCC should not be permitted to analyze and judge content.
Said John Chancellor:

One function of the FCC which sometimes runs
into my ideas involving freedom of the press
is that the journalism side of television has
to be journalism. As such it should not be
regulated in any way, nor should there be
any prior restraint on it, nor should there
be what the lawyers call the "chilling effect" of a previous decision. . . . I think
the fairness doctrine is probably wrong. I
think the idea of fairness is just fine.
But the principle of giving smaller political
groups an opportunity to use the electronic
media should be our responsibility. (Penthouse, 1972, p. 44.)

While giving Congressional testimony Walter Cronkite
stated that potentially broadcast journalism was not free
"because it is operated by an industry that is beholden
to the government for its right to exist. . . . The mere
existence of their power is an intimidating and constraining threat in being." (Rugabel, 1971, p. 24.) However,
only 20 percent of those interviewed felt that the FCC and
the legal ruling posed an actual threat or "chilling effect." There seems to be a disparity between what the
correspondents say in public in their effort to rid themselves of these potential legal constraints and how these
rules actually affect their activities at the moment.
There does not seem to be any significant constraint in
the newsgathering process that can be discerned to be imposed only on this medium.

There is, of course, the professional criterion of
balance; of the good with the bad, the combat footage
with the pacification report, or the right with the left.
Network policy supports this concept, independent of any
legal requirements. "Whenever possible, you should as a
matter of NBC policy, try to include the view necessary
for balance within the same program or, if that is not
possible, then within the same series." (NBC Policy Book,
1972, p. 35.) Coverage of dissent, minority views, and
the like receive air time as a result of this criterion,
in spite of the implied constraints I have discussed
earlier.

In summary, the legal restrictions on television do
not at present constrain the journalist. They are perceived more as a potential threat, employable by "irre-
sponsible political forces," more than as an actual constraint on their practice. Balance is considered something

106

indigenous to the medium, and if it were not prescribed by law it would be, and is, prescribed by network policy positions:

THE CORPORATION

The television network is part of a corporate, conglomerate structure that houses many disparate interests. By and large the news departments function within an organization of which the corporate executives are not professional journalists and indeed have virtually no experience in journalism at all. In 1959, Edward R. Murrow wrote on this subject that

> One of the basic troubles with radio and television news is that both instruments have grown up as an incompatible combination of show business, advertising, and news. Each of the three is a rather bizarre and demanding profession. And when you get all three under one roof, the dust never settles. The top management of the networks, with a few notable exceptions, has been trained in advertising, research, sales or show business. But by the nature of the corporate structure, they also make the final and critical decisions having to do with news and public affairs. Frequently they have neither the time nor the competence to do this. (Lyons, 1965, p. 188.)

For example, NBC News is one of six divisions of the National Broadcasting Company,* which is only one division within the RCA corporate structure. RCA is one of the giants of the electronics industry, a manufacturer of consumer goods that range from washing machines to color television sets, and is involved in secret government installations and products contracted by the military. CBS is not such an enormous corporate structure and is less involved in the electronics-military complex, but it too is a conglomerate with interests in such disparate areas

---

*The other divisions are the NBC Television Network, NBC Television Stations, NBC Enterprises, NBC Radio Division, and RCA Records.

as CATV systems and Creative Playthings toys. CBS once owned the New York Yankees and was a major investor in "My Fair Lady." It owns an amusement park, a television tube division, an electric guitar factory, and the Holt, Rinehart and Winston publishing company. A similar list of diversified holdings could be made for ABC as well.

Whether one reads the prideful yearly statement of the corporation or studies the percentage profit increase year after year; reads the literature of both its supporters and detractors; or observes the patterns of diversification and conglomeration, one must concur with Fred Friendly that "the quest for new properties continues lest the future not provide anything to grow on, as the profit centers continue to produce excess cash that must be invested." (1967, p. 169.) Whether or not this phenomenon has subverted the medium's service to the public for the needs of profit, is a question that far exceeds the capabilities of this study to provide a definitive response. Nicholas Johnson, a critic of the corporate, profit-driven communication system, concurs that it is "often difficult to uncover documentary proof that the content of the media is affected by the corporate interest of those who are in a position to exercise influence" (Barrett, 1970, p. 38), but rightfully observes that concern should be placed on not the "inevitability but the risk." (Ibid.)

The reality of the situation is that the primary source of our information about the political and social events of our time is set into the corporate structure of our system, the objective of which is to make money. The issue that this limited study must deal with is, in what discernible ways does the corporate structure constrain the electronic journalist as he carries out his information-dispensing function? To answer this question three areas of investigation were pursued. (1) the corporate attitudes toward the news; (2) how correspondents perceive the influence of the corporate hierarchy; and (3) what corporate, structural characteristics there are and how they affect the newsgathering and disseminating processes, that is, the role played by local affiliate and advertising demands.

To answer the first question the focus of attention quickly turned to a particular network which had, late in its operation, decided to build a serious and competitive news division. Why? The initial response was the FCC requirement to act in the "public interest, convenience and necessity," interpreted to include the obligation to offer news programming. However, it quickly became apparent that for any network to consider itself clearly competitive with the other two, it had to have a viable news division. "For us," said one of its high corporate executives, "news is a pain in the ass. What difference does it make if news is taken out of television. It makes little difference! News is not integral but has been adapted to television. Newspapers can't exist without news. But if we are going to be first, we need to be first in news as well."

Most executives, at least among those interviewed or whose opinions are expressed in writing, are not quite so negative in this area as the one quoted above, but competition and public responsibility are vital for explaining the corporate attitude toward the news. Fred Friendly put his finger on the more substantive and practical attitude of the corporate hierarchy when he wrote: "Television news gets the attention it does, at the compensation of profit, because of the prestige factor." (MacNeil, The People Machine, 1968, p. xxi.)

In 1963, when the CBS Evening News was expanded, the following were deduced as contributing to the decision, in order of importance:

1. Prestige: CBS had won awards and acclaim for its coverage of the 1962 elections and wanted to maintain the momentum of its primacy position;
2. Ratings: News was doing well in audience totals, and the increased time would increase the audience for the entertainment programs that followed the news broadcast;
3. Money: The news broadcast was gaining more financial revenue from advertisers and thus enabled them to cover the news with greater depth (MacNeil, October 1968, p. 73).

Said a foreign correspondent with many years of experience, "There is still the feeling around here on the corporate levels that the classiest thing they do is the news. The money is made available because they don't want it to be bad." Another foreign correspondent who is now a news executive said, "Last week we did the 'Conversation With The President.' It got a very small audience but it's important that we do that kind of program. It's important for our image." Robert MacNeil concurs with this observation: "In this war of corporate image, news programming is the touchstone of prestige." (The People Machine, 1968, p. 24.)

In general both discussions with corporate executives and their public statements reconfirm or at the very least reflect the same general perceptions as the correspondents toward the virtues of television news, when the news is the sole, noncomparative topic of discussion. They perceive television news within a predominantly visual medium "to be able to communicate clearly in pictures and to get people interested in things"; that television does not take the place of newspapers or magazines or books ("if people want more information they will go to the New York Times"); and that the level of influence of television news is not at all specific. For our purposes here an elaboration of their attitudes can tell us little; the more important question to pose is: How do the correspondents perceive the influence of the corporate hierarchy?

The response to this question, as it relates specifically to newsgathering activities, is uniform: The news division is a separate division of the corporation, and it is not corporation executives but the president of the news division who has responsibility for the news operation. Walter Cronkite succinctly focused upon this point once again during an address when he said:

> In my nine years as managing editor of the CBS Evening News, the CBS management has not once--not once--suggested to me in any manner whatsoever--by memo, friendly telephone call, a dropped hint at lunch, or in any other fashion--NOT ONCE have they ever suggested that I include in the CBS Evening News, or delete from the CBS Evening News, any item. Nor have they suggested any particular treatment of any story. (1971, p. 5.)

A Washington correspondent who throughout our interview was very critical of the shortcomings of television news and its superficiality, stated,

> I am not aware that . . . [the network] bends its policy to accommodate itself to the government. They have demonstrated a high degree of independence from the government and have never interfered with the way I handle my stories, or to my knowledge, with the way my colleagues handle theirs. They just leave us alone.

Indeed, there is a high respect for the management of the networks, and they are perceived to be steadfast in the support and defense of journalistic integrity in this medium. Walter Cronkite wrote:

> Our network and station owners are no more or less inspired by the profit motive than are the publishers of newspapers and magazines. I can testify that the executives--of my network--are far less meddlesome in the news process than the publishers for whom I've worked.
>
> When the history of our branch of communications is written, the names of William Paley and Frank Stanton of CBS and David Sarnoff of NBC should loom large. They came to the ownership and management of the most powerful communications medium ever without journalistic background--just as have some publishers. But by their wisdom they have created one of the freest news systems yet.
>
> From the very early days of radio they kept the advertisers and the political power wielders off our backs until today we have established our independence and that tradition of objectivity. (1969, p. 5.)

Reuven Frank of NBC concurred:

> Although I believe that most of the development of American television has been inevitable, the adoption of newspaper rules by television news people was in large part a conscious act by a small group of men, principal among them my predecessor and teacher, the late William McAndrew. He and some others believed, when it was still conceivably a matter of choice, that the only alternatives to carrying over into television the traditions of American news would be bad alternatives, which imply a superior wisdom to filter news, and objectives inimical to journalism's tradition. (Winter 1970, p. 13.)

Alexander Kendrick in his biography of Edward R. Murrow describes how during his tenure with CBS Murrow maintained a personal friendship with William S. Paley, chairman of the board, and how correspondents and executives were all on familiar terms with each other before CBS became the enormous corporate conglomerate that it now is (1969, p. 18). That contact no longer exists. Today most executives see the evening news broadcast at the same moment it is being transmitted across the nation.

Generally the executives' concern is with the broad principles of freedom of the press, television camera access, and governmental and national responsibility, as shown by Frank Stanton, president of CBS, in his testimony to Congress and his public exhortations, and by a special Emmy Award given in 1972 by the industry to Stanton to acknowledge his forthright defense of television's rights and privileges under the First Amendment. Indeed, the diversification of the industry has created many more executives, with more limited powers, and it might even be hypothesized that this diversification has had the effect of decreasing the direct influence that any one executive might exercise over the news division.

There is, however, one important area in which the network hierarchy does exercise substantial influence, and that is in the allotment of time for news broadcasts. Very often these are commercial decisions. All the correspondents and producers interviewed stated that they would like a 60-minute broadcast, and most said that they would prefer a 10 p.m. time slot. The first is unlikely, and the second would be in prime time, which seems to be reserved for the more profitable entertainment shows.

The time period designated for the evening news, however, although not prime time, is prescribed and regular. June 5, 1967, was one of only a few exceptions to this regularity of broadcast schedule. On that day it was announced in New York that the local news would be telecast one-half hour early, ostensibly because of the Middle East crisis. The network news would therefore also be broadcast one-half hour earlier. However, the actual reason for the change of schedule was the plan to telecast a baseball game scheduled to begin at 7 p.m. Occasionally the weekend report is canceled for one reason or another, usually a conflicting baseball or football telecast.

The problem is not so much with the regularly scheduled weekday news program but rather with the broadcast of documentaries, special half-hour or hour reports of major news events during the week, and the extension of the half-hour evening news to an hour. It is in these latter cases that Robert MacNeil's criticism seems to apply,

that the network news departments often
have no say in decisions about when news
programs will be shown, when they will be
preempted or killed off, how long they
will run and who will appear on them.
These decisions are made quite often by
men who are not journalists or who have
other concerns in mind. (The People
Machine, 1968, p. 26.)

This is the entertainment-journalism-profit oriented dilemma of American television, best illustrated by a comment of James Aubrey, president of the CBS television
network, to Fred Friendly, who was at the time the new
producer of CBS Reports:

Look, Fred, I have regard for what Murrow
and you have accomplished, but in this adversary system you and I are always going to
be at each other's throats. They say to me
(he meant the system, not any specific individual), "Take your soiled little hands, get
the ratings, and make as much money as you
can," they say to you, "Take your lily-white
hands, do your best, go the high road and
bring us prestige." (Friendly, 1967,
pp. xi-xii.)

Andrew Rooney, former CBS writer-producer lamented: "Everybody in the news division assumes that they are the
only honest people. Everybody in entertainment assumes
that they are the only ones who can attract an audience."
(Barrett, 1970-71, p. 14.)
    There remains one more area in which the executives
do affect the news, and that is their budget allotments.
The general theory is that when times are good the news
department benefits. When times are bad, being a division
whose profit margin is not so wide and which is often in
the red, the news department is among the first to suffer.
News gets the budgeting it does primarily because it
brings "prestige" to the network.

The Local Affiliates

    Local affiliates are an important constraint on the
corporate structure that further inhibits it from providing

additional time for news programming. Each network is limited to ownership of only five local stations. For program dissemination the networks are dependent upon their nationwide affiliations; for example, CBS has some 250 local affiliates. Local station ownership is a very profitable enterprise. Observed Marvin Barrett: "In what other business can a moderately astute operator hope to realize 100 percent a year on tangible assets, or lay out $150 for a franchise that in a few years time he can peddle for $50 million--should he be so foolish as to want to sell?" (1970, p. 4.)

In general, for profit reasons, the affiliates oppose more network news. From the network news program they receive only 50 percent of the profit from advertising fees, while they receive a full 100 percent from locally produced news or entertainment programs. Concludes Fred Friendly: "The harsh fact is that most affiliates are too profitable under present circumstances; mining gold from ether as they are, they have no incentive to tamper with the magic results of 'giving the people what they want.'" (1967, p. 275.)

Local affiliates also resist the idea of network editorials and pressure the networks to keep analysis and criticism to a minimum. When these are broadcast, many affiliates have been known to superimpose on the screen "Network Analysis," or "This Does Not Represent the View of this Station." Poor clearance with the local affiliates was reported each time the Cronkite Evening News was extended to an hour. Robert MacNeil summed up the problems in this relationship when he wrote:

> The affiliates chronically feel that they
> are being milked for their audience by New
> York, while there is much sorrow on Sixth
> Avenue that the affiliates constantly demand
> a larger slice of the pie. Affiliates em-
> barrass the networks by refusing to carry
> public affairs programs designed to improve
> the network's public image. It is, while
> conducted with the diplomacy of a strained
> marriage, a greed-hate relationship. (The
> People Machine, p. 278.)

Edward R. Murrow said of this problem:

> If we were to do the Second Coming of Christ
> in color for a full hour, there would be a
> considerable number of stations which would

decline to carry it, on the ground that a
Western or a quiz show would be more profitable. Forgive the irreverence, but there
are times when I think that the Lord is
wholly indifferent to this business of television and this is why. (Kendrick, 1969,
p. 458.)

Advertising

There remains one corporate, structural factor yet
to be discussed, and that is advertising. American television is privately owned and operated, and since the
early days of its inception it has depended upon advertising revenue to finance its activities. Television news
is no exception, although traditionally the news division
has not been a profit-making operation and has not been
required, like most other television programming, to function on a profit-loss basis. This does not mean that
profits are of no concern for the news division; indeed,
its budget and time allotments are in part the result of
its merchandising potential. There is a cross of interests between the commercial nature of the medium and its
informational responsibilities, as reflected by Alexander
Kendrick's remark: "There are those in the industry who
believe broadcasting can move men, and even some who believe it could move mountains, but they are outnumbered
by those who believe all it has to do is move goods."
(1969, p. 458.)
    Commercially, ratings are important for any program
that seeks advertising revenue. The total news audience
is fairly stable. If one news program does substantially
better in the ratings than the others, not only can it
demand higher rates from its advertisers, but because of
the constancy of the total audience available, the other
news programs are forced to lower their rates. Also important for programming purposes and audience delivery is
the number of viewers that will be carried over to the
entertainment that follows the news broadcast. The larger
the news audience, the greater the probability that part
of that audience, through sheer laziness in turning the
dial, will be carried over to the next program.
    Ratings and audience delivery, therefore, are im-
portant corporate considerations, and not simply a question of evening news profitability. The evening news
programs do show a profit, but from the perspective of

115

growth potential, news is not profitable to the extent
that it greatly increases network profits. Said one network executive producer just returned from a cocktail
party with advertisers and salesmen (a social obligation
of the profession),

> My impression was that I was sure that if it
> were left up to them (the advertisers and
> salesmen), if the FCC did not exist and if
> the corporate heads of the networks were not
> good and responsible men, that there would
> not be any news on television. I felt that
> they really don't like us, that we are time-
> money potential that is wasted.

At the same party a corporate executive was reported to
have uttered to a news executive this view of the dollar
situation: "You see, we are a money-making operation;
the news is a money-spending one." Often when it is a
question of extending the half-hour newscast, providing
extended live coverage of a major event, or scheduling a
documentary, the decision comes down to weighing the
scheduling of the news program against revenue that will
be displaced. For example, it was especially expensive
for CBS to provide live coverage of the Watergate hearings, not because of the cost of production but because
of their particularly profitable afternoon programming.
These, however, are not such prominent concerns for the
evening news as they are for the other news formats.

There is a growing interest among individual stations
in longer local news programs, usually at the expense of
the time allotted for documentary broadcast. The reason
for this is that advertisers have shown an increased interest in the evening news as its audience totals, and
therefore their profits, have increased. The 1963 increase in time from 15 to 30 minutes was in part attrib-
utable to increased advertising revenues.

For the advertiser, television news has become a good
buy for a specific type of product, in cost per thousand
viewers. The news audience is generally very constant,
loyal, and mature. This offers the advertiser not the
widest of all possible audiences but greater frequency of
contact with one audience, which is valuable for an advertiser who is interested in increasing the consumption
of his product and less concerned with finding new cus-
tomers for that product.

What effect does this have on the news operations
themselves? For the practitioner, the man who gathers

and produces the news, it has seemingly no effect. These
men are virtually, and intentionally as a matter of network policy,* free of advertising pressure. No correspondent even hinted of commercial pressure. "Reporters
are remarkably free on news content and how it should be
given. Advertising is a consideration on a level higher
than mine. I don't even remember who our advertisers are."
Comments Walter Cronkite:

> The remarkable thing is that in a short time,
> relatively, the best broadcast news organiza-
> tions have established a total independence
> from advertisers. The wall between sales and
> news content . . . is quite impregnable. Ad-
> vertisers have no rights of approval, no
> rights of review. Our journalistic indepen-
> dence of advertisers is a good deal greater
> than exists in many magazines and most news-
> papers. But the truly remarkable thing is
> not our insistence on independence--but that
> advertisers have come to accept this indepen-
> dence in broadcast journalism. (The Chal-
> lenges of Change, 1971, p. 78.)

Even Fred Friendly, although he has accused the
broadcasting industry of becoming the servant of merchandising, has written:

> Although it has become difficult to uphold a
> high standard of broadcast practices in radio
> and television, the news division's insis-
> tence on maintaining the separation between
> sponsor and program has been sacred, and in
> my tenure as President the support from Paley
> and Stanton was usually unflinching, even
> when it cost the company money. (1967, p. 206.)

This observation is confirmed through an independent study
conducted by the Columbia University sociologist Herbert
Gans, who also observed that

---

*The NBC Policy Book states: "NBC News observes two
inflexible rules on advertising messages in news programs:
the news content must be unmistakably separated from advertising messages, and the NBC staff newsman or correspondent reporting the news is not permitted to read
advertising material." (p. 12.)

despite the old stereotype that media employ-
ees report the news as their owners and advertisers see fit, this is not true on national television . . . however true it may
be of the local press. People who work in
the media I have studied so far are surprisingly free from outside interference on the
part of non-professionals and business executives, and can decide on their own what
to cover and how to cover it. (Small, 1970,
p. 279.)

Financially, the evening news can afford to be independent. It has more advertising offers than it has time
to broadcast them. One producer after another denied advertiser influence with the obvious satisfaction of having
the freedom to say, If they bother us we drop them and
get another sponsor. No evening news program is dependent
upon revenue from one advertiser, and usually they have
four or five. It is fairly easy to find one as substitute
for the other should there be any hint of editorial interference by an advertiser. Indeed, so stable is advertising revenue for the evening news that Bill Leonard, vice-
president of CBS News, could foresee a time "when the
stable mainstay for broadcasting. . . . I don't mean the
biggest money maker, but the stable support, the thing
that leavens bread--will be news." (Myer, 1968, p. 34.)
This has enabled and probably will continue to permit the
news to maintain its immunity from advertiser pressure.

5

REPORTING THE
TELEVISION NEWS STORY

We have discussed the correspondents' definitions of
the news and their views about the mechanical and structural characteristics of the television medium. Almost
3,000 people are deployed throughout the United States
and abroad in one capacity or another in order to record
and transmit the electronic message. News bureaus are
maintained in most major capitals of the world. With increased time and money, the electronic medium claims that
it leaves less to the work of others and that its networks
have become major newsgatherers, with increased utiliza-
tion of their own on-the-spot correspondents reporting the
major events of our times. How do the television correspondents get the news? Three areas will be discussed:
(1) the correspondents' sources of news stories, (2) the
distinctive manner in which the television news story is
prepared and written, and (3) the way television covers
different types of news stories.

SOURCES FOR THE NEWS

Anyone who sits before three television consoles in
the early evening, each tuned to a different network news
program, will, perhaps surprisingly, see not only coverage of the same stories but a similarity of placement
within each lineup as well. After having spent the day at
one network and observed the composing process for the
evening news program, I sat in the office of the executive
producer and watched with him, simultaneously, the broadcasts of all three networks. Ten minutes into the broadcast, two networks (his and one other) were broadcasting

a film report of a speech given by Vice President Agnew. This congruence in placement was not an unusual occurrence. What was surprising, however, was that both broadcasts, the format of which had been composed in the absence of any contact whatsoever with the competing network, had timed their film stories for telecast so that at this moment of actual transmission the words emanating from the Vice President's mouth were in synchronization with one another, although broadcast over two separate channels. If you were to compare the front page headlines in a newspaper with the lineup of an evening's television broadcast, a close similarity would also be found. How do these congruent judgments about the news, especially foreign affairs news, come about?

The producer in New York, by the time he has reached his office, has read the New York Times, the Daily News, and probably the Wall Street Journal. On his desk, waiting for him, is the Washington Post. Over the weekend he had read the advance copies of Time, Newsweek, and U.S. News and World Report magazines that are due to reach the newsstands on Tuesday. If he missed the competitors' broadcast, their lineup has been recorded. He also has the lineup of the morning news broadcast. In the afternoon he has at his disposal the Christian Science Monitor, the New York Post, perhaps also the London Times, and in some cases the Boston papers and some Midwestern newspapers.

The correspondent in the United States has also read the New York Times; the three news magazines; and if in Washington, the Washington Post. The correspondent abroad reads the International Herald Tribune if he is assigned to Europe and the major newspapers in that particular country. Each day in the foreign bureau a telex arrives from New York, listing the lineup of stories broadcast the night before. However, the most pervasive reading in every news department and domestic or foreign bureau is the AP and/or UPI tickertape. Television journalists and producers are tuned into the wire services, of which the sounds and the streams of paper are ever present. In short, the television correspondent and producer begin their day by reading the products of their own and their competitors' staffs, both in the electronic and print media, to see what they and others have considered to be news as it was reported the day before. Yesterday's stories were begun in the same manner, by reviewing the stories that were reported the day before.

It is through the observation and examination of their own and their competitors' previous work that there develops this congruence of news judgment. This corresponds to Cohen's observation that "each of them [the foreign correspondents] is shaping both his news sense and his working day by examining the output of his professional colleagues, all of whom are simultaneously doing the same thing." (1963, pp. 58-59.) That is, the correspondent and producer have a frame of reference within which they operate that is predominantly the product of their (the press's) prior judgments about stories that have been considered important. In that regard, news is highly imitative. Concludes Cohen, "News takes on a kind of objective reality: what was reported was news; what was not reported--for whatever reasons--is not news. And once it is news, it exercises a powerful claim on the attention of reporters." (Ibid.)

This is essentially how news judgments come to correlate with one another, but it must be asked what resources are available to, and predominant for, the television correspondent and producer, from which they determine which stories to report and what information will be contained in those stories.

WNBC News runs a local New York advertisement publicizing its anchorman and picturing him as a man who selects the news each day only after going through thousands of reports from all over the world. Ostensibly the advertisement was correct, but what it failed to include was that over 80 percent of those stories were not submitted by the news department staff but were taken from the major wire services. In that sense television is not a major newsgathering operation. For the general reaction story, such as a plane crash or a premier's resignation, the story is initiated from the wires; if it is deemed important a correspondent and film crew are sent to photograph and record the reaction of witnesses or of an aide.*

---

*While engaged in research at one of the Paris bureaus a radio correspondent was preparing a story on a controversial scheduling of nuclear weapons tests by the French military. His story was taken entirely from the AP wire, simplified, and capsulized for a 45-second report. The story was recorded by him in Paris and transmitted to New York for broadcast. Earlier that day New York wired Paris that they had read about the nuclear tests in the AP wires in New York and requested from them a 45-second spot. The reporter, using the same AP wire report quoted by New York, condensed it for radio broadcast. New York

Again, it may be the practice in Brussels or Paris to "stake out the picture" as insurance (visual insurance) that there will be fresh film footage for a story that takes place behind closed doors in a conference room. The facts are usually reported by the wires, and it remains for the film crew to get the participants coming and going and leave the network to "voice over the story." There is an international airlines strike: the correspondent is instructed to get pictures of the planes in their hangars and get the inconvenienced passengers to say something on camera; the wires will report the issues in the settlement talks and the progress achieved. The wire services constitute the primary source of the day's hard news. About 70 to 80 percent of the stories read on camera by the commentator are gleaned from the wire services. They provide the basic skeleton of the news for the television broadcast, along with, though less significantly, the New York Times and the Washington Post.

Increasingly, however, television news has become an independent gatherer of the news. In Washington its correspondents cover regular beats and submit stories, including mini-documentaries, that they have gathered on their own. Sometimes the evening news, as a member of a news wire service, contributes stories to it. Television correspondents are consulted by the bureau chief and the New York producer about whether there is an important story that day coming out of State, the Senate, or the White House. For the most part, however, correspondents in Washington and on assignments abroad complained that there is not enough of this exchange of information and that their input, their on-the-spot interpretation of what is important and what should be broadcast, is insufficient. One Washington correspondent explained it this way:

> It's deeply demoralizing. There is a deliberate shelving of a reporter's input into a story, and the producer has been elevated into a super editor and genius in everything. To get a piece on the evening news I never speak to the managing editor (in this case the commentator with the theoretical editorial responsibility for the news broadcast).

---

asked for it that way. No more information needed to be gathered. It was the voice transmitted via cable from Paris that was important.

I talk with the producers here and those in
New York--I have to speak with four producers to try to get a piece on. They control,
run, dominate, shape the content of the
evening news. Somebody has to control the
shape of the evening news. But the reporter
who knows the story should control content
(of the program), but he doesn't.*

A major problem, in Washington, for example, is that
there are only five camera crews available. Five stories
are therefore chosen to be filmed, and the crews are then
assigned to the correspondent. Rarely does the producer
call the White House correspondent to ask what is important and which stories to cover. More often, if there is
communication between the two, it usually finds the producer saying "AP has a story in its Day Book on Senator
M----, is it worth a film story?"
News departments plan their calendars well in advance,
usually on a monthly basis; hard-core planning occurs on
a weekly basis; and the news editor analyzes bureau reports once a week for upcoming stories. These are supplemental to the wire reports and the advance copies of the
news magazines, which are quite important. For example,
said one foreign news editor, "Brandt's problems with the
peace treaties will be an important story that we are going to cover even though it's not really a direct concern
for an American audience. _Time_ is doing a big series on
it and so we are going to cover it." Television likes to
see it first in _Time_ or _Newsweek_ to know that the story
is there: "It costs a lot of money to follow a 'sense'
in television."
After a day of analyzing the bureau reports and the
other materials, the overall week's plan is sent out to
the various bureaus. These are directives, not on events
but on situations. They include fixed calendar stories
that must be covered, such as a presidential State of the
Union Address, the opening of the U.N. General Assembly,
or a German-French Summit Conference. Then there are the
day-to-day stories, which are discussed and handled on a
day-to-day basis. At the end of each day a tentative
schedule for the next day's stories is drawn up, with a
residual to cover the unplanned events.

---

*This criticism is substantiated in Chapter 6.

For assignments abroad, more than 50 percent of the stories emanate from New York. In this case many of the directives are merely congruent judgments, since every foreign bureau has at least one wire service teletype, and usually both American services and one foreign service, such as Reuters or, in Paris, Agence France Press.* Most of the foreign stories assigned are those that must be covered, as when the EEC was enlarged from six to nine, or when there is a change of government. The stories that originate from the foreign bureau staff are predominantly feature subjects, film stories on events or situations that show the world in a more relaxed light. They are expressions of the human experience, of the life and ac-tivities of people, to set against the more weighty events that are at the top of the news. These are stories about divorce laws in Italy or life along the Volga; they are films of the First Lady visiting a dancing school when she accompanies the President on a foreign trip, of the city policeman who rides a bicycle on his beat and comes to know the people better, or of the "typical German family." Occasionally there is an important mini-documentary to be done, such as a three-part story on agricultural problems in Europe or on the Common Market; if New York can be sold, the story is filmed and gathered.

Dependency on the wire services, whether in New York or Washington or at any foreign bureau, is largely a prob-lem of television's small news staff. As already noted there is but one correspondent at State, one in Paris, one in Italy, and so on. In Washington there is little wandering among departments by the correspondent to put a story together, but in Europe the correspondent is often out of the bureau covering a story in Malta, Northern Ireland, or West Germany. Research staffs are small; often at the foreign bureaus they are nonexistent or un-professional. At the networks the facilities for back-grounding a story are inadequate. In broadcasting there are no clippings files to speak of and there are no news morgues.† One correspondent said as she prepared to

---

*Networks seldom have foreign-language press services in either New York or Washington.

†One Washington correspondent responsible for regu-larly interviewing Washington officials on the vital is-sues of the day has his office piled high with back issues of the New York _Times_ and Washington _Post_ with large index tabs sticking out from the seven-foot piles listing the

accompany the President on his trip to Canada,

> I've got this call going through to the State
> Department. I'll get the official point of
> view. I have some clippings from this week's
> newspapers. . . . [The White House correspon-
> dent] has clippings too. I'll fly down to-
> morrow and we'll spend the evening "rappin."
> That's enough.

When a television correspondent is on a particular beat,
he compiles his own resources and is well-read in the
area. It is only when the unusual happens, or for correspondents on general assignment, that the inadequacy of
resources becomes a major obstacle and cause for wire-
service dependency.

Academics, or experts on a subject, are not important
sources for news, or as a background resource for a news
story. Indeed, there is a perceptible bias against them
among the correspondents, who see the academic profession
as almost antithetical to theirs. Said one well-known
correspondent,

> We just wouldn't use an expert as a corre-
> spondent. Take, for example, a China
> watcher. He has his passion and that's
> all he sees. A correspondent's training
> is different. The correspondent is trained
> to observe and see everything, to come up
> with the factual report, and find what the
> truth really is.

No less than a vice-president in charge of news with
over twenty years of correspondence experience was asked,
among others, why a China expert who speaks Chinese was
not sent with the news team on the President's trip to
Peking instead of sitting in the news studio in New York
telling the correspondent, who was in Peking, what it was
he was seeing. The vice-president responded, reflecting
this general attitude,

---

date and the major headlines. He saves them for two
months, at which point he runs out of space and throws
some away.

Look, during the President's trip we had a
panel of six academic experts on China sitting around a table and discussing China and
the implications of the trip for an hour on
the air. They couldn't agree on anything.
By the end of the hour you forgot what the
issues were. Now, our correspondent over
there can spend a day or two talking to
people and asking questions and so on and
get at the truth of what's happening. That's
why we send a correspondent and keep the expert in the New York studio.

Another correspondent explained her hesitance in
calling for an academic for background on a story because,
she explained, "Academics give you too much and more than
you want to know. They'll also give you political interpretations. It is rare to find the academic whom you can
phone and get concise facts."

Whatever contact there is between the television
journalist and the academic, exists on a personal and
often social basis. Academics are sometimes interviewed
on camera for comment on a major political, economic, or
social event on which they have expertise. Who is used
is a matter of the "photogenic" quality of the individual
as well as the level of his expertise. New York academics
especially those at Columbia University, are particularly
in favor because of their proximity to the New York recording facilities and the availability of news teams.
This is not true for academics in Washington. Abroad it
is more difficult to use academics for comment on camera
because of the language problem and the disdain in which
simultaneous translation is held, particularly if the expert is not a direct actor to the event.

In summary, we have found that congruent news judgments result from the daily immersion of the participants
in similar news sources and publications. In television
news there is a major dependency on the wire services,
resulting from the limitations of staff and crews and the
absence of backgrounding facilities. Finally, academics
are not an important resource for background information.

COMPOSING THE NEWS STORY FOR TELEVISION

There are essentially three discernible types of
television news story formats: (1) the story read by the

commentator on the air; (2) the "standupper" or "talking
head," and related to this, the stakeout and the recorded
interview story; and (3) finally, and most important, the
television film story. Each format requires some discussion for a satisfactory comprehension of the television
news broadcast.

The first two formats are very much alike in structural form and will be discussed together. It has already
been noted that because no film may be available or taken,
or possibly because a story does not warrant the extra
time that it might take to do it on film, many news stories are just read over the air by the anchorman. The
standupper is done for similar reasons, but either orig-
inates on the specific beat covered by the regular staff
correspondent; is a story he or she initiated and gathered;
or involves a correspondent's interpretation. For this
type of story the correspondent is merely photographed
talking, sometimes in the studio but more often in front
of the Pentagon, on the stairs of Capitol Hill, or before
the Eiffel Tower in Paris, telling (usually reading) the
story. Both the anchorman's story and the standupper are
considered nonvisual stories that nonetheless contain important news information. Mechanically they are the same
type of story, since both involve a single person talking
on camera; only the setting varies, not the format.

There are special compositional criteria that affect
the writing of these two types of stories. The correspondent is aware that his audience is national and that the
message cannot be recalled. The story, therefore, must be
readily comprehensible, and the electronic journalist's
enemy becomes complexity. He has less than one minute in
which to tell this story: usually as little as 45 seconds,
often only 30 seconds. The format provides little room
for interpretation, and the amount of background information that can be included is severely limited. Oversimplification becomes a necessity, since much of the analytical material is cut.

> In broadcast news there is not the room--
> or time--for background that exists in
> print journalism. When a story has been
> in the news for days, even weeks, it is
> assumed that the listener knows the back-
> ground. Only the latest developments in
> these so-called "running" stories are
> reported. (Bliss and Patterson, 1971,
> p. 108.)

A television correspondent must know the same amount
of background information as the newspaper reporter and
gather 10,000 to 20,000 words just the same, in order to
do the story correctly; but for the story he records he
seldom writes more than a page. The objective is to report the essential facts accurately and briefly within
the allotted time. The story must be clear and comprehensible because the viewer must understand at once what
he says. "The problem is to get that key sentence to the
guy who does not really comprehend the story." Bliss and
Patterson, in Writing News For Broadcast, wrote that "the
guiding rule in writing news for television . . . is to
tell your story clearly and accurately--as effectively as
possible--in the fewest number of words." (Ibid.) Style
is for clarity, not literary purposes; it is conversational: "The best TV writing is when you don't notice
the writing," commented a Pentagon correspondent. "You
don't look for that memorable phrase or good line like
they do in a newspaper art section. It's not effective
on television. That's the secret of . . . [our commenta-
tor]--he is the teller of the news, not the great phrase
maker. He is clear and simple." Clarity of style is important, but it is also necessary that the report be concise. The NBC Policy Book explains: "There is no open
and shut answer to this problem but it helps if the reporter keeps in mind that he is filing a piece of journalistic enlightenment and is not dumping his notes on the
listener." (P. 56.) The whole process is nicely described
and analogized by Bliss and Patterson:

> Just as the person who writes science arti-
> cles for a popular magazine must be able to
> translate complicated scientific data into
> layman's language, the stories sound simple.
> Few listeners, for example, have the back-
> ground necessary to understand the workings
> of the Common Market. A story concerning
> the Market must be written in such a way as
> to be universally meaningful--i.e., meaning-
> ful to the mechanic in Youngstown as well as
> to the economist at Yale. (1971, p. 108.)

The key terms are clarity, comprehensibility, accuracy, conciseness, and conversational tone. The report
tends to be on a surface level, headline in nature, and
comparable in length of composition to the first few paragraphs in a newspaper article (which is about the amount

the average reader consumes of the newspaper article). It
is an "all-purpose" story for an audience that is plural
and national: a report that justifiably corresponds to
the criticism that television news is a headline service.
The correspondents make no pretense about the superficiality of this form of the television news story. Critics
who voice this complaint fail, however, to distinguish the
different news formats, particularly the longer television
film report, called the mini-documentary or pocket documentary, which runs from two to four minutes of broadcast
time.

The stakeout, the interview-response, and the press
conference film report should also be included in this
grouping. This is typically the report of a reaction or
planned event to which the correspondent is assigned.
For example, there may be a controversy that involves an
American general who has knowingly disobeyed orders: the
correspondent stakes out the general's home or his super-
visor's with the hope that he will get a filmed response
from one of them of his opinions on the issue. This film
is not to be made part of a larger film story on the subject, but will be broadcast as an isolated reaction to a
news event, introduced by the anchorman and broadcast,
after which the program will turn to a different item of
the news. Although it is not actually written by a member of the news staff, the editing of this filmed interview is subject to the same criteria as the writing of a
"talked" news story: it must be concise, clear, edited
to accurately reflect the opinion of the person interviewed, and readily comprehensible. The NBC Policy Book
suggests

> that news spots based on such things as news
> conferences, briefings such as those held in
> Saigon, and even reports from regular beats
> should adhere as closely as reasonably pos-
> sible to one subject and one idea. It is
> only confusing when a reporter tries to cram
> three or four subjects into a spot which may
> run no more than 45 seconds. (P. 56.)

Many of the 20 items covered in the daily news broadcast are of this nature, but they do not represent the
typical, distinctly visual television news story. The
news story that television prides itself on tends to be
somewhat longer, usually between one minute thirty seconds
and three minutes in length, and often as long as four or

five minutes, depending upon the importance and complexity of the story as well as on the news policy of the particular network. These are the television film reports, mini-documentaries, pocket documentaries, features, or enterprisers.

It is this form of story that is the product of the real, or perceived, distinctive characteristics of the medium. It is different from the television "talk" story and the print story because of the way in which it is written and composed for television. The verbal demands are the same as those already described (clarity, comprehensibility, accuracy, conciseness, conversational tone), but the important difference is that the correspondent is writing for film, not to be filmed. That is, it is a visual subject for which there is film available to illustrate the story, and the correspondent writes the story and edits the film with the visual in mind. The war in Northern Ireland is a representative example. The film crew has taken fine film of a funeral march of Protestants through the Catholic section of Belfast. Another cameraman had gotten permission to follow a police search party through suspect districts of the city. The correspondent screens the developed film, edits it, and writes his story for the film: "It's like writing long cut-lines [captions] for photographs in a newspaper." The difference is that this caption is also the whole verbal story.

However, it is not always so simple. The Common Market story provides a good example: the action is behind closed doors, or perhaps one delegation has walked out of a meeting while the film crews were not there. The event happened, but there is no film showing it happening; the correspondent still needs a picture for his story. The crew photographs the conference building, the limousines coming and going, and the Brussels streets. The film is edited, and the correspondent writes his story as a peg to the visual images: the pictures do not reflect the actual news event, but the story becomes visual. It is difficult for television to reconstruct an event. It can create the impression of having been there, but in reality it is after the fact, and often there is a wide gap between the film of the place of the event and the facts of the event itself. However, "it is visual and that's not quite so boring."

The picture, however, has its advantages for telling a news story and often helps the correspondent make his report concise and comprehensible. The correspondent does not need to tell his audience that the victim is male, white, elderly, nervous, or sickly; a close-up picture will tell it for all to see, and he need not expend a single word. We might also be able to tell if he is a business leader, student radical, or foreigner. What is the issue? The reporter will tell this to the viewer, but viewers who miss the first words explaining the situation may be brought back to the story's text by reading a placard carried by a protester, or they may associate the locale with a story that has been current for the past few days. The viewer can "see" what is happening. The electronic journalist composes his story not only with words and sounds, but also with silence, because pictures alone can often tell the story.

Because television is visual, because it is evanescent, and because the audience is national, the news story must be composed differently from that of a newspaper. The newspaper press has developed a format for writing a news story that in the trade jargon is called "inverted pyramid": this calls for the newspaper reporter to write his story in such a manner that the essentials of the story, the who, what, why, when, where, and how of the event, are all contained in the first few paragraphs. The balance of the article is background information that varies in its direct relevance to the event. Generally the newspaper editor can edit out any part of the story at almost any point after these first initial paragraphs without doing serious damage to the substance of the news, in order to fit it into the layout of the printed page. There is no "inverted pyramid" in television. Each correspondent has his own way of describing how he writes the story, but some general characteristics can be observed and analyzed.

Order of Presentation. A television news story has a beginning, a middle and an end. It reflects Aristotle's dictum for persuasive speechmaking: tell the people what you are going to say, say it, and then tell them what you have said. The reason is mechanically determined: the television message cannot be recalled. If the television correspondent were to employ the inverted pyramid, he would have no way to insure that the viewer would catch the first few lines of the story and therefore be able to grasp the important facts that follow. Commented one correspondent: "The story has to lead up to a conclusion, the key sentence in your story. You almost have to lead them by the hand." This varies with different individuals; some begin with a key sentence, explain the different components of the story, and repeat the key sentence again at the end; others follow the more traditional introduction, middle, and conclusion; while others choose a variation of the two that calls for an introduction by the commentator, who presents the main facts in the story, while the correspondent follows with a film survey of the scene that concludes with a picture of the correspondent on camera summarizing the story. The story is simple and usually reflects one event or one idea. It is visual; the ideas are repeated; the language is conversational. All this is necessary, so it is reasoned, to maintain the non-selective, often wandering attention of the viewer.

Reconstruction of Events. Because the camera has difficulty capturing the actual events as they are happening and usually arrives on the scene at its aftermath, reconstruction becomes a problem. This does not pose a difficulty for the newspaperman. He asks his questions, surveys the scene, collects his data, and writes and reports his story in much the same manner (although perhaps relatively faster) as he and his predecessors have done for almost 400 years. It is more difficult for the television correspondent. For television it is much easier to report a plane crash (you photograph the burning debris and interview some witnesses) or a press conference or the itinerary of a visiting dignitary, than to report an ongoing, continuous story, particularly if events are occurring in different places simultaneously.

For example, the newspaperman could spend his day covering the Middle East war in Jerusalem, or maybe venture into the field, or check the wires and contact a few sources in government. At the end of the day he could sit down, put it all together, and cable the story to his editor. The television correspondent cannot do that; he needs a film story. If he is in Israel and there is an important news story that week, New York expects at least one mini-documentary a day and two if possible. The television correspondent must also check his sources, the wires, and so on, but he needs film footage as well, and that requires a crew and an array of equipment. His mobility, therefore, is limited. It is a handicap, not for the covering of one story but for covering the Israeli side of the story. The newspaperman can write, Today there was fighting in the Golan Heights and on the West Bank; but the television correspondent cannot record, This is what the battle looked like at Golan Heights, but we couldn't get our cameras over fast enough to photograph the story at the West Bank--the news departments are not quite so modest about the limits of their mechanical capabilities.

Television newscasters, however, feel that they have solved this difficulty. The camera cannot cover all events of the war story, such as the movements of troops from four different points, military confrontation at two other locations, or a United Nations observer shot while on patrol, and so many of these stories must be "talked." The recitation of the day's events, the first paragraphs of the newspaper's inverted pyramid, is presented by the anchorman. The correspondent in the field probably could not do it any better, since the best he might be able to do is to film a "standupper." This, of course, is non-visual and would probably be simply a recording of what is already on the wires, and there seems to be little interest in expending so much time and effort for a shot of the locale. The large amount of money required to satellite this story to New York to keep it current, further constrains this effort. The anchorman in New York can read the story just as well, using graphics of the map of Israel, freeing the correspondent to pursue the more pictorial story. It is a constraint of visual worthiness, timeliness, and the enormous cost involved in transmitting the television news story.

It often happens that the correspondent does try to film all the events, but by the time he has gathered them the situation has already become a different story. As a result, the television journalist needs to specialize, to select a specific incident at a specific time, one idea that is concise and comprehensible. Almost without exception it must be visually interesting and is chosen for its impact. (New York determines whether or not to approve satellite transmission based on the weightiness of the issues and the quality of the film report.) The correspondent will focus on the activities of the resettlement program as it is working today, soldiers out on patrol today, or refugees in a war camp today. The camera is directed toward recording a single moment.

The Vietnam war was illustrative. On Monday a correspondent recorded a three-minute film story on ARVN troops leaving Hue for the north: that was the major event in the news at the time. On Tuesday the troops had progressed ten miles: it was again the major event of the day, but the picture story would have been very much the same as Monday's, and therefore the anchorman in New York "read" that story. For a newspaper it was still

news, as it was for television, but in the newspaper the
same correspondent was reporting the story with the same
tools, using the same format: it was still page one,
column one. For television it was still item one, but
without a picture. The question for the television correspondent out in the field became, what story to gather
today? There were a number of alternatives. There were
the refugee camps: they had always been news, especially
since the offensive: what were things like at the camps
now, and what hope did the refugees have of returning to
their homes? The story was gathered and recorded.

That night, in the United States, the major story of
that day, both for television and the newspapers, was the
progress made by the ARVN troops going north. In the New
York _Times_ this story was on page one, column eight; the
story on the refugee camp was at the bottom of page one,
columns two and three. On television the movement of
troops was reported during the first minute of the broadcast, the refugee camps during the second. The difference? On television, troop movements were given 30 seconds of reportage time, while the refugee camp was given
3 minutes 45 seconds. The news stories were reported,
but the mirror does not quite reflect the same image.

Both media present their stories according to a prescribed hierarchy reflecting the stories' importance, but
newspapers present their stories concurrently, television
sequentially. The newspaper reflects its image on paper
through placement in space; television through placement
in time via the orthicon tube. The newspaper reinforces
its placement hierarchy through variations in the size of
headline print and space allotment, making its layout
readily distinguishable as a hierarchically delineated
map of the day's events. Television often is subject to
distortion of this hierarchical map because it employs,
not space and paper, but time and visual fields. By the
very nature of its mechanical intentions, the picture
story eats up more of the broadcast time than the reading
of a news story on the air by a correspondent. Although
the film story represents only one issue or a single-
moment news event, this fragment will consume four to six
times the amount of time that is devoted to the balance
of the event. Metaphorically, the television format in
time tends to refract as well as reflect the day's events.

Thematic Character of the Story. The television film
story is thematic. There is no inverted pyramid; the
story has a beginning, a middle, and an end. It is diffi-

cult to visualize the whole "event" for television, and
decisions must be made about where the equipment should
be allocated and what segments of the story should be
visualized; this determines which stories will have pictures and which will be read. Cost, equipment, and time
require that it be so. Because the correspondent perceives these technical demands of his medium, he must compose his film story in such a manner that it is thematic.
That is, the audience's attention span is limited, or
perhaps the audience is inattentive, while his message is
evanescent. He must therefore abandon the inverted pyramid and compose a film story that deals with one idea and
offers the viewer an opportunity to grasp the essence of
his story quickly. At the same time, because the camera
mechanically and logistically cannot record the whole
event, the correspondent must select a segment of the
story that is visualizable, focus on this fragment, and
depend on the anchorman in New York to provide the balance
of the story. He is required, however, to briefly explain
why this fragment is important to the viewer and how it
fits into the overall event. That is, he must state the
theme behind the selection of this filmed segment.

For an example, let us take a story of the ARVN
troops moving out of Hue. The scene was visually active
and easily photographable, but it was fundamentally unin-
teresting as merely a three-minute film piece without an
accompanying description. What was left for the correspondent to objectively describe? the uniforms? the
equipment? the topography?--all that was already there
in living color. He could talk about where the troops
were going, what the objectives were, or why this was an
important move at this moment, but this would be inherently interpretative, or what the New York *Times* clearly
labels "News Analysis."

At the time of broadcast, the commentator reported:
"Today 4,000 ARVN troops moved out of Hue to relieve the
city of P---- held by enemy troops. Here is T---- with a
film report." The report that followed was not assumed
to be a consecutively recited description of the event.
It did not ask where the troops were going (which had
already been stated by the commentator), but tried to
delve beneath the surface of this movement (which was
graphically portrayed in the accompanying film) and explain what it meant, what had caused it to occur then, or
what its chances of success were--that is, why the report
was focusing on this fragment of the event and why it was
important.

The refugee story I mentioned was similar to this.
The pictures were vivid and "good television," but what
were the reporting options open to the correspondent? The
major story, about the troop movement, was virtually the
same. If the correspondent chose to record this story
again, it would also require him to choose a different
theme to "talk over" the same film footage of yesterday.
The refugee story, on the other hand, offered a new locale, fresh pictures, and a new story option. The correspondent could put the story into perspective and describe
how these refugees were the victims of the war. He could
humanize the story and show the sufferings of these people
forced from their war-torn villages with only the things
they could carry on their backs. He could ask why they
were there: was it Vietcong shelling or American bombing
that had frightened them into fleeing from their homes;
or was it a lack of faith in the Saigon government? He
could also take the longer view and ask what the future
held for these people. In each case the correspondent
could select a theme that looked beyond the surface of
the recorded visual image of the refugee camp and explain
how it fit into the overall scene that remained unphoto-
graphed. In New York the anchorman talked for 30 seconds
about the troop movements:

> Today ARVN troops advanced ten miles in
> their effort to relieve Quang Tri. . . .
> South Vietnamese refugees have been among
> the major victims in America's bombing ef-
> forts in support of Saigon ground troops
> during earlier confrontations along this
> same route a few months ago. Here is a
> film report from B---- with a closer look
> at these refugees.

The film story was three minutes long. It was concise and
comprehensible and contained only one idea: these refugees
had been victims of American bombing raids. It was thematic, and it was an analysis of the news, but it was labeled simply, "a filmed report from . . ."
    The Vietnam story has been isolated only for purposes
of illustration. The same is true for most film reports;
that is, they have similarity of form and are made under
comparable mechanical difficulties of mobility and limited
recording capabilities. They are also thematic.
    Examples can be drawn from any European beat. It is
January 1972, and Prime Minister Heath is in Brussels to

sign the agreements that will bring England into the Common Market. The television anchorman informs the audience that the Prime Minister is in Belgium to sign the documents: "We have a report from B---- in Belgium." The report is the first of a two-part series on the Common Market. This mini-documentary is four minutes long: for the first one minute and thirty seconds we see the prime minister with the ministers from the other member countries signing the agreements, and it is explained to us that Britain will enter the Market with three other nations over a gradually-phased period of years. Then the correspondent states, "Agriculture was the key stumbling block for both parties and still is a heated issue for both sides to the controversy." For the next two minutes and thirty seconds the countervailing arguments of both sides are presented, with a pictorial backdrop of horse-and-plow farmers in France juxtaposed against mechanized farming elsewhere. National self-interest and consumer pocketbooks are the themes that simplistically sum up the dispute: "the key sentence to the guy who does not really comprehend the story." In short, the correspondent reporting on British entry into the Common Market has offered the American viewing public his interpretation of why Britain had difficulty gaining entry into the Market. It was a complex dispute in which two French vetoes blocked British entry, but for the television viewer the theme of national self-interest and consumer pocketbooks summed it all up. It should be recalled that one of the objectives in composing the television news story was to "humanize the news" for the viewer. How important national interest and consumer pocketbooks were in the actual dispute is open to question, but the preconceptions of the television correspondent concerned with the inherencies of his medium potentially directed him toward the "human" and readily comprehensible interpretation of the news story. Part Two of the series looked at the implications of British entry. The report was a news analysis, an interpretation and not a description of the event. However, it labeled and considered "a film report from Brussels of today's events."

In other words, whether it be a story about the strong and individualistic Basques fighting for their identity in Spain; about the loneliness of an American soldier at Checkpoint Charlie on the Berlin Wall; about whether the Gaullist Party survives as a political party; about what the North Shore oil discoveries will mean to the British economy; about why the Soviets support détente; about the role the Shah of Iran is likely to play in world politics;

or about what the non-oil-producing nations can do to protect their economies, the television film report is not
simply the record of an event; the mechanics of the medium
prevent this. Rather, it is a focus on one segment or one
idea or fact that is thematic and often interpretative and
analytical, although labeled "film report from . . ."

These observations tend to support criticism that
television news reports are fragmented and give only a
partial image of the news event. Critics fail, however,
to distinguish among the different formats and their potential impact. The information is there and the event is
described, usually by the commentator. The thesis here,
however, is that the television film story that is introduced as, and is perceived to be, simply a filmed account
from the scene of the event is in reality a thematic, interpretative analysis of one segment of that event; that
is, it is unlabeled analysis, not by reason of deceptive
intent but because of the actual and perceived mechanical
and structural characteristics of the medium.

Subjective Use of Pictures. Television news tries to
visualize its stories, and because the correspondent pur-
sues the story with this frame of reference there is at
times a tendency to "let the camera tell the real story"
without modifying its message with words. This is what
Kendrick described as the "treatment of public questions,
. . . [as] subjective, instead of as objective," a "kind
of cinema verité that substitutes impressions for points."
(1969, p. 36.) It is faith in pictures, a fascination
with being able to capture the mood of the moment and the
belief that the picture can transfer the experience.
Reuven Frank spoke favorably of this ability when he wrote:

> What is it like to starve to death in Al-
> geria because they can't make up their minds
> about the kind of government they want? Now
> we could find the symbolic thing that opens
> this up, that illuminates it. Television
> does it. It illuminates the news. It
> PICTURES much better than it EXPLAINS. You
> can pick on little things, and by examining
> them you cast light over a larger area.
> This is the function of pictures. (Bluem
> and Manvell, 1967, p. 13.)*

---

*Edward R. Murrow believed "that the medium made it
possible to convey and interpret the message, but that

In television the correspondent often tries to provide the viewer with a first-hand account of the news and tries not to be as indirect as a newspaper. He tries not to quote a news source but to get the individual to speak on camera. It may be a comment that is only a few seconds long, but it leads to a conclusion or represents a point. The correspondent's role in this collage of actualité is to provide the weaving and the structure. "He is the tourist who orders and captions the photographs in his scrapbook." However, he is being selective; his verité is the subjective selection of impressions edited into a whole.

However, in order for the selection to represent the whole, the image often becomes a stereotype, such as of the typical German, Italian, or Russian. Observed one Paris correspondent, "The picture is to capture the stereotype of the object. If you do an interview, or photograph famine, you shoot for the stereotype." However, there is a potential danger of letting the mechanics control the story because the film story can inform by reaching the emotions of the viewers rather than their intellects, by touching their emotions rather than by telling them the facts. Are the people in Algeria starving simply because of indecision by their government? Is the flamboyant George Meany the best spokesman for labor on presidential politics? Was that really the typical Swedish housewife? What are the exceptions and how significant are they? From what part of the whole is the "slice of life" taken? Do people's discussions of their problems resulting from a natural disaster help the viewer in any way to comprehend what has happened or to consider what might be done about the situation? These are all potential perceptual shortcomings in television's mirror image.

THE CONSTRAINTS ON COVERAGE OF VARIOUS TYPES OF STORIES

Attention has been directed at television correspondents, their attitudes and role conceptions and how they view mechanical and structural characteristics to facilitate and/or constrain their newsgathering activities.

---

there had to be a message to start with, that in the beginning was the Word. Otherwise, he said, 'all you have is a lot of wires and lights and a box.'" (Kendrick, 1969, p. 11.)

How the foreign affairs film story is composed has also been described. The picture of this entire process would be incomplete if attention were not given to some of the different foreign affairs beats and to how some of the mechanical and structural characteristics of television affect the gathering of their news stories.

The following observations do not constitute the conclusions of a series of case studies, although the Washington and Paris bureaus were studied in great detail; rather they are conclusions drawn primarily from interviews with at least four, and usually more, correspondents who are either presently or were at one time assigned to one of these beats. We have already observed that certain subjects do not readily lend themselves to television news; philosophy and pornography are examples. What are the specific difficulties that are encountered by the electronic journalist as he or she gathers the Washington foreign policy story, the story abroad, the investigative report, or the news commentary?

The Washington Story

Unless there is a major foreign event, such as a conference, a Presidential trip, or a flareup in a major world capital, in terms of television news coverage there is more activity to be found in Washington than in virtually any other spot in the world for news on foreign affairs for the American audience. Each day the bureau in Washington staffs about eighteen news stories. The evening news is the dominating influence at the Washington bureau, with its own producer, and the major source of money. Of the eighteen stories covered, some three of them will find broadcast time on the evening news. The others are syndicated or used on the morning show.*

---

*The existence of a morning show is an important factor in a network's ability to cover a wider range of stories. One of the three networks does not have a morning news program, and its Washington bureau is at least one-third smaller than the others and therefore able to staff fewer potential stories. The morning news programs are longer and have a different type of audience makeup, watching at a different time of day. The producers are able to permit longer news stories that do not necessarily demand the currency required for broadcast on the evening

The Washington producer and bureau chief are in continual contact with New York. Their advice includes recommendations to the executive producer in New York that include which four or five stories are most important in Washington that day, what they have, and what they can get. They keep their fingers on the pulse of the Washington story, with New York making the final decisions. Said one evening news producer in Washington:

> I'm a salesman. New York can't use all our stories but we can't wait until they make up their minds if they want the story and then try to cover it. We send the crews out, cover more than New York can use, and then I become the salesman at this end and try to sell New York on using our stories.

On both ends of the telephone the producers have read the same newspapers and followed the wires. The Washington bureau, in addition to sending film stories to New York, also at times feeds information to the New York writers working on stories to be read by the commentator. Washington checks out stories that have appeared on the wires that might possibly develop into important leads for larger stories. Correspondents within the bureau compete strenuously with the other Washington bureaus, and among themselves to get on the air.

There is an important perceptible discontent among Washington correspondents, who by and large (75 percent) complain that New York is not attuned to Washington and the other sections of the country. This attitude was also found in Paris and seems to be a natural phenomenon among the correspondents who reside away from the decision-making center and who, because of their own local perspective, see their stories to be the most pressing and demanding of air time. This is true of most news organizations, whether they be newspapers, magazines, or the electronic media, and probably true of most large organizations in other areas as well. The discontent in the Washington

---

programs. This enables the correspondent to engage in more interpretive reporting, to compose more "page two" stories, and to get on the air more often. Correspondents in the network without a morning show uniformly regret its absence and acknowledge its handicap, which is that there are fewer shows to feed their stories to.

bureaus results from a particular problem beyond that of simply different social and cultural atmospheres, however. It is a mechanical problem: foreign affairs news in Washington is not visual. Often the foreign affairs event does not occur in Washington, but it affects and relates to the various parts and departments of the government there. Said one White House correspondent, "In Paris the film comes first, the writing comes last. In Paris as I filmed the story it took its shape. In Washington it is hard to film, and the stress is on the importance of the word and the writing of the story." Correspondents complain that they are at a handicap because "New York wants the picture first."

Most Washington stories are "talking heads" and "standuppers"--the White House correspondent with the Presidential mansion in the background talking his story into the camera. The format is basically the same; only the building in the background and the faces of the correspondents are different. "It's not interesting film," said a Pentagon correspondent, "but there is much below the surface in this town that is subtle and it does not lend itself easily to film or short stories."

Accessibility is a problem that inhibits a pictorial medium even more. Particularly in the foreign affairs area, it was reported, it is more difficult to get decision makers to talk on camera. "They are a little more sensitive to the camera, they weigh their words more."

Finally, the television format inhibits the Washington correspondent. Correspondents complained that the foreign affairs story is usually very complicated and difficult to handle in one or two minutes and particularly problematical when the correspondent must consider the "one idea per story" demands of the television film story. Geoffrey Cox illustrated this dilemma in his discussion of the "situationer," a story that tries to provide background and perspective for an updated story that lacks form and ambles.

> This is a story which the cameras cannot tell, and for which television is forced back on to what is virtually a radio report with the reporter in vision. A certain amount can be done by the use of the sound camera to give atmosphere and authenticity, so that the reporter delivers his report against the background or the place where the conference is being held, or by bringing up film underlays to illustrate his point. But even if this

is done very skillfully the viewer's attention is liable to wander unless the report
is kept short and pointed. Probably the
most effective way with this type of story
is to do these reports only at intervals,
and then to give them a good spread of space,
with the full complement of diagrams and
maps. (Swallow, 1966, p. 46.)

The latter suggestion, however, has a potential for fragmentation of the story, especially if the viewer misses
one of its segments.

To compensate for the nonvisual quality of most Washington stories, the electronic journalist tries to personalize his story; that is, "there is a need to get personalities to comment on the news." For this reason accessibility becomes an even greater concern, not merely
in getting information, but in getting an informant to
discuss or describe it before the television cameras. One
White House correspondent provided an illustrative example. In midwinter 1971 price control hearings were held,
and 30 witnesses were called over a period of 20 days
to provide testimony; the problem was how to handle this
as a two-minute film story. This correspondent chose to
take the testimony of a housewife who spoke before the
group. He was asked why he made this choice and responded,
"I tried to dramatize the story from her point of view.
She was the only one who did not represent a pressure
group and would be readily identifiable with the viewing
audience." The need to visualize and concurrently to
dramatize, simplify, and make identifiable to an audience
(to increase attention and comprehension) mechanically
biases the television news story.

Whether or not the housewife's testimony was representative cannot now be proven. However, the attitude
among the correspondents that they are at a pictorial disadvantage and that their most effective means to visualize
their stories is to personalize, and their attitude toward
the New York producers that "they want the story more
spicy," create the potential danger of a bias toward over-
dramatization and unrepresentative personalization.

Relatedly, there is another potential danger that is
mechanically caused. The Washington story is political
and complex. It often takes place behind closed doors
through which the camera cannot follow. Very often, for
example, the story of détente with the Soviet Union is not
only at the State Department but at the Pentagon, the

White House, and the Senate. Even if the correspondent
drifted from department to department, which he usually
does not because he is often the only one covering the
one beat, while the other correspondent is jealous of the
exclusiveness of his, he would not be able to take with
him the tools of his trade, the camera and sound equipment. The producers in Washington and New York try to
compensate for this problem by tying together 45-second
"talking heads," with each correspondent contributing his
part of the story. For example, there is the military
story from the Pentagon, the diplomatic story from the
State Department, and the political story at the White
House. Each commentator is limited to one idea. The
intertwining thread is mechanical: it is simply the back-
to-back placement of the reports. However, although the
viewer has learned that a picture dissolve represents a
passage of time, it does not follow that in a back-to-back
film report the viewer will be able to discern a uniting
theme. Indeed, very often the correspondents do not con-
sult with one another about the content of their segments,
and their only common frame of reference is their perception of the event itself. Again there is potential danger
of distortion through fragmentation.

Finally, the event may be photographable, but what
is photographed may not represent the story. Most Washington stories occur in the minds of men and within the
decision-making chambers not ordinarily acceptable to the
television lens. For example, there may very well be good
film footage of the Cuban foreign minister denouncing the
American "imperialistic forces" at an annual meeting of
the Organization of American States. The real story, however, may be occurring behind the closed doors at the
State Department, as decision-makers plot a series of sig-
nals aimed at better ties with the Castro government.
Very often, covering public conferences has little to do
with the politics of foreign affairs.

Relations with the Government. In Washington the business,
and therefore the news, is government. Television correspondents in Washington do feel that they are listened to
and seen by members of the government. President Johnson
used to monitor the evening news broadcasts, and if he
disliked a report the correspondent was soon to find out.

> There was the summons to his office for
> sorrowful rebuke. There was the word from
> the press secretary to the local Bureau

Chief. As the weapon of last resort there
was the word from the President to the network chief--with whom he might have personal
as well as business links. This is an artillery that no reporter could hope to withstand.
If an American President chooses to see his
relations with television as war, then it is
one war he can win. (Whale, 1969, p. 147.)

The public information operations of the executive
branch of the government have been estimated to cost $400
million annually. This is more than three times that of
the combined news budgets of the three networks. Dale
Minor in his book The Information War concludes from the
increased centralization and control in government for
the shaping of news information, that "the instinct of
government is not to provide information but to 'manage'
it, to manipulate the information the public receives in
order to elicit a desired response." (1970, p. 4.) Television correspondents are unanimously adamant that the
government must be prevented from deliberately distorting
or omitting information through its control of access to
its personnel, agencies, and the like. Said one veteran
Washington correspondent, "They often try to mislead us
but it is our job to check out the information." Criticism from government is often the payment the correspondent receives for his disclosures. Commented one Washington bureau chief:

It's the great Washington hangup--there's a
touch of incest in this town--correspondents
and government officials intermingle all
the time. There's some danger of being
seduced by cocktail parties, etc. The correspondents rarely go to these parties and
the good correspondents don't get involved.
The correspondents' role is one of distance.

Nevertheless, the Washington correspondent enjoys dining
at the same restaurants with top government officials and
being seen with them and calling them by their first names
and being called the same way.
The correspondent on the beat interacts regularly
with his sources, and it is obviously not easy to face a
source, whether a department head or a press secretary,
the day after a critical report or the disclosure of secret information. In this respect the television corre-

145

spondent faces many of the same problems experienced by reporters from other media, but the television correspondents, like the others, are conscious of, and insistent on, maintaining their distance, although this is not meant to imply that there are not exceptions at times. As David Brinkley stated about this general idea, "Anyone who can't stand the criticism should not go into journalism, as I think anyone who can't stand criticism should not go into politics." (1971, p. 95.) Also, Walter Cronkite observed, "Somewhere in the history of our Republic there may have been a high government official who said he had been treated fairly by the press, but for the life of me, however, I can't think of one." (December 1970, p. 53.)

Television, to some degree, needs more cooperation from its subjects, if only to get them to comment on camera. The print journalist can compile a rather comprehensive report without the actual participation of the central news figures; the same story that a newspaperman gathers can be written for television but the demand for pictures remains unsatisfied. Television would like to have the newsmaker on camera, but this usually requires his cooperation.

At the same time, however, television might have a degree of independence not available to the newspaper. Many local newspapers have problems getting the story because they lack a wide enough audience to gain or demand the attention of a department head. They are often more dependent upon or afraid of the power of the local government or community and are inhibited from reporting a particular story. Television correspondents, on the other hand, often provide examples of their ability to gain access because they represent the major networks and large, national audiences. "We have more clout around here," said a White House correspondent. The most prominent example of television's independence from local governments has been its coverage of the civil rights movement, which has often been ignored by the media in the very communities on which a decision made in Washington had direct bearing. In these instances the national character of the medium facilitates the dissemination of important information.

The State Department Story. The State Department is an example of a Washington beat with stories that are not readily visualizable. It is an important newsgathering point, especially for leaks and background information. The department's personnel are mostly career people and

146

are more likely to believe in candor, particularly if the
decision is one that was made by the White House without
involving their services or if it overturned their recommendations. There is an almost daily news conference that
has its own code. To the layman it means little, but to
the trained correspondent the intentional twist of a phrase
tells the story. It is a long and laborious process
to arrange television recording of this press conference,
and because of the code its pictorial recording has limited news value. Moreover, the department personnel tend
to prefer the pad-and-pencil correspondent; New York _Times_
and Washington _Post_ reports provide maximum impact for
their story, for a good leak, or for a policy plant. The
source of a news leak obviously doesn't want to be visually identified, and television provides too wide and
diverse an audience for the interest-group reaction they
desire from the story plant. The preference, therefore,
is for the print journalist.

The State Department television correspondents have
not always been the happiest of men. During the Kennedy
and early Nixon administrations key foreign policy decisions were made in the White House. Moreover, one Secretary of State was afraid and nervous of the television
camera. Therefore the State Department correspondent did
not find himself on the air as often as he would have
liked. There were stories at State, and they were being
reported, but by the important newspapers, since they
were page two or page ten stories in the paper and television has only a page one.

With Henry Kissinger as Secretary of State, more
stories are coming out of the State Department, but the
packaging of the story is still very difficult.

> It's not visual but New York wants it to be
> dramatic. I wrote that there was a "major
> change in policy." New York called back
> and asked if I would change "major" to
> "drastic." I had the power not to, but
> there is the pressure. I did a story on
> the walkout on trade with the Soviet
> Union, but they chose the one from Moscow
> --it was more dramatic.

On the other hand, because there was very little picture
value at the State Department and under Rusk and Rogers,
it was not a very busy beat, and there was time allotted
occasionally for interpretive stories on such matters as

the U.S. position toward Latin American countries, Cuba's isolation, the department's underlying pessimism about the cost of oil, and lower-echelon discontent with the Secretary of State.

The Pentagon Story. The Pentagon story is nonvisual too, notwithstanding there are five possible angles of the building to speak from instead of the ordinary four. Today the special problem the television correspondent has in covering the story is the distrust they have for him in this organization. Commented one of the network correspondents assigned to this beat, "The basic feeling here is that television was responsible for their problems in Vietnam. That we're the guys who showed the burning of villages, that we oversimplify and overdramatize. They are convinced that we have an enormous impact."

It is particularly difficult to get an interview at the Pentagon, and when an interview is granted it is monitored by the Public Affairs Office. It often takes weeks to set up, as did one interview with the Secretary of the Air Force, which when it finally occurred was simultaneously recorded by a Pentagon official in front of seventeen observers. Private telephone calls to or conversations with members of the press are looked at askance. Leaks are very few for television at the Pentagon. Investigations are immediately held, and although they have no possibility of finding the source, the intensity with which they are carried out discourages other leaks. Most information about the Pentagon's military intentions comes from Capitol Hill through the budget, from the Senate Arms Services Committee, and from contacts with individual members. Select members of Congress are well informed through closed-door hearings on such matters as what weapons systems will be pushed or what the present state of the Salt II talks is.

The Pentagon has often made this beat especially difficult for television. Frequently a story is not released until 4:30 p.m. or later, when no television personnel are left in the press room and it is too late for the evening news. It appears the next morning in the newspapers, but by 7 the next evening its currency has faded and it is generally not broadcast. Officials may return a call that attempted to get confirmation on a tip at 6:28 p.m. Television too has some leverage, however. Because like any news medium it can make people aware of certain deficiencies of information by broadcasting the fact, television can enlarge audience awareness, forcing the Pentagon to respond. Some stories are not covered that the television correspondents think should be done, including the arms race and strategic balance; they are not done for various reasons, the most prominent of which are that "the American audience is not interested"; "it can't be made simple"; and "we don't know how to do it."

The Congress Story. Congress also poses certain problems. Much of its work takes place in committee rooms and on the chamber floors. Reporters and cameramen are only occasionally permitted to transcribe and photograph the proceedings of the committees and are specifically forbidden entrance into chambers. For committee coverage the success of the film story often depends on the cooperation of the chairman and thereby is often biased toward covering the cooperative ones. For example, Senator Fulbright has been described as particularly cooperative with television correspondents. After a closed committee hearing he would meet with correspondents in a pad-and-pencil session and then, afterward, step before the waiting cameras in the corridor and try to repeat his comments for television and radio recording. Said one Senate correspondent, "You never come away from a Fulbright hearing without a film story." Television is often naturally susceptible to the cooperative personality, and it requires extra effort to record the views of personalities who are not so conscious of the media.

However, all Congressional correspondents mentioned that it was much easier to cover Capitol Hill for television than to cover a city hall. Commented one, "If a local paper goes against City Hall, the legislature will not talk. Here we have an easy relationship with the legislature, and it is better to deal with the senator himself than with his staff." Correspondents covering this beat complain of the little coverage their stories receive in actual broadcast time. A lot happens there, they say, but it is not interesting television. It is not always easy to find the right spokesman on an issue, and when they do focus on someone it is usually for his "Congressional" or "opposition party" reaction to an event. Many of the legislative maneuverings are not visible, and, it is a slow and uneven process. Commented one correspondent, "The White House story is much easier; there is one man and it is easy to humanize."

The White House Story. The White House beat suffers all the problems of secrecy, distrust, need for permission to

149

photograph an event, and dependency on sources and on getting people to talk, as well as its own distinctive ones.
Its advantage over the Congressional beat is the ability
it gives the correspondent to focus on one man holding the
highest political position in American government; but
that, too, creates its own difficulties. In a sense,
whatever the President does is regarded as news, and the
problem is how to cover and handle the story.

Television is particularly tied to the activities of
the President: the President may take his family on a
sailing trip, pull the ears of his dog, or get a cold, or
he may spend his time with certain people when he stays
at the Southern White House; whatever it is, the equipment is there. It is good television: easily humanized,
dramatic, visual, and a subject identifiable with American
interests.

Television journalism has a tendency to overreact.
Nixon's China trip is an illustrative example. Not only
did almost every major correspondent cover the trip, but
top corporate executives and executive producers went as
well, filling roles as soundmen, cameramen, and other
technicians. Russell Baker commented humorously on television's almost total reaction, succinctly represented in
his article's title, "No Harry? No Walter? No John?
No . . . ?"--the first names being those of the networks'
commentators. What he says in the balance of the article
is humorous not for its fantasy but for its true reflection.

> There are a few people, however who will be
> in trouble. All those people who are run-
> ning for President, for example. What's the
> point of running in the U.S.A. if all the
> television is over in China?
>   The same question--"What's the use?"--
> confronts Congressmen, people who blow up
> buildings, writers with new books to be
> flogged--everybody, in short, to whom tele-
> vision exposure is life's blood and mother's
> milk. . . .
>   The President flying about the earth
> to engage in pageant diplomacy, like a Tudor
> king on a royal progress through the realm,
> provides the spectacle story which televi-
> sion reports incomparably.

While this example may represent an extreme case, its
manifestation is by no means isolated, as Bernard Rubin

reported about President Johnson's speech before the United Nations General Assembly on December 17, 1963.

> The address was extremely pedestrian in content. His purpose was merely to be seen before the international body and not to ruffle feathers. But television, on the theory that ANY major appearance of the President is intrinsically important, dutifully presented the speech as a MAJOR international event. (1967, p. 118.)

Although the President can also exert influence on the networks through legislation and the like, if his purpose is simply capturing the attention of the news media he can generally have it. The television correspondents see the President as the chief source of domestic legislation and the chief architect of American foreign policy, and they consider the White House "good television." Therefore the President is the recipient of frequent and extensive television coverage.

In short, the Washington story has one major constraint for the television journalist: it is not visual. This handicap potentially, if not really, tends to promote the personalization of the news and an increased dependence on the cooperation of news sources to agree to have their comments videotaped, while certain advantages of exposure on the medium accrue to certain branches of the government and certain disadvantages to others.

The Story from Abroad

On almost any day the television viewer may have visualized before him fighting in Belfast, ARVN troop actions in Quang Tri, a trial in Israel, and pictures of Soviet agricultural operations. This is television's special function: to pictorially bring the outstretched world into the living room. How does it go about carrying out this task?

There are a number of technical advances that have greatly enhanced television's ability to report the news. The most important include more mobile equipment, which permits the correspondent and his crew to photograph hitherto untapped areas; the satellite, which permits faster transmission of the story; and, very important, the jet plane, which enables the correspondent to arrive on the scene a very short time after the news story has broken.

Much has happened in the short history of television journalism, the technology of which is only part of the story. America has changed from a country of the vast involvements across the globe and strong interest in international affairs that followed the victories of World War II, to one of self-doubt and internal turmoil. Whether some pundits are correct in saying that the American people have moved from internationalism to isolationism, will be for future historians to determine. That there is an increased turning inward to confront our own domestic problems and a concomitant turning inward among the broadcast journalists, cannot be doubted. More and more the television journalists point to problems at home and their concern about them: "This is where it is happening. This is where the story is."

More correspondents are becoming interested in the domestic story, yet they equally lament the drop-off in interest in the foreign story. Just as one generation of American journalists were brought up and trained in foreign affairs news in the European theater, the new generation of journalists gained its seminal training in Vietnam. These two generations, for the moment, coexist at each network. The older generation's frame of reference is Europe, the second world war, and the aftermath of peace and reconstruction. It was the time of the "European dateline," and the pattern of foreign bureaus reflects this frame: London, Paris, Rome, Bonn, and so on. The younger generation's frame of reference is Asia, and its training ground was Saigon. Its time is now, the daily report from Saigon, Hong Kong, or Tokyo. They know the back streets of Saigon better than they know the tourist attractions of Paris; they can shop in Hong Kong but know nothing of Regent Street; they are more familiar with the taste of saki than that of chianti. If you pursue the issue with those under 40 years of age, their interest lies in Asia; they see China as vital; and their focus is the Pacific Ocean. Said one of these correspondents: "I have been five times to Asia and only once to Europe. When we are in their positions [the older generation's] there will be more bureaus in Singapore and all over Asia."

The Foreign Bureau. The foreign correspondent abroad is responsible for covering a particular country or area in the world, rather than a particular story. His or her center of operations is the foreign bureau. Generally two or three rooms in size, the foreign bureau has one and sometimes two correspondents assigned to it, one or two film crews made up of nationals of the foreign country, and perhaps a radio correspondent and a few stringers, an office manager, and two or three secretaries who also substitute as researchers. Each bureau usually has a minimum of one American and one foreign wire service. There are facilities for processing and editing film and usually a small studio for television and radio recording.

Traditionally the foreign correspondent has been the bureau chief, although there are some indications of change. Especially at the European bureau, the correspondent is likely to travel outside of that country and to spend as much as half of his time away from the bureau. Field producers and administrative bureau chiefs have recently been assigned in an effort to relieve the correspondent of the administrative responsibilities and free him from chores that do not relate directly to a story. While theoretically the correspondent has final say on stories and content, the new administration aide is responsible for equipment allocation and satellite feeds and is the one most often in contact with New York.* This is a trend most prevalent at one network, although discussed and being planned by other networks as well. This phenomenon is easily explainable by the changes that have come about at the foreign bureaus over the past few years. As mentioned above, when television came onto the scene the focus of the news was in Europe. As a result, today most foreign bureaus are located in Western Europe; but the "European dateline" has vanished and the story is not always there. Perhaps there is a story or two every month out of Paris, but that alone is not enough to justify the cost of a correspondent and his attendant staff. However, there are stories in Northern Ireland, Malta, the Azores, Spain, Libya, and so on, and the Paris correspondent or the correspondent in London or Rome is sent via jet plane, to cover these stories. For the moment at least these stories do not warrant a bureau, but perhaps they will require a three-week stint by the Paris correspondent, who will do three or four film reports from Belfast, spend four weeks in Malta for another four or five stories, and then be off to another story in Munich. Paris is quiet, and although the bureau is located there and that is his home base, the correspondent's absence may leave a potential story uncovered or delegated to a stringer, or the

---

*See the discussion of the role of field producers in the first section of Chapter 3.

radio correspondent may be substituted. Said one foreign
correspondent, "I'm on the road most of the time. I carry
two suitcases, one with clean shirts and the other with
research materials to prepare myself for the next story,
wherever that may take me."

In the 1950s this was not the case. If a correspondent's assignment was Germany, he remained in that country
most of the time and became an expert on Germany and Eastern Europe. The story was there as well. Said one veteran of this period,

> That was the era of Hottelett, Leiser and
> Schorr. We were much more expert on Germany
> than our correspondent there now. Our beat
> was Germany and Eastern Europe. His now
> ranges as far as Bangladesh and the Middle
> East. There is no longer the threat of World
> War III in Europe. The story is elsewhere.

It was also a smaller news operation, and the correspondent knew the man in New York personally and was in contact with him directly. This is not always the case today.
Now there is often an intermediary in the form of a field
producer on the beat or a European producer located in
London. This movement tends to cause the correspondent
to follow the events and limits his time to do non-event
stories within a country.

Most of the ideas for foreign stories come from New
York, and an elaborate and effective system has been established to keep the foreign correspondents attuned to
the attitudes operating there, although this varies among
correspondents. The more well known have greater independence as a result of their stronger personalities and
the leverage of their national prestige. "There is a
jealous news hierarchy in New York," said one Paris correspondent. The bureau chief or his representative is in
daily contact with New York either by the telex or if very
important on the telephone. The bureau receives daily
logs of the stories broadcast on the evening news programs
of its own network and on those of the competitors. Very
often there is an accompanying note on one of two themes:
(1) "Good film last night. We beat the opposition." or
(2) "They had good footage on that story yesterday. Where
were you?" From this log the correspondent can evaluate
which stories made the broadcast and which did not, which
gives him a further indicator of the selection preferences
exercised in New York. Once a month a filmed selection of

an evening broadcast is sent to each bureau to help the
correspondent see the visual product as well and judge the
selection criteria employed. At 10 a.m. each morning the
"daily insight" is telexed to New York, indicating what
stories are being covered, what the correspondents are
intending to do, and how the stories will be transmitted
to New York and giving some evaluation of their importance.
There are also weekly reports and evaluations from New
York. Although most of the stories were earlier suggested
by New York, the correspondent does retain a degree of independence, particularly in the editorial content of the
story. This independence seems to increase the further he
is from New York and the more vital the story is, especially when edited abroad and transmitted in edited form
to New York by satellite.

New York is concerned lest the correspondent abroad
lose contact with the climate of interest and attitudes
prevalent in the United States. To prevent this "foreign
isolation," each network has an elaborate rotation system.
Bureau chiefs, and often correspondents, are rotated every
two or three years. The correspondents are brought back
to the United States at least once every two years for
special "exposure" tours of the United States. These last
a number of weeks, and the correspondents tour six to ten
cities across the country watching the local and network
news broadcasts, participating in seminars, and giving
speeches to local organizations. This is a relearning process for the correspondent and a valuable public relations
effort for the network. Commented a correspondent in Paris,

> Living abroad gives you a wider spectrum,
> and you naturally read the local press and
> see points that a skilled French correspon-
> dent has done that the American press might
> not have covered. While abroad you naturally
> read the local papers, which when living in
> New York becomes a chore. What you have to
> guard against abroad is to make sure that
> your standards remain American ones.

Indeed, the foreign news story seems to be a reflection either of American interests or of American stereotypes. Very often correspondents indicated that French
prison reforms, for example, or Sartre's dispute over Le
Peuple, did not conform to what Americans were interested
in and therefore stories were not done on these subjects.
And, of course, how do you illustrate them? "Ecology is

big," said the correspondents, and international reaction to the Angela Davis trial and an all-woman slate in a small-town French city were uniformly mentioned as important news for an American audience. Only major flareups or unavoidable historic moments, such as the 1968 riots in France or a national election, can supersede these criteria. "New York tends to run into stereotypes," commented a Paris correspondent. "For example, I was sympathetic to de Gaulle's foreign policy. He was a shrewd man. But New York regarded him as unfriendly to the United States and jealous of this country. That's the story they wanted covered. We contribute to the stereotype." Another observed, "we serve up to their clichés."

Correspondents reported that it was very difficult to get a piece broadcast that opposed American viewpoints. For example, they observed that it was always easy to get a story broadcast on a German beer festival or on German war crimes "because the United States sees the Germans as either beer drinkers or war criminals." There is also the European "slice of life" feature on a "typical Italian family," an inherent stereotypic format. Other examples include the French concern over the rise in the price of bread; the first drive-in theater in Paris; the Italian family celebrating Christmas eve; the English and the modern beer pub; and the modern Swedish woman--that is, the stereotypic peculiarities of life and attitudes in the European country. It was more difficult to get approval for a story on German youth unless it in some way corresponded to the problems of American youth. These perceptions seem to cause the television journalist, and therefore the American viewer, to miss important developments within a country, unless they have a perceptible direct bearing on American interests and stereotypes.

There is one important editorial tool available to the foreign correspondent that facilitates his efforts in reporting foreign news and mitigates the otherwise constraining influence of writing for an American audience. Of the use of interpretation in the foreign news story, William S. Paley was quoted to have said to a group of CBS News executives, "In this country play it down the middle. Overseas you can be tough." (MacNeil, 1968, p. 75.) This attitude was discernible among television's foreign correspondents.

> In the foreign affairs television story we
> can make an interpretive point much easier
> because there is less sensitivity to the

subject than there is to a domestic subject.
In the United States you have to be con-
cerned not to offend the Democrats or the
Republicans, for example.

The European Story. Television faces some important problems that are distinctive to the medium in reporting the
European story. The camera poses important constraints,
particularly since it is dependent upon the cooperation of
a foreign government. By and large, as Europe has entered
the era of modernization, the people have become more and
more familiar with the roving television news team with
its strange and complicated equipment and do not shy away
when approached. This is not always the case with their
governments. After the events of May 1968 the French government of Georges Pompidou distrusted the television
medium and was not especially cooperative about participating in talks or discussions on camera. In semidicta-
torial countries like Spain and some Eastern European
nations, the governments are more suspicious of the camera
than they are of the pad and pencil. Commented a correspondent with experience in Spain, "If you report for the
New York Times you go to an event and if you are really
smart you don't take your pad and pencil. But when you
arrive on the scene with a camera you are a clear target
for the police." There is a suspicion of cameras in these
countries.
     Moscow is a particularly difficult beat for televi-
sion because there, too, the government has a distrust of
the camera. Indeed, many correspondents commented that
there was greater freedom for the television correspondent
in the People's Republic of China than in the Soviet Union.
There is no direct transmission from Moscow, Nixon's 1972
visit being the major exception. A story told by a former
Moscow television correspondent illustrates this problem:

     When I arrived at the assignment in Moscow I
     checked in at the Foreign Ministry and I met
     Mr. K----. I said to him that I was here
     because I'm interested in the Soviet people
     and I want to do "feature stories" about
     them. He asked me for an example. I looked
     out the window and told him that I would
     like to do a film story on that woman in
     the street putting snow onto a conveyor belt
     to be cleared away by being dumped into the
     river. His reaction was that it was not an

objective story. I asked why and he said
because the woman <u>will not</u> be down there.
That was the problem of a dialectical view
vs. an objective view of reality. The picture conveys the reality of the moment.
The Soviet government wants to convey only
the dialectical reality. They are very
short on cooperation toward the candid
conveyance of the picture's reality.

It is difficult to get pictures, especially since the
American correspondent is dependent upon Russian camera
crews to film them. Often permission to do the story is
given but no camera crew is made available. The same
difficulties do not exist for the newspaper reporter.
There are virtually no film reports from Eastern Europe.
   "Talking heads" are often the only pictures available
for a European story, and they are not only nonvisual but
also less likely to be transmitted by satellite. The
story will therefore lose some of its currency. Language
poses a problem with a "talking head" piece, and it is
sometimes difficult to find an expert or "man on the
street" who speaks English well enough and who is also
willing to talk on camera.
   In Europe the story is the Common Market and the
monetary crisis but it is uniformly agreed that the economic story is difficult to do for television. NBC had a
special economic correspondent stationed in Brussels to
cover the EEC story, but the bureau was closed within one
year.
   The economic story is more abstract or theoretical,
and most information is given out in conferences with reporters while the decisions are made behind closed doors.
It tends to be esoteric, as in the debate on the duty to
be placed on cheese dependent upon the altitude in which
the cow grazes, and there is very little visually. The
story is perceived to be very remote from the people, not
only in America but in Europe as well. "It's important,"
said a Paris correspondent preparing to do a story on the
Common Market, "but it's hard to grab. There's no picture, no action, only a conflict of ideas or the exchange
of money and goods. You have to distill it and simplify
it. They are stories that correspondents hate to do--
there's not good film in it." The story is reported,
therefore, in one of two ways: (1) the economic issue
takes on an important political significance that breaks
out into the open, and is then reported as a political

story; or (2) it becomes personalized into how the individual shopper will be affected, as a "slice of life" or as a stereotype.

Economics is reported on television only when it is vitally important and front-page news. Important economic news that would find space on the financial pages of the New York _Times_ or Washington _Post_ finds no time on the evening news broadcast. A correspondent commented that television "has never covered a national budget and it never will."

Competition is also an important factor abroad. This occurs not just in the coverage of the stories in the daily log reports of the three networks, but also in deciding the means of transmission. For example, two networks might have film reports on the presidential election in Paris. If one network discovers that the other has reserved time for a satellite feed, while it is planning to send the story to New York by plane, it is quite probable that the latter will alter its plans and also reserve satellite time, so as not to be found at a competitive disadvantage.

Cost is an important consideration in satellite transmission. Generally one story produced in Europe would not warrant a satellite, but two might. For example, a network might have coupled a story on bombings in Northern Ireland with Heath's signing of the EEC agreements. For a short period of time Europe was averaging two to three film stories a week, satellited to New York. None of these stories warranted single transmission, but this was the period of the India-Pakistan war, and film footage was satellited to New York by way of London and the European stories were tied on. During that period the networks very often had their European film reports on the air before the same stories appeared in the newspapers. Without the tie-up, the individual European story was considered too expensive for transmission.* "It has to be visually big to be sent out by satellite," commented a Paris bureau manager.

The Latin American Story. Television news has always given Latin American affairs sporadic coverage. Three

---

*The first three minutes of satellite transmission are much more expensive than the next three minutes. Very often the networks will agree to transmit their stories back-to-back to cut down on costs.

periods can be said to have represented high points of television coverage from that area: the Castro revolution in the late 1950s and early 1960s; the 1967 Punta Del Este meeting; and Allende's election in 1970 to the presidency of Chile and his overthrow and death in 1973. During the early Castro period there were foreign bureaus in some Latin American capitals, including Rio de Janeiro, Mexico City, and Buenos Aires. However, with the exception of a skeleton bureau in Mexico City, these were closed until 1967, when NBC and CBS each assigned a permanent correspondent to Latin America, located in Mexico City, in response to what appeared to be increased American concern and activity in this part of the world. Within 13 months the NBC bureau was closed; during this period the correspondent had spent some months in Korea and in Hong Kong and had covered Humphrey's presidential campaign and the second marriage of Jacqueline Kennedy. The CBS correspondent had spent most of his tenure as Latin American correspondent covering the India-Pakistan dispute, the Middle East, and Vietnam. Ultimately this correspondent was also reassigned. Since 1970 there have been no permanent foreign bureaus in Latin America. One network maintains a skeleton bureau, but it is located in Miami.

Both Allende's election and his death caused a stir in this country, and correspondents were sent out to cover these stories. Most Latin American stories are covered in this fashion. They are considered spot stories. The correspondent goes out for about three weeks to cover the Peru-U.S. fishing dispute, Nelson Rockefeller's Latin American trip, or the visit to Cuba by Senators Javits and Pell. He files his story and returns to home base either in Washington or New York.

There are a number of reasons for the scarcity of coverage and the absence of foreign bureaus in Latin America.* The jet plane is one. Because the north-south flight routes are more frequent and direct, it is generally easier and faster to get to a capital in Latin America from New York or Miami than from another Latin American city. For instance, it is easier to go from New York or Miami to Uruguay than it is to get from Rio to Uruguay. The other is the perception that Americans are not interested in Latin America unless "their ox is being gored." Said one veteran Latin American correspondent, "It's still

---

*There are stringers kept on retainer in virtually every major national capital.

160

back to the old story--the red menace. A stringer once said to me: 'the only thing you Americans are interested in is earthquakes and revolution'--and he's right." The first Latin American bureau was set up because of Castro. News from Latin America declined, so the interpretation goes, as Castro ceased to be news.

There are stories in Latin America that are crucial to that region, including the Brazil-Argentina power struggle, land reform, and runaway inflation; but as one former Latin American correspondent said,

> If I called the producers and told them about the interesting and subtle maneuverings for influence on the continent between Brazil and Argentina they would not be interested. But if I said they were going to have a war I would be on the plane within an hour. Why? It can be told in the simplicities of struggle and it's good film.

Another experienced journalist in the area stated,

> It's a problem because most of the issues there are economic and social. Take for example ITT communications control in Chile. It didn't become news until it became political (because of the ITT letter to President Nixon recommending U.S. interference). News is predominantly political.

When the bureaus existed in Latin America, feature and mini-documentary stories were broadcast because the correspondent was there and sent them in. One correspondent commented that while he was on assignment in Latin America he had 14 stories in New York unused; however, he did have more than 15 broadcast over a period of six months. Information was being disseminated, but not enough to warrant the financial outlay and the time and interest of the correspondent. The same correspondent said:

> I left because my stories were not being aired. People don't care about Latin America unless it's anti-Americanism. My colleagues at the New York _Times_ would get their stories printed on page two. . . . I go back occasionally to cover a spot story, but I would resist a permanent

161

assignment there. It's an exercise in frustration. Eventually they ask why you are
there and they fire you. It's not competitive. The other network had a man there at
a time when we didn't and had some stories
we missed, but we weren't too upset about
it. Your stories don't get on the air.

The American audience is interested in Latin American
news if it is political or anti-American or directly affects American foreign policy, but not in news indigenous
to the area or about relations among these countries. It
is a noncompetitive sphere, and for television it is a
dark continent. When a story breaks, a correspondent is
sent to the area to cover the event. If he has time he
collects some additional stories that surround the major
one. But there is no permanent or continuous Latin American newsgatherer at any of the three networks.

The African Story. A news department president commented,
"We did a special on Africa because we happened to hit on
it at a good time. There was a certain mystique about
this area that does not exist in Latin America." However,
there is no foreign bureau in Africa either. Travel is
a problem here too, and the question is, in which country
should the one or two correspondents be located? When
the continent is covered it is from Rome. Furthermore,
because of the diversity of the area many correspondents
resist assignments there because of the amount of leg work
involved in preparing to cover a story in this complex and
unfamiliar continent. There is almost a perceptual iner-
tia running against this area of the world. Said one
correspondent, "We don't cover the Third World revolutions
because Americans really aren't interested. The perception is that we are so far removed and these flareups have
left a bad taste. We should cover them but they don't
get air time."

Logistics, of course, create a problem. There are
no central transmission points. Color processing requires
much more complex equipment, and facilities are not available in these countries. It is difficult for the story
to be current. In the less-developed countries there is
greater suspicion of the press in general and toward television in particular. A First Lady's trip to Africa is
covered if and when it occurs, but only a national disaster or perhaps, though certainly not always, a revolution
is covered: Nigeria, for example, is far better covered

than Burundi, which receives virtually no film coverage.
Burundi is also a country that has few Western residents,
that is not cooperative toward the press, and that has few
facilities for transportation or communications transmission. Africa remains, for television, another dark continent.

The Asian Story. Finally, if one talks to the average
correspondent hired after 1963, he or she will reflect in
one manner or another a preference for Asian news and will
predict that the news of the next decade or two will come
from Asia.* Most correspondents in this category received
their seminal training in Vietnam. Toward the end of the
1960s the Saigon bureau had become the second-largest
television news bureau, that is, second only to Washington. The networks spent more than $5 million per year to
report this story. This is too complex a story to be
dealt with in any great detail here, and the influence
that television played on the outcome of this war will be
a fundamental question that communications specialists
will be struggling with for years. In an earlier section
of this chapter some of the problems of writing the film
story in Vietnam were described; but the other biases
created by the mechanical and structural characteristics
of the medium also have come to play an important role in
the Vietnam story. A sampling of these constraints, although it is not intended to be exhaustive, will show the
representative highlights.

1. The television format tended to promote a fragmented, segmental approach to coverage of this big, continuing story. As reported by Michael Arlen,

> Television, with all its technical resources
> with all the possibilities of film and film-
> editing for revealing fluid motion, continues
> for the most part to report the war as a
> long, long narrative broken into two-minute,
> three-minute, or four-minute stretches of
> visual incident. (1969, p. 108.)

---

*It should be noted that this perception was recorded
in early 1972, when most of the American population, and
in particular the journalists on the scene, had soured
toward American involvement in Southeast Asia. The perception, nonetheless, prevails.

This observation was prevalent among veteran Vietnam correspondents, and interviews with them elicited responses
that concurred with Leonard Zeidenberg's finding that
"there is among the newsmen an undercurrent of dissatisfaction. Some say that massive as television's effort
already is in reporting the news and its collateral aspects, its coverage should be enlarged." (1968, p. 31.)
    2. Combat footage was consistently mentioned as
good television news. William Small, the CBS Washington
bureau chief, wrote:

> The pursuit of the big battle has been the
> heart of one of the greatest controversies
> involving television in Vietnam. Many corre-
> spondents and producers, despite disclaimers
> from New York, insist that the "name of the
> game" is to "shoot bloody," to get the good
> battle footage. Sometimes it is not that
> direct. Sometimes it is a cable saluting a
> good story on pacification or the upcoming
> election or refugee problems and there is the
> added note: "By the way, the competition got
> some great battle footage of the Marines near
> Hue." (1970, p. 96.)

Mike Wallace, a CBS correspondent, was reported to have
said:

> Some of the correspondents kept a kind of
> scorecard as to which pieces were and were
> not used and why, and it did seem as though
> an inordinate number of combat pieces were
> used compared with some first-rate pieces in
> the political area or the pacification area
> and non-bloody stories. (Minor, 1970, p. 155.)

The NBC Policy Book states with regard to policy on Vietnam coverage:

> There is a ground rule against reporting the
> size of the units engaged in an action--pla-
> toons, companies, etc.--or the unit strength
> in numbers of men unless this information is
> released by an appropriate unit commander or
> by a military authority in Saigon.
>   Casualty figures in an action are sub-
> ject to the same security rules. Casualty

figures for the U.S. troops are acceptable
as given in official U.S. announcements.
Casualty figures for enemy troops by an ap-
propriate unit commander or by military
authority in Saigon.

Acceptable film showing identified
American dead or wounded is subject to a
check with a designated Defense Department
office to make certain that the next of kin
have been notified.

A designated Pentagon office is notified when we are going to show film from
Japanese, Chinese, French or other sources,
exposed in North Vietnam and identifying
American prisoners of war. The Pentagon
then may notify families of the prisoners
prior to the showing. Such film is identified on the air as to its source.

It is important, where the fact is
clearly established, to designate whether
enemy forces are North Vietnamese, Viet Cong
or mixed units. Specify also whether an
engagement is fought by South Vietnamese,
Americans or units of allies such as the
Australians and South Koreans.

Be careful when offered film made in
North Vietnam or under North Vietnamese control. Part of the war is a propaganda effort. We do not want to be an instrument of
policy.

Editors are asked to consider whether
the naming of specific units in an action
is essential to understanding the story
since it may cause needless anxiety to
relatives of the men. (p. 85.)

3. The political story on Vietnam tended to end up
as a "standupper." The economic story was not always
visual, and compared to the combat story it was not very
dramatic. The social story was visual and dramatic but
fraught with hazards: the cameras did not have access to
the activities of the North Vietnamese; they would accompany the American troops into battle or follow them into
a village after a search-and-destroy operation. Said one
correspondent, "Television, because it focuses on humanity, has been critical of the United States in Vietnam."

165

For the most part there was no front line in the
Vietnam war. The story was to be found on the company
level, not the command level. The correspondent went out
with the troops, and the story became a personalized,
humanized story, a slice of life. Said another veteran
Vietnam correspondent, "We follow the troops and assume
that we are after the combat or the personal story and
that the others in New York will do the other parts of
the story."

Vietnam, however, has not been the only story in
Asia, but it initiated, trained, conditioned, and accul-
turated a generation of correspondents to the region.
For them China and the Far East loom ever present in their
political maps of the world. The big question that must
be raised, the answers to which will have to await the
passage of time, is: What shape will foreign affairs news
take when this generation assumes the editorial direction
of television?

Alternative News Formats

The foreign affairs story poses many problems for the
television correspondent. The mechanics and structure of
the medium affect how he covers the story, whether in
Washington, Europe, Asia, or Africa. Different news formats offer alternative approaches for completing the foreign affairs picture, however. These additional formats,
the investigative report and the news editorial, which
are traditional to the press function, are available to
the television correspondent only in a very limited way.

When the nightly news increased its time allotment,
it was hoped that the new possibilities for mini-documentaries would enable the television correspondent to engage in more investigative reporting, but this did not
happen to any great extent. Said one former Vietnam
correspondent responsible for some major investigative
disclosures from that area, "We just don't have the time
to do investigative stories. We should, but with television it takes too much time, and we don't have the
excess staff to do it." Cost is a major factor. Investigative reporting takes time, and it is very expensive
to release a correspondent and crew to spend several
months on a four-minute film piece that may or may not
work out. Time plays an important role. With their large
though limited staff, the networks already have difficulty
covering the basic news and do not have the comfortable

margin necessary to allow the temporary loss of one or two correspondents and crews. John Luter analyzed another constraint as follows:

> Some investigations obviously depend on the kind of detailed information and documentation that can be obtained only through a painstaking search of records, or from informants who are unwilling to be identified. This is often true, for example, of exposés involving official corruption, shady financial manipulation, or conflicts of interest. In such cases, the camera is more of a hindrance than a help, and it would be reasonable to expect television in most instances to leave this kind of exposé to the print media, which also usually have larger news staffs at their disposal. (Barrett, 1970, p. 71.)

Investigative reporting is not a major consideration abroad because the findings would generally be of more interest in the local country than in the United States. If and when foreign affairs investigations do occur, it is most likely to be in Washington. None of the correspondents were able to think of an example of a foreign affairs investigative report.

In 1973 the Washington *Post*, as a result of the determined investigative reporting of two of its correspondents, re-focused attention on the Watergate scandals. This eventually led to the appointment of a special prosecutor, additional investigations, the presentation of charges against the alleged conspirators, and the resignation of the President. The network news departments were clearly embarrassed by the initiative taken by the print media and their own "reactive" reporting of news uncovered by their newspaper colleagues. In the aftermath of Watergate the networks have assigned one or two news teams to engage in investigative reporting. At the time of this writing, it is too soon to evaluate the success of these efforts. Nevertheless, the mandate is domestic investigative reporting, and foreign news stories, if they emerge, will come from the Washington scene. The mechanical constraints in television journalism restrict its investigatory role abroad, and it has not yet become an important factor in foreign affairs television reporting.

Commentators used to be a frequent and familiar sound on radio news programs. Elmer Davis, H. V. Kaltenborn, and Cecil Brown, among others, were well known for their positions and points of view. This tradition did not carry over into television until the early 1970s. One network newscast has introduced a commentary on the news as a regularly scheduled conclusion to its broadcast, while the other two networks have one veteran journalist each who comments periodically when there is a subject he sees demanding further analysis. Eric Sevareid, who plays this role for CBS News, explains its reintroduction into television as follows:

> Our problem is to find the techniques that will balance the spot picture and put them in proportion, and without letting hours or days go by until we can do a special report or a long documentary to explain it all as it really is. (1967, p. 14.)

The subject of the commentary varies with the news of each day. If the week is heavy with news from abroad or because of an election period, the subject matter will vary accordingly. Discussions with these commentators did not indicate any concerted effort to concentrate on analysis of either foreign or domestic issues, one at the expense of the other. The analysts are forbidden to endorse political candidates, and their commentaries tend to be well-balanced and, with few exceptions, interpretive in nature. Their analysis is not perceived to correspond to the editorial page of a newspaper.

The preceding chapters have considered the foreign affairs correspondent, who he is, how he functions within a group setting, and how he conceives his role in the overall political system. The newsgathering activities have been examined, and we have analyzed how the mechanical and structural constraints of the medium affect the way the correspondents collect, prepare, and record the news story and how these constraints help determine what kind of story is produced. The correspondents' concern is to get their stories on the air. How the half-hour news broadcast is put together, which stories are selected and why, and where they are placed in the overall format are decisions taken by the executive producer and the associate producers. This is the news composing process, and the people responsible for this activity; their attitudes toward their work; and how they handle, adapt, and organize the news broadcast is the subject of Part III.

PART

III

COMPOSING THE
NEWS BROADCAST

6

The heart of broadcasting is in New York City, in the broadcast centers located on the west side of midtown Manhattan. The nerve center of the newsgathering operation is to be found there. Its structure somewhat resembles a pyramid with the correspondent at the base, for it is he and his crew, once assigned, that are the first to take the actual measure of a story. On this level the primary judgments are made and the initial actions taken that will ultimately determine the perimeters of the story as it appears on the air: the pictures of the event will be selected and fixed by the cameraman; the correspondent's interview questions will limit what can be employed from the audio tape; and the accompanying narration to the sound and film report is for all practical purposes immutable. The television correspondent, unlike the newspaper reporter, cannot simply call back the person interviewed and ask an additional question to fill a gap in his report. The omitted question requires a comparable illustration of picture and locale and would require more than the few moments of the subject's time that can be gained from a simple telephone call. In short, the correspondent's conception of the story in the field and the cameraman's video documentation of it are important decisions made at the bottom of the pyramid.

On the highest level of the pyramid, at the point of program composition, is the production staff, comprised of an executive producer and his associate producers. They measure the pressures of time for the broadcast, make the final determination among competing stories, decide the program's content, and draft the actual perimeters of the broadcast on any given day. Their role is important because the number of reports gathered in the field exceeds the amount of time available, and theirs is the ultimate responsibility for shaping the content and hierarchy of the news that will be received by the viewing audience.

It has already been noted that while the structure is pyramidal, the process is not linear but circular: the broadcast content is both an end product and the starting point for the correspondent in gathering the next day's news. The correspondent in the field does have important editorial responsibilities, but within this formal organization the major policy-makers are located at the top. The circularity provides a number of inherent opportunities for the executive producer to secure and maintain conformity to his selection criteria at the lower levels.

A number of avenues have been noted by which the correspondent learns these criteria:

1. The apprenticeship period offers financial incentives to the reporter that promote the habit of gauging the selection biases at the New York center in order to insure the broadcast of his news report.

2. The high competition among correspondents to get themselves and their stories on the air causes them to gauge the producer's criteria closely.

3. These criteria are reinforced through the employment of previous broadcast lineups as the starting point for the next day's newsgathering activities.

4. The telephone permits the producers to be in constant contact with the correspondents in the field.

5. Field producers, who have closer links to New York and who are more likely to reflect the selection criteria of the executive producer than those of the correspondent in the field, are employed.

6. The dependence on the wire services and the limited number of crews available to the correspondent limit the newsgathering activities that can be initiated. This, therefore, increases his dependence on New York for decisions and directives on the stories to be covered as well as for the allocation of crews to record those stories.

It has been observed further that there are a number of reasons why the correspondent is willing to follow these criteria. Competition to get on the air is the most important. Although no one tells the correspondent what the network's selection criteria are, they are something he learns very rapidly in order to maintain his position, to fulfill his mobility aspirations, to establish his professional reputation among his colleagues in his own news department as well as among his competitors, to develop a national reputation among the viewing audience, and to uphold his own professional regard for the importance of his story and the necessity for its broadcast. Indeed, there are no alternatives. The correspondent is drawn to this medium because of the distinctive mechanical and structural capabilities of the medium to dispense information. If his report is not broadcast it can not be regarded as "in the news," he does not capture the attention of his viewers or colleagues in a positive way, and his own worth as a television correspondent is not reinforced.

In summary, the executive producer and his staff at the production center in New York have an important influence on the gatherers of news as well as on the news that will ultimately be received by the viewing audience. It is important, therefore, that we investigate who these people are, what decisions they make, and how they define and shape the television broadcast.

ROLE CONCEPTIONS AND CHARACTERISTICS

The executive producer is responsible for the interpretation of the rules governing news policy and for the operations as they are determined by the executives in charge of the news department. This is achieved through his role as the final determiner in the news selection process. It is his job to decide what final order the news stories will take, how much time will be allotted to each story, and which ones will receive visual complements. He is assisted in this operation by his associate producers. Usually one is in charge of production, including editing of film, time specifications, and ordering of transmission lines. Another is responsible for news control and content, including negotiations with the correspondents in the field, the constant monitoring of the wire service reports, and the timing of the written reports. The activities of these three producers overlap, and only the ultimate decisional power and responsibility is clearly in the hands of the executive producer. Said one network executive producer, "I'm the one who makes the decisions--it's a divine dictatorship."

Each domestic news bureau has a producer, often in addition to the bureau chief, specifically assigned to it for the network evening news program. There are also

field producers who go out into the field with the correspondents. In all there are about 40 people at the three
networks with one title or another of producer that are
responsible to the network evening news programs.

Statistics on the producers indicate a marked difference in some crucial categories from those on the correspondents discussed in Chapter 1. A division between the
years before 1963 and after did not indicate any important
variations in employment patterns. The reason for this
appears to be that the promotion lines from writer to associate producer to executive producer take place over a
longer period of time than the pattern from recruitment
to reporter to correspondent, the latter taking place over
a period usually not longer than three years. The average
age of the producer is 45. The average age at the time
of employment was between 25 and 30 (both ages representing important age clusters). Similarly, the producers
have been employed at the networks for a period of from
15 to 20 years. Of the 95 percent who were graduated from
college, 20 percent have advanced degrees. The important
difference is one of training. Only 20 percent began in
television as correspondents, and this was usually at a
local station. By the time they were recruited to the
network it was either as a writer, a bureau chief, an
associate producer, or for some other nonreportorial position such as news desk editor. Only 30 percent had any
experience in newspapers, while 60 percent gained their
experience in television, either at the local or network
level.

The profile of the average executive producer, from
statistics gathered on the present three and the past
three executive producers, shows that they are about 48
years old when they hold that position and have a college
degree and have engaged in some graduate studies. Two of
them hold advanced degrees. They were employed by the
network for a period of 20 to 25 years before they finally achieved this position. Of the six men, four have
received their experience solely in television. The general pattern is from television news writer to bureau
chief to associate producer and then executive producer.
One of the six was a television correspondent, but not
for a network.

A few comparative observations can be made. The
producer comes to the network television news department
at a slightly earlier age than the correspondent. The
level of education is comparable. Fewer producers have
newspaper experience, and those who do, because of their

slightly earlier employment, have spent less time working on a newspaper. More than half of the producers gained their experience in television, less than one-third have been television correspondents, and not one of the present three executive producers was at any time a network television correspondent.

Both from discussions with the producers and from the training patterns as represented in these compiled statistics, there seems to be support for the observation that the television producer is essentially a product of the medium, has long experience with one network, and is recruited and promoted on the basis of his ability to deal effectively with the mechanical and structural characteristics involved in the composing of the television news broadcast. He is a journalist, not in the sense of having correspondent experience, but in composing the network broadcast, whether it be in writing the news in the newsroom, managing the logistics and equipment while accompanying the correspondent in the field, directing the operations of a news bureau, or assisting the executive producer in New York. That is, his experience is predominantly in the newsroom or with the television equipment, rather than out in the field as a gatherer of the news story.

TABLE 2

Television Producer Profile

	Producers[a]	Executive Producers[b]
Age at time of appointment	25-30	25
Present age	45	48
Education (in percentage)		
BA	95	100
Postgraduate work	20	33
Training (in percentage)		
Newspapers	35	40
Television	65	60
Percentage who were television correspondents	30	15

[a] A total of 42 producers were analyzed.
[b] Six executive producers were analyzed.

The producers are a cohesive group and interact
closely with one another. The executive producer and his
associate producers are a finely-tuned team that has been
working together for a period of years. "We don't have
to use many words around here," said an executive producer. "I start the sentence and they finish it. It has
to be like that in this business. The pressures are too
great." They are in constant contact with one another,
and the executive producer's office belongs to all three
and is their central meeting point. The producers at the
different bureaus are in constant telephone contact with
the New York producers, and it is part of their job to
know what New York wants. The Washington producer, for
example, is in telephone contact with the New York producer at least ten or fifteen times each day. The field
producers' home base is New York or the bureau they are
assigned to, and they too are in constant contact with
the New York producers.

The duration of this group varies from five to eight
years, depending on the stamina of the executive producer
and on good ratings. His associate producers generally
retain their jobs for as long as his term lasts or until
they choose to go elsewhere. The duration of the assignments of the other producers depends on their capabilities
and on the availability of positions for advancement. It
generally takes fifteen to twenty years for a field producer to be promoted, if he is, to executive producer.
The executive producer may be recruited from among the
producers assigned solely to the evening program, but may
also come from the documentary and special events division. Whoever it is will have many years of producing
experience, however.

There are few clearly discernible positions for promotion beyond executive producer. A producer may become
executive producer of the special events division, of the
morning news program, or of public affairs programs, or
possibly one of the two vice-presidents in charge of news.
Some simply retire or are retired.

The group is open for admittance and promotion to
other producers and bureau chiefs and, on the lowest levels, to newsroom personnel: writers, copy editors, and
desk men. It is not a group to which correspondents as-
pire for admittance, nor do the producers desire to engage in correspondence activities. Both groups, in training and interests, have distinctly different career objectives.

By and large, the producers are competitive with one
another for promotion to higher levels of producing with

greater decision-making authority. They are not before
the camera and therefore do not compete for media exposure. They are very satisfied that what are nationally
known as the Walter Cronkite; John Chancellor; and Harry
Reasoner and Howard K. Smith news reports are the responsibility, and indeed the product, of their labors and decisions. They tend to quietly lament the public's almost
total ignorance of the magnitude of their efforts in composing the finished products, but are compensated with
the satisfaction of knowing that the professional staff
is aware of the real extent of their exercise of power.
In their early careers most of them seem to have come to
the conclusion that their influence on camera had inherent limitations and that if they were to pursue their
careers in television to the full extent, it would have
to be off camera and in the production area. The producer
role offers the most power, next to the actual news role
of the broadcast medium. Executive producers are at the
top level in the structure of the television news production process. They are basically independent from the
news executives who determine the outlying perimeters of
news policy. The producers are the predominant inter-
preters of that policy on a day-to-day basis. The correspondent in the field is dependent upon them for the
broadcast of his stories. As of this writing, to be sure,
the evening network news might justly be called the Paul
Greenberg, Lester Crystal, and Av Westin reports. How,
then, do these three men and their associates go about
composing the news broadcasts that become the "reality"
of the day's events, the shape of which forms the "map of
the world" for so many millions of viewers throughout the
country? What are the variables that affect their judgments, and ultimately what judgments are employed to shape
the television news broadcast?

COMPOSING FOR THE MECHANICS OF TELEVISION

Allocation of Time

The newspaper reporter competes for scarce space, the
television correspondent for scarce time. Ostensibly the
evening news program is 30 minutes long, but after station
identifications and other intrusions the program is left
with approximately 28 minutes 50 seconds. Each program
has five and sometimes six commercials, which when de-
ducted from the whole leave two networks with an average
of 23 minutes 35 seconds and the third with 22 minutes of

actual time for the news reports. There is altogether a loss of from 7 minutes 25 seconds to a full 8 minutes of broadcast time.

By and large this time is inflexible and cannot be expanded. Unlike a newspaper, a few pages cannot be added, financed merely by adding one or two commercial ads. Furthermore, the deadline is constant. The evening news is always broadcast at 6:30 or 7:00 p.m. The presses cannot be held up; the papers cannot arrive late to the newsstands. The alternative to missing television's deadline is a blank television screen, a totally unacceptable alternative. Additional time is lost through the slow presentation of visual news. Each film clip must be introduced in order to prepare the viewer for what is coming. The viewer cannot select the story by its headline; he must be informed of what is to come. Often the film piece must be rounded off with a summary sentence from the anchorman before the show can pass on to the next news story. Precious seconds are lost simply for the introduction of a film story.

As a result of the constraints of time, the operating mode for the television producer is one of elimination rather than inclusion. The biggest difference between the composing processes of newspapers and those of television is that the newspaper is editorial (it rearranges and distills the story) and television is selective (the story is included or excluded). Said an executive producer, "You can put into a newspaper any small item that will conceivably attract a small audience. If you include a regular story on stamps in television you lose the majority of your audience, and also potentially more important news stories may be excluded."

The line-up is the projected guide for the broadcast of the leading news stories of the day. The television broadcast is not a concurrent use of space, since television can deliver only one news item at a time. The line-up provides the frame of reference for that day's potential news stories in terms of the time factors involved for the total broadcast and the probable time allotments for each story. Arithmetically the total time of the line-up must equal, to the second, the actual time available to the news program. It is the daily map for all concerned in the news process and their guide to what areas will receive focus and what actions they must perform within the system to insure an efficient broadcast. (For an example of a network news line-up, see Appendix C.)

Within the mechanical limitations of time, there are further policy considerations that determine the actual time allotted to foreign affairs news. One might argue that an international story is the most pressing item in the day's events, or perhaps that a national event should usually be given the highest priority for the allotment of air time. However, there were no discernible policy priorities favoring one category of story over the other among the television producers. All the producers inter-viewed regarded foreign affairs as one among many cate-gories competing for attention. According to the produc-ers it is how a particular story stands up in competition against the day's other important stories that determines its selection, not any special news category under which it may fall. Representative of this conception is a com-ment by an associate producer about a Common Market story: "Should we tell them the story? Yes, in the best of all possible worlds, but at the expense of what story? It is always at the expense of something. We only have a half-hour."

Because of the limitations of time and the competi-tion for its allocation, the "bad" news often tends to drive out the "good" news. Walter Cronkite discussed this problem as follows:

> It is possible that some news editors have
> enough time allotted by their managements to
> cover all the significant news of their
> areas--much of it, presumably, in the "bad"
> category--and still have time left over for
> a "good news" item or two. But for many
> and certainly those at the network level,
> that is not the case. To crowd in the
> "happy" stories would mean crowding out ma-
> terial of significance. Some good-news ad-
> vocates know this, and it is precisely what
> they want: to suppress the story of our
> changing society in the hope that if one
> ignored evil it will go away. (December
> 1970, p. 54.)

The Vietnam war, the Middle East crisis, or any major, continuous news story also tends to limit the amount of time for the broadcast of other news, particularly foreign affairs news. The producers cited Vietnam coverage, re-garded as both a foreign affairs and a domestic story, as the major cause for fewer stories on the Third World or from Spain or Eastern Europe. While the Vietnam war loomed large over the country and demanded more and more air time (once or twice it filled the entire broadcast period), no additional broadcast time was added to the news program to compensate for the heavy flow of news from this one area. Inclusion of the Vietnam story, almost on a daily basis for seven or eight years, had to be at the expense of some other stories. The cost of Vietnam coverage was also an important factor that drained network resources and tied up personnel and equipment that might otherwise have been sent to cover other stories.

In summary, the selective character of the medium has a tendency to cause the broadcast of bad news at the expense of good news and the large and continuous, hard-news story at the expense of the more reflective, less immediate spot story. When increased broadcast time is not made available to the evening news program to report an important story, and decisions are made in the newsroom to focus attention on that story, the inclusion of this additional material is at the expense of other stories, not in addition to those stories. Thus the map of the world created by the television news broadcast becomes skewed in the direction of that event because the gain in one story, by its very mechanical nature, is a loss in another.

The Foreign Affairs Allocation. The producers agreed on two policy conceptions that affect the allocation of time to the foreign affairs news story. (1) For the moment, public interest in foreign affairs as opposed to national concerns has diminished. The producers believe that recent events of the past five to ten years have caused the American people and therefore the press to be more interested in U.S. news and less concerned with foreign news. (2) As a result, in the competition for time the foreign news story probably has to be a little better than the domestic story to get on the air. This latter perception is reaffirmed by the correspondents abroad. As one correspondent said, "Ultimately we record what is interesting to the audience and the editors in New York. There has been a change and they are now more interested in what is happening at home, and I had better have a really good piece before I consider recommending it."

Depending upon the researcher's items of comparison, television fares either poorly or well in the allocation of air time to foreign affairs stories. Adnan Almaney compared foreign affairs news stories in the New York Times with those reported on the network news broadcasts. His study found that for the given month of investigation "the New York Times reported an average of 19 international stories per day compared with an average of 1.4 stories on

TV, and an average of about 42 foreign stories per day
compared with 0.7 stories on TV." (1970, p. 508.) With
regard to subject emphasis, Almaney observed:

> The degree of American involvement in world
> affairs was clearly reflected in the pattern
> of TV coverage of international affairs.
> Thus, the U.S. position in the Far East con-
> stituted the dominant element. The three
> networks devoted 52% of the total number of
> international stories and 65% of the time
> to U.S. involvement in this region. (Ibid.,
> pp. 502-503.)

This study failed, however, to distinguish page one
New York Times foreign affairs stories from those on later
pages. This is a crucial factor in the perception of content objectives for the television producer. In addition,
the study fails to add the second dimension, which is percentage of newspaper space devoted to foreign news compared to percentage of air time allocated. Cohen quotes
a Wisconsin study* that compared total news space (in
column inches) with total foreign news (in column inches)
and concluded that the Chicago Tribune, the Milwaukee
Journal, and the New York Times contained a total of foreign news space of 5.8 percent, 6 percent, and 10 percent,
respectively (1963, p. 117). Malcolm Warner found that
55 percent of total broadcast network news was devoted to
foreign affairs news (after adjustments for period of time
analyzed and comparable studies) (1968, p. 61). Independent samples I made myself over a one-week period confirmed this 55 percent foreign affairs news allocation.
(The samples were taken during mid-May 1972, between the
previous month's escalation of the Vietnam war and the
commencement of the Democratic Convention, and again in
the fall of 1974.) The stories reported and the percentage of time allocated correspond within 5 percentage
points to the front-page space allocation to foreign affairs news in the New York Times the day after each broadcast.†

---

*James F. Scotton, "Foreign News Presented to News-
paper Readers in Madison, Wisconsin," Masters Thesis
(Madison: University of Wisconsin, 1960).
†This does not appear to be the situation in local
broadcasts. William Wood reports that an early 1967 study

In short, in a comparison of the total number of news stories printed in a newspaper with the number broadcast over television, television does not compare well. However, in terms of percentage of foreign affairs news compared with percentage of domestic affairs news, and even more in terms of percentage of front-page foreign affairs space allocation compared with percentage of television news time allocation, television scores considerably higher. Furthermore, that the "front-page" character of the television news program causes important measurement problems for a comparison with newspaper content cannot be ignored. Despite all these reservations, however, it can be said that television network news devotes an appreciably higher percentage of its total content to foreign affairs news than do the local newspapers and local television stations throughout the country.

Attention to Pacing

Because the audience is national and cannot select which stories it wishes to concentrate on and because the producers desire to maintain audience attention throughout the news program to its conclusion, it is important that they give attention to the pacing of the news program. The concept of "program pacing" is comparable to the layout of the newspaper, not as it affects the hierarchy of news stories but as it is intended to promote reader attention and ease of comprehension, for which the newspaper varies the size and character of type and picture placement. The CBS News staff wrote of news program pacing that:

> The distribution of film and the length of
> film and audio stories may have much to do
> with the overall effect of the program.
> Short film clips and punchy stories may
> help to produce a show that "moves," that
> keeps viewer interest up and insures a

of the CBS-TV news program showed the following time allocations to different categories of news: New York City, 37 percent; regional, 14 percent; Washington and national, 10 percent; world, 9 percent; and the remaining 30 percent for science, the stock market, sports, and the weather (1967, p. 40).

182

proper urgency for the news. It is hard to
maintain pace with just a few long stories
unless the film itself is very good. Features and sidebars may be used to change the
pace if needed. (1958, p. 111.)

Examples of adjustments for pacing illustrate this point:

1. An important story on an agreement in the Soviet
Union is at the top of the day's events, but it is all
"talking heads" and the story will need at least 4 minutes
to tell; but 4 minutes of one talking head is slow and
dull. The producer will direct the Pentagon, State, and
White House correspondents each to do 1 minute 20 seconds
of the story, and they will be edited back-to-back for
broadcast. It is still a talking head, but this time it
is three different heads speaking from three different
locations, making it less slow and less dull.
2. There are a lot of middle-important stories in
the news on this day, and the middle 10 minutes of the
show have the anchorman telling most of the news. There
is no good film available to accompany any of these stories. This is slow television. The middle will be re-
adjusted, and a film feature from the last third of the
program will be pushed up into the middle to move the
program along. Film increases the movement of the program.
3. There is a good film story on Australia, but the
accompanying commentary is long. It can be edited into a
good 8-minute story, but that would be almost one-third
of the entire program. The film story will therefore be
broken up into two or three segments to be broadcast on
separate days. Two reasons prompt this decision: First,
it is insurance against a large segment of the audience
not being interested in the subject, which would be more
likely to turn the program off if it is a particularly
long item than if it is a short one. Second, it is perceived that the audience's attention span does not extend
for a period of more than 5 minutes for any one news
story, no matter how valuable it is or how good the film.
4. Some news programs use two anchormen, one in New
York and the other in Washington. Pacing is achieved by
limiting the amount of time each anchorman talks on the
air, as they switch from a story in New York to one in
Washington and into a film report from somewhere else.
5. ABC has a specific policy that assumes that the
audience's attention span is very limited, and it is the
rarest of occasions when an ABC correspondent's story runs

as long as 3 minutes and even rarer when it exceeds this
time. Excerpts from a manuscript written by ABC's present
executive producer illustrate this concept of pacing.

> At ABC News the basic approach to presenting
> the news--this, of course, affects the line-
> up--is to divide the broadcast into segments.
> A segment is the air time between commer-
> cials. In each segment, a narrative of all
> stories that relate to one another is woven
> together. Then, as a punctuation mark, a
> commercial is inserted. . . . Stories--both
> film and the anchorman's scripted on-camera
> material--are combined into a logical thread,
> leading the audience through the news so that
> their distracted minds do not have to make
> sharp twists and turns to follow what is go-
> ing on. . . . Pacing, in my view, means
> letting the audience breathe a little be-
> tween periods of high and intense excitement.
> A vivid pictorial report of battle action
> should be followed by an interlude of less
> exciting material, enabling viewers to ab-
> sorb more of the information they are seeing
> flash by. Setting the pace is a producer's
> function and the line-up, of course, is a
> guide-line to him and the staff of how the
> broadcast is expected to zip along.
> (Westin, 1972, pp. 11-12.)

Although ABC News is the most extreme of the three networks in its concern for pacing through the use of shorter
news stories, the network policy is reflective of the concern about story length as it affects pacing, about the
sense of forward movement, and about the ability to maintain audience attention through change and variation
within the program format.

The style of the television broadcast is an important
adjunct to the concern for pacing. Each of the networks
has its own style. CBS projects the image of efficiency,
a slick, fast-moving news operation with a strong correspondent press corps that is, among the three networks,
the most frequently called upon to present its news reports on the air, under the guidance of the experienced
and trusted anchorman, Walter Cronkite. NBC projects an
image of informality, which John O'Connor of the New York
Times describes as follows:

While being tagged with labels like "profes-
sorial," Mr. Chancellor stresses a concept
of informality, comparing his approach to
the lecturer who, after a speech, mingles
casually with his audience and is confronted
with such questions as "What is Henry Kissinger really like?" (October 1971, p. 83.)

ABC, which has a newer and less experienced press corps
and finds itself more often dependent on the anchorman to
tell the story, has developed a style that gives particular emphasis to the visual impact of its presentation.

Graphics play a key role in the presentation of the show and the line-up organizes
their production and indicates how they are
to assist the flow of the narrative. . . .
The audience can catch with a glance the
overall theme of the narrative being constructed. (Westin, 1972, p. 12.)

The placement of film stories, the employment of
feature material, the use of the correspondent on camera,
and the style of presentation are all important considerations for the producer as he goes about the formulation of
each day's line-up of the news. The need to pace the news
broadcast is a potential mitigating factor against a truly
representative hierarchical presentation of the major news
events of the day. "Basic understanding comes first,"
said one producer, "but then there are the cosmetics--
informality, believability, looks, and good sounds. The
three networks produce much the same product, and we vary
as to our personalities and images, and not so much in our
content." Defending the consideration of these factors,
Av Westin said: "If show business techniques can be used
to convey information without distorting it, then I believe they are perfectly all right." (Ibid.) It is generally not the content of the news that is threatened with
distortion, but rather the hierarchy of importance in its
placement in the overall picture of the day's events drawn
by the news broadcast.

Cost Considerations

The high cost of television news production as it
affects the newsgathering process has already been

discussed. Cost also has a subtle but discernible influence on the composing process. It is the executive producer and his associates in New York who have the final decision regarding a story's satellite transmission from abroad. If the film is transmitted, then money has been spent; and there develops a pressure to broadcast the film story. However, on a number of occasions I have witnessed an executive producer rejecting a satellited film story, or a cabled story from California or Canada, because it was inferior reporting or because more pressing news had developed. Nevertheless, executive producers acknowledged the difficulty of justifying transmission expenses when these stories continually do not receive air time. The same potential constraint is imposed when the producer is deciding to make an initial outlay of expenses for what may turn out to be a mediocre film story, such as the assignment of a correspondent and crew to cover a story in Africa. Once the network has gone to great expense to get to the story, film and record the details, and transmit it to New York, the pressure is on the producer to broadcast the story in order to justify the initial decision.

The consideration of cost is an additional potential constraint. The producer has only the telexed verbal report, if that, with which to judge the worthiness of a proposed film report. He has, of course, the recommendation of the correspondent in the field, but the correspondent does not generally have the understanding of the flow of the day's news that the producers have. Very often film reports will be rejected because of cost factors although, for the very reason of cost, the actual visual content of the stories has not been judged.

Once the cost is incurred, there is pressure to broadcast the story to justify the expense. In either case, the enormous cost involved in the transmission of the television news story is a characteristic constraint of the mechanical structure of the medium.

The Picture

R. Smith Schuneman found that over three-fourths of the producers he interviewed agreed that news film is the major reportorial tool of television news. This was confirmed by the findings of this study. Producers were more often likely to mention the importance of visual content over verbal content in a news story (30 percent for only the visual, 70 percent for varying degrees of words and pictures). This reflects Alexander Kendrick's observation that "most television news producers, intent on pictures, believe that spoken words are a mere accompaniment and should not 'fight the picture.'" (1969, p. 32.) The availability of pictures has certain advantages: it makes the need for adjustments solely for pacing less likely; it enables the correspondents to participate in the television news broadcast and satisfies their professional and personal objectives by getting their stories aired; and it fulfills the producers' professional interest in fast-moving visual television productions.

Because of his training and experience, the major concerns of the producer are the visual and mechanical capabilities of the medium. If he can tell the story in pictures it is, by his criteria, good television. If the pictures are in color it is even better. If there is action or movement, still better. If it is in color, has movement or drama, and is satellited from a distant place, then given the present level of technology, this fulfills the producer's criteria for "good television news." The mitigating factor, the crucial element distinguishing the producers' activities from the show business activities of television, is its content, the news. The producer walks a tightrope that demands on one side that he be a journalist fulfilling the responsibilities of his profession and on the other that he be the composer of a television broadcast with all television's mechanical ability, and inadequacy, to transmit its message to its characteristic audience. The method by which he can fulfill the demands of both these responsibilities is the use of pictures. Therefore producers become intent on using pictures to facilitate the presentation of the product, the evening broadcast.

Pictures are what television can do best, they argue. Pictures distinguish their news reports from newspaper reports. Pictures are what the audience wants. Sometimes this perception causes a dilemma for the producer: not all stories are visual, and on a given day there may not be film available for the most important stories. The producer can not choose to ignore that prospect; he must somehow resolve the problem in a journalistically responsible manner and at the same time remain true to the mechanical and structural demands of time, pacing, competition, and audience maintenance. To maintain journalistic standards, the day's most important story, the lead, even if nonvisual, will probably be aired first. However,

in order to maintain the pacing and the visual component
of the broadcast, if the second story is nonvisual as well
the producer will probably drop the piece to the third or
fourth level in the line-up and substitute in its place a
less vital but more visually interesting news item. The
lead story, because of its overriding importance, is seldom compromised for mechanical or structural reasons. It
is at some point after that story that nonjournalistic
criteria may be employed that could distort the producer's
professional judgment in presenting a journalistically
determined hierarchy of the news.

One additional impression was discernible as a result
of interviews with producers and their staffs concerning
the way the mechanical characteristics of this medium affect the composing process. Because of the nature of this
impression, I hesitate to conclude that it is an actuality,
not because proof of its occurrence cannot be found--it
can be--but rather because I question how inherent it is
to the mechanics of the medium or how permanent the actual
perception is, or what its future effect on the behavior
of production personnel will be. Nevertheless, it was
mentioned quite frequently by producers and warrants discussion, if only as a description of the past, as a passing phenomenon, or as a warning for the future. Television is a comparatively new medium. Its equipment is
ever-changing and its true capabilities are just becoming
known. The idea of visualizing events captured the imag-
ination of the world, but it also drew people to this new
medium who had a special fascination with these new capabilities provided by television. Producers at the three
networks, drawn to the medium because of its technical
characteristics, became specially trained to understand
and effectively employ them and were promoted on the basis
of their successes on the production side of the process.
Accordingly they acknowledge that they have a propensity
to become fixated, initially, by new mechanical abilities
as they are periodically developed and added to the medium. They have a tendency to overreact, to immerse themselves in the new mechanics, becoming overly indulgent in
their use and for the moment too fascinated with them to
be able to perceive the concomitant distortion they create. Said one executive producer, "We have a fixation
with the new, and it takes us a while until we adjust to
it and are able to control it and put it in proportion
to the whole."

There are many examples illustrating this phenomenon.
Television's ability to transmit pictures from Europe dur-

ing the early period of its development led to the creation of the "European dateline," a regular, daily report from Europe. Its regularity was the product not only of events taking place in Europe at the moment but also of the fascination with the ability to have a correspondent reporting directly from the scene of an event that took place thousands of miles away. Even if the story had limited news value, and sometimes even if the visual component was undramatic, at least it was an on-the-spot report. Fascination with this capability prolonged and overemphasized the news transmitted from Europe. Said one veteran European correspondent of this period,

> I had a heck of a time finding a really
> worthwhile story to report once or twice
> each week. When something was happening it
> was fine, but to report a story every week
> out of Bonn that would be of interest to an
> American audience really distorted what was
> happening here and elsewhere.

Vietnam coverage also became a victim of this fascination with new mechanics. While television did cover the Korean War, in terms of actual coverage Vietnam was television's first war. As the war began, television entered its second generation of technological development. Color film made the war more vivid and real. Lighter and more mobile equipment could accompany the troops in the field and film the story as it was occurring. Satellites could bring the war home the very same day. So fast was transmission that networks had to hold back some film that showed dead American soliders because the military had not had time to notify the families of the deceased and it was felt to be an impropriety to have the family learn of the death on the evening news. Said one associate producer:

> It's fascinating to be able to show the war
> and what it's like in people's homes--to be
> able to bring it to them live. The other
> day we had film on American bombing of a
> Vietnamese village with scenes of children
> running away from the bombed village (straight
> toward the cameras) covered in flames and
> with screams of fear and agony. It was ter-
> rible, but that happened, we had it on film,
> and the people have a right to see it. But

it's true, we still have a hangover from
this fascination with our new capabilities.

To show it as it is, particularly the human tragedy
of war, to bring it into people's homes, is the most prevalent tendency among television producers, especially
among those who have actually been assigned to Vietnam.
It is a component in the electronic journalists' neutral
role conception as visualizer of the news. A comment by
the commentator Frank McGee represents this attitude:

> While I wouldn't want the civilian population
> involved in a war, I see no reason not to
> let them know what it's like. If they can
> sit in front of their TV set and see what
> the kids are going through--and I'm not say-
> ing whether you agree with the war or not--
> then they'll have a better understanding of
> all wars. (Zeidenberg, 1968, p. 56.)

The producers, through their professional training
and job responsibilities, are likely to be more concerned
about, and to put a greater emphasis on, the pictorial
worth and mechanical components of a television news story
than on the work of the professional correspondent in the
field. Their concern is not with the individual story
but with the whole broadcast, including the placement and
juxtaposition of film and talk stories, the pacing, and
the visual style, and with the audience attention span
throughout the duration of the news broadcast. It is this
concern that causes them to emphasize the visual, to encourage the correspondent in the field to "shoot bloody,"
to make the story more "spicy," or to try to package the
story with dramatic impact. Their intent is not news
distortion or nonjournalistic concerns, but rather a concomitant responsibility for the flow and movement of the
total broadcast product.

COMPOSING WITHIN THE STRUCTURE OF TELEVISION

Television is a highly competitive medium, and the
television producer is constantly attuned to the product
of his competitors. If their show contains an important
story that his does not, if theirs moves along faster or
has better editorial content, it is the producer that is
judged for the product and not the individual correspon-

dents. If ratings are low and a change of anchorman is felt to be necessary, the producers of the unsuccessful program are generally among the first to be replaced.

A similarity was manifest about the production levels of the three networks: their production concerns (time, pacing, equipment, picture) are the same; their competition is essentially for the same national audience; and they employ basically the same criteria. Deviation from these ground rules, that is, less emphasis on the mechanics of the broadcast, runs the risk of losing the prize, meaning the audience, not because journalistically the broadcast may be less sound (on the contrary) but because, in the perception of the producers, the audience expects what it presently receives and will not accept a less medium-oriented production.

Editorial content and other professional journalistic standards were consistently mentioned by the producers as important criteria employed to judge the importance for inclusion of a television news story in a broadcast. Their ideas about what constitute these criteria closely resemble those of the correspondents, which are discussed in Chapter 2. However, because of their distinctive composing responsibilities, the producers are disproportionately concerned with the audience. Both the correspondents and the producers compose for an audience, but their responsibilities to that audience are different.

The correspondent must effectively communicate a particular news item to the audience in three to four minutes. He wants the audience to be able to easily follow and comprehend his story. The producer, on the other hand, must communicate an entire program to an audience and sustain its attention throughout that program. Writing his story, the correspondent is concerned that it be comprehensible, simple, clear, and conversational. The producer must consider many of the same concepts, but he does not write a story; he composes a production. His concern is not with a thematic presentation of one idea but with the fluid pacing of a combination of many ideas that are separately gathered and separately written. He has different assumptions about what he wants to give his audience. One executive producer commented about these assumptions:

> I believe that the audience is interested
> in having the answers to three important
> questions: Is the world safe? Is my home-
> town and/or my home safe? If my wife and

children are safe, then what has happened in
the past 24 hours to make them better off or
to amuse them?

Another executive producer put it this way:

> I want the audience to have a map of what
> has happened that day, not to give them
> answers but to get them thinking about what
> is happening. I want to include one or two
> stories in each show that they will talk
> about the next day on the subway. I think
> there is something to be said about the
> success of a program and the word of mouth.
> We also try to humanize our program--to
> relate it to our viewers' lives. News
> events are people, and they become signif-
> icant to the extent that they become con-
> cerned with them. The viewers become
> concerned about the fighting in Belfast if
> they can identify with the people there.

Commented the third executive producer: "We want to give
them some feeling of what has happened that they should
know about. That's what they're looking for." Audience
evaluation (or ratings) is an important criterion by which
executives evaluate the producer's product, and it is
therefore important that the producer's evaluation of his
audience be examined.

The National Audience

Television producers know very little about their
audience other than that it is national, heterogeneous,
and large. They do not really know why some people watch
NBC and others CBS. ABC believes that it attracts a
younger audience, but its findings are based on a 1966
study conducted before they entered the news competition
and before the success of their local news format employed
on the affiliate level. Mechanically, the producers believe they cannot appeal separately to individual group
interests within the audience because neither the audience
nor the program can be selective. "After all," said one
producer, "how many people buy the Wall Street Journal?"
They aim at the broad middle.
They do have criteria, however, whereby they measure
audience interest. It should be noted that these criteria

are based not on actual data gathered on their audiences but only on subjective impressions of what that audience wants or should have. The underlying assumption is that it takes two people to communicate. The network can broadcast, but someone must be watching. It follows, so they reason, that the news must be interesting. Reuven Frank reflects this perception: "All criticism of television news . . . postulates television news would be better if it were duller. Because television news is so important it must also be a bore. But television news had to be interesting before it became important." (Winter 1970, p. 22.) To be interesting, the reasoning continues, the news must relate to people's lives. One executive producer ranks news stories in three categories listed by degree of interest to the audience: (1) stories that have a direct effect on the viewer, such as those about meat prices or wages, which have a priority over almost anything else; (2) stories that do not directly affect the viewer but are presumed to have some intellectual interest, such as one about the death of a queen; (3) stories that do not directly affect the viewer and are not expected to have much interest, such as one about a military coup in Togo. "Beyond that," he said, "I look to see how important the story is, how dramatic it is, what kind of film we have, and what obligation we have to tell the people this story."

Another producer, with an advanced degree in international affairs, after declaring his special interest in foreign affairs news lamented that for the mass national audience with which he must be concerned, foreign affairs news had little interest because of its limited effect on people's lives. The television audience, he said, prefers domestic news to foreign news, and unless the foreign story bears directly on the average American it is seldom broadcast. Certain types of stories generally fail to have an obvious effect on the viewers' lives, and their inclusion in the television broadcast is very difficult. These include stories about the federal budget, internal events in foreign countries, international events that do not directly involve the United States, science, intellectual or abstract ideas, and ideological debates. There are no network reports on the press, for example, as explained by Reuven Frank: "People are not interested in our covering the problems of the American press. If we were to put stories like these on the air people would switch us off." One story must sustain audience attention to carry that audience into a second story, the second

into a third, and so on until the conclusion of the broadcast. The stories must be interesting and must move
quickly. There is, as a result, a temptation to include
the abnormal at the expense of the normal, the latter
being more dull.

Furthermore, there is thought to be a large segment
of the audience that is made up of nonreaders, as William
Wood confirms. "They are recognized by television news
directors, who have been around long enough to know their
audience, as a significant part of their viewership--a
group large enough in itself to give television an edge
as the leading news medium for most people." (1967, p. 8.)
This group is important in the ratings competition among
the networks and cannot, therefore, be ignored. Non-
readers should not be chased away by reports that are too
intellectual or abstract. Repeatedly the producers voiced
the opinion that "you can't force-feed the people information that they don't want." Confirms Reuven Frank, "It
seems to me axiomatic that you cannot take advantage of
an audience by driving it away." (Winter 1970, p. 22.)

Keeping the audience is also a personal objective
for the producer. As Leo Bogart observed,

> The media decision-maker feels he must re-
> spond to what the public wants, and he
> senses that the public wants drama, excite-
> ment, titillation, wants its curiosity
> piqued. The editor or program producer
> must somehow satisfy these interests, not
> merely because the economics of his job
> require the satisfaction of his audience,
> but because in human terms he needs their
> approving response as much as does the
> actor on the stage. (1969, p. 38.)

In short, the producer is concerned not simply with
the transmission of some abstract concept of the news,
but with gaining and maintaining a diverse national audience, and they perceive that the way to achieve this
end is to provide that audience with what it wants and to
try to relate the news information directly to its experience. Through these considerations the audience will
be attracted, its attention sustained, and communication
with it fulfilled. The competitive factor that is constantly operative among the networks is perceived to prevent alternatives to this behavior. "In the audience-
delivery business, you do not have the luxury of setting

either your standards or those of your audience. Instead, they are set for you by the relative success of your competitors." (Eck, 1967, p. 49.) Very often the producer justifies the exclusion of a seemingly important news item on the grounds that the audience would not be interested in it.

Ratings

Television is often criticized for its concern about the ratings of its news broadcasts. The networks do not deny the importance of ratings for the commercial viability of the programs. Hugh M. Beville, Jr., former Vice-President for Planning and Research at NBC, provided testimony before the FCC on the question of ratings on behalf of the NBC management, explaining the reasons for using a ratings system:

> Basically there are two reasons why broad-
> casters use ratings. Primarily we use them
> because they are the only means we have for
> gauging the extent to which each of our
> programs is being accepted by the public.
> Since the broadcaster undertakes the respon-
> sibility to serve the public, he would be
> remiss in his duty if he did not also assume
> the responsibility for using every valid
> means at his disposal to determine the re-
> sponse of the audience to the programs he
> offers. . . . Analysis of audience response
> is also necessary because viewer patterns
> are extremely fluid. Unlike the relatively
> stable circulation figures of printed media,
> changes in audience behavior take place
> from day to day, week to week . . . with
> considerable rapidity when there are pro-
> gramming changes. . . .
>   The second basic reason why we use
> ratings is that television is intensely
> competitive and centers on competition for
> audiences. The only value a broadcaster
> has to offer an advertiser is an audience,
> and proof of audience deliverance is essen-
> tial to the networks' economic survival,
> in competition with other networks and
> other media. (1962.)

Ratings are repeatedly compared to reader surveys, subscription data, and the like. Network spokesmen insist that ratings do not affect the content of the news story or the news selection process.

No evidence was found to substantiate the criticism that ratings affect the correspondent in his newsgathering activities. Producers, however, were very conscious of the ratings battle; one network even has hanging in its newsroom a "win, place, show" chart to record the latest Nielsen reports. Ratings do not "directly" affect the daily program format to the degree that the producer could quote actual figures, and none were able to do so. They do influence the program to the degree that executive producers perceive audience attention to be the product of pacing and mechanical capabilities and not just news value and informational content. Ratings are more closely watched, particularly by the executives, when the news program is doing poorly, or its position is slipping, in the ratings. Again, these findings indicate that the producer is located somewhere in the middle of two pressures and that through his job responsibilities and training he is inclined to lean toward the mechanical attributes of television whenever there are no clearly distinguishable judgmental lines between the content and the form.

Balancing the News and Legal Considerations

The Fairness Doctrine was not considered to be an important consideration for the executive producer as he carries out his daily activities. Said one producer, "It's something that the executives point out to us after it has happened. It is not something we keep in mind as we put the pieces together." Balance, on the other hand, was regarded as an important professional consideration, although in actual practice it seemed to play a small role. Most producers concurred that it was virtually impossible to ensure that each broadcast be politically balanced. They were vague about what political balance actually meant and were unsure how it might be achieved. For example, feature stories on the candidates for the Democratic nomination for President were being prepared for broadcast on consecutive nights prior to the 1972 primary vote. Two of these stories were dropped from the line-up, one at each of the networks on different days, because of what was considered more pressing news or a

better film report on a major news event. At one network
the feature was broadcast after the primary, while the
other network never did use the feature. When questioned
about the deletion, both producers resisted the obligation
to provide equal time or equal exposure to rival candidates or opposing issues at any one time or on a particular news broadcast. Content, they insisted, was the
choice of the producer, determined by his criteria of
news worth and program needs and not by some arbitrary
measure of balance.

The producers generally felt that their reports were
balanced over a period of time, if not during a particular
program. The sheer volume of reports that are broadcast,
they reasoned, would result in a balanced presentation.
A representative response to criticism of an excess in
combat footage was as follows:

> There are inevitably stories that are mis-
> leading. One story one day, with limited
> time on the air and restricted focus, may
> be off the mark. But there are many stories
> on many days and focus shifts within subject
> matter. . . . In the long run I believe the
> public gets a pretty fair overall picture.
> (Zeidenberg, 1968, p. 57.)

In short, while there was a positive response to creating
a balance in the news, the criteria for balance were not
explicit and did not seem to be a conscious consideration
as a producer worked to compose the actual broadcast.

One impression above all pervades this research on
the producers, and that is that the producers' belief that
the audience is attracted and maintained through the visual and mechanical characteristics of the medium is in-
stinctive and based on faith, not research or knowledge.
Not one producer could document this impression of his
audience, either with studies conducted by the network or
independently. That the audience is national, diverse,
and large is shown by the Nielsen ratings and the Roper
studies. Why people watch one news program instead of
another; why they remain interested throughout or lose
interest midway; whether they truly like the dramatic and
lively; whether the news must appeal to their own lives;
or whether, indeed, it must conform to that vague criterion of being "interesting," are things the producers say
they "intuit." They possess no studies, nor are they
aware of any data that confirm their intuitions. It is,

however, through the employment of these criteria that
they judge their own product, and it is the same criteria
that each employs to evaluate the others' product. It is
the continual and daily employment of these criteria
through practice and observation that reinforces the perceived validity of the criteria. It also reinforces the
high degree of competitiveness among the networks and the
high cost of failure, which inhibits deviations from these
norms and, in fact, inhibits experiments.

The basic mechanical and structural considerations
of the television medium have been analyzed as they seem
to affect the composing of the news broadcast by the network producers. Mechanically, the primary considerations
are time, pacing, logistics, and the visual. Structurally,
the major considerations are competition, the national
audience, and secondarily, balance. There are other considerations that are taken into account and subtleties of
those already mentioned. These can best be exhibited
through a re-creation of a typical day in the newsroom of
a network television station. The way an executive producer decides what is to be included and what is to be
deleted will shed additional light on the medium's composing processes.

At what point and under what conditions does the
executive producer make his decisions? An understanding
of this is crucial to the overall picture of the process
that began with an event in the field, was gathered and
written by the correspondent, and has now been transmitted
to New York. This is the last point before actual disper-
sion to the national audience. This last question will be
approached through an hour-by-hour account of a day in the
network newsroom, taken from the vantage point of the executive producer, the man invested with the authority to
make the final decisions determining the content of the
news broadcast. The following is a composite of two weeks
spent with the executive producers of the three networks
from early morning until after the evening broadcast. The
limited accounts available in print are also employed.

Although there are some variations among the networks, the processes are so similar that the differences
are insignificant. For example, while ABC considers itself a headline service and CBS insists that its objective lies somewhere between a journal of record and a
headline service, the methods and processes are the same
whereby they fulfill these objectives, with varying degrees of competence and success. ABC tends to choose
shorter stories than CBS and NBC chooses longer and more
serial stories than the other two. But the criteria for
selection, the pressures for exclusion, and the constraints on inclusion operate in fundamentally the same
way.

The following description combines the events of
many days into one. The times, the particular stories,
and the reactions are drawn from among the three. networks, each story illustrating a different decisional

problem. The prime considerations, mechanical and structural, have already been discussed, but a description of the actual process will provide a more complete impression of how these variables interact to produce the final product, the news broadcast.

The typical day begins at about 9:30 a.m. The executive producer (EP) and his associate producers (AP_1 in charge of the flow of the day's general news and AP_2 in charge of film and equipment for the production) arrive at the broadcast center already having read the New York Times and listened to the news on the radio. Over the weekend they have read the advance copies of the news magazines. They arrive, greet one another cordially, hang up their coats, roll up their shirt sleeves, loosen their ties, and are now in uniform, prepared for the day's work.

The newsroom is about the size of a classroom. It contains seven or eight desks, wire service teletype machines, bulletin boards, maps, and other informational aids. Arranged in various orders, sitting at and sharing the desks in the center, are the AP_1, two or three news writers, the graphics man, a news editor, and two or three secretaries. There are empty seats waiting for the EP, the anchorman, and a copy editor. Within view are two or three separate screening rooms, each with three projectors and a table and chairs for viewing potential film stories during the day.

The EP's office, the only separate one, is just off the newsroom, with its open door giving him full view of the proceedings. The office is spacious, with a couch; five chairs; a desk cluttered with seven or eight telephones, in and out boxes, and a typewriter; maps of the world on the walls; three television consoles lined one next to the other; and the newspapers and magazines of the week strewn on the floor, in boxes, and on shelves. There are few books, if any, on his book shelves. On one wall is the "bank," a list of the stories in the house already recorded. The bank is a reserve of stories prepared in advance in the anticipation of upcoming events or of features used as time fillers or pacers if the news is light or particularly full of nonvisual news. The following is an example of the bank at CBS one day in 1972:

Stories and Correspondents	Minutes
1 How Green (Wagner)	5:15
2 RMK (Simon)	5:33
3 Son of Smog	4:37
4 Ski-Kite (Kalish)	1:47
5 Teaching (Chase)	5:33

Stories and Correspondents	Minutes
6 Child-God (Kurtis)	--
7 A. F. Academy (Turkl)	6:27
8 Gold Coast (Duvall)	3:37
9 State Department (Kalb)	5:45
10 Deserter (Kalisher-Young)	5:00
11 Stockyards (Kuralt)	3:30

It was observed that at this time the bank was quite heavy and also that the stories were rather long. Before broad-cast, for example, Son of Smog was edited to 3:50 and A. F. Academy was cut by one minute.

ABC tends to have many more items (generally 30) in its bank, but only one or two were as long as four minutes. Commented Av Westin, EP of ABC:

> The "bank" at ABC News contains an average of 30 pieces, all edited and ready to go, cover-ing a range of subjects from divorce regula-tions in the Soviet Union to the problems of educating migrant workers' children. It has been my experience that in any 30-day period, a news development will come along to provide a new peg for any bank story. Very rarely does a "bank piece" disappear unused and out-dated into the limbo of the film library morgue. (1972, p. 15.)

NBC has fewer items in its bank than CBS, but they tend to be longer and to have two or three parts.

Actual planning for today's broadcast already began, immediately after last night's broadcast. Potential stories were assigned by the assignments editor to the correspon-dents, who have begun their activities this morning in the field. The first order of business each morning is to read the wires, check the newspapers, go over the line-up of the morning show, and perhaps discuss the previous show. Morn-ing is a very quiet time at the networks. AP_2 is in the editing room checking the film stories that have been brought in and assigning his film editors to different filmed reports; he wanders in and out of the EP's office reporting to him about what they will have and inquiring which stories from the bank the EP wants to screen. AP_1 sits at his desk in the newsroom or in the EP's office (the office door is always open and it is accepted that the EP's office is the APs' office as well) and reads the rolls and rolls of reports just off the teletype. Every 15 to 20 minutes an aide comes in with a fresh supply of news stories just off these machines.

In the newsroom itself the writers are perusing the newspapers and the wires, talking with one another, and generally taking it easy. Multiple copies of the New York Times, The Daily News, the Washington Post, and the Wall Street Journal are piled high in the center of the newsroom for their use. There is a constant and pervasive sound of the pounding keys of the teletype, but the atmosphere is relaxed and almost leisurely. At 10:30 or 11:00 a.m. the "excitement" and "glamor" of network television is nowhere to be found.

The EP checks the traffic chart to see what stories are being gathered abroad and at what time cable or satellite feeds or film shipments are expected in. He comments to AP_1, "The Times had a story this morning that we missed yesterday." AP_1 concurs and explains that it was probably an oversight. At 10 a.m. AP_1 types up an "outlook." This contains the stories in the house and the assignments of all the network correspondents. This is then telexed to all the news bureaus.

At 12 noon the secretary comes in and announces that the important conference call is on Line 4. This is the daily telephone call with the evening news staffs in New York and their producers and bureau chiefs at the various domestic bureaus. Listening in in New York are the EP and his two associates and the anchorman (if he is in by that time); on the other ends of the line are the bureau chiefs and/or the evening news producers in Washington, Los Angeles, Chicago, and Atlanta (and various other centers depending on the network). They all identify who is listening in at each point. "It's going to be tight tonight," the EP begins. There will be three film reports satellited in from Vietnam (the North Vietnamese offensive seems to have begun), and it is also the day Charlie Chaplin returns to the United States since his less-than-voluntary exile years earlier.

"O.K." he says, "what do you have going?" On the other end, each in turn discusses the stories he has, what is being gathered, and what the news looks like for the next few days. The EP listens and takes notes, as does the AP_1, and asks their evaluation of their stories' importance and whether the stories will be good enough to carry into the evening broadcast. "It's a good piece," the EP may say. "I like it. Let's use it on Wednesday." Washington reports that R__ has a hunch that Humphrey has used ITT planes and is checking that out. The EP suggests that crews be sent out to the airport to photograph the planes and to see if they can get interviews with a

few of the pilots. He will wait to see what R__ finds.
"Get S__ at the Pentagon to check on the air war and see
what effect it is having. We might be able to tag in onto
the film reports from Vietnam if we are running 45 seconds
short. Let me know if he gets anything. See if you can't
work something out with a map for graphics." The conference call is over in less than 20 minutes.

Having read the day's morning newspapers and wire reports and consulted with his associates in New York and at
the domestic bureaus about their assessments of the day's
news flow, the EP now busily occupies himself with formu-
lating the first line-up. That is, by 12:30 a reasonable
picture of the day's news has already emerged.

At one network the line-up is composed in segments,
while at the other networks it follows an "above line,
below line" format. The stories that are the most important that day and will most assuredly be broadcast are
placed above the line. Those that are marginal, depending on time availability, are below the line. There is
almost always one film piece from the bank above the line
and a second below.

The line-up is shown to AP_1. Very often AP_1 writes
up his own line-up simultaneously with the EP and they
compare the two; in each case that I saw they were virtually the same. It is quickly typed and immediately
wired to the various bureaus. Each line-up contains the
exact running times of the film reports and the approxi-
mate allotted time for the anchorman's talked pieces.
They must add up to the "magic number" that equals the
actual broadcast time, to the exact second.

If the EP and his associates stop for lunch, it is
at this point. This is not often the case. Throughout
this period, between conversations, food, telephone in-
terruptions, and the like, the EP and APs are reading the
wire reports as quickly as they are brought in. A correspondent comes into the EP's office. He has a piece in
the bank and lobbies for its broadcast. "I don't know,"
says the EP: "It's an awfully heavy day, and five minutes is a very big chunk of air time. We'll see how the
day progresses." The correspondent leaves unassured.
AP_2 enters the office and informs the EP that the Chaplin
film story is ready in Screening Room 2 and that if he
wants he can see it now. He agrees, but he also wants to
screen another story in the bank at the same time.

The screening room is about 12 x 8 feet in size, and
viewing the film with the EP are AP_2, a film editor, a
writer, and the film projectionist. The Chaplin piece is

2 minutes 10 seconds long and will be used to close the
evening's program. The EP likes it but laments that it
is entirely composed of old footage. It has been reported
that the local New York affiliate has one of its correspondents on the plane with Chaplin with some exclusive
interview footage, but they won't know its quality or content for another three hours. Furthermore, they will be
unable to get the film until after the affiliate broadcasts it locally at 6 p.m.* The second film story is
viewed and timed. The EP suggests a deletion of one scene
and asks for an updated timing with a possible "go" for
the evening's broadcast.

By 2:30 or 3 o'clock a second, more accurate line-up
is prepared. By this time the writers have been at work
on the stories that will be talked, and the film stories
are beginning to take shape. Earlier, Chicago called that
one story is being written and edited for approximately 2
minutes 10 seconds; the Chaplin story was clocked at 2
minutes 10 seconds; and so on. Adjustments are made in
the line-up to accommodate these new times. The bank
piece above the line is for the moment a negotiable item
with the bank piece below the line. It will depend on
the length of the stories from Hong Kong which one will
be included, the one below the line being 1 minute 5 seconds shorter. AP_2 comes into the office and notifies them
that his editors are having trouble putting together the
film story on one of the Democratic candidates in the Wisconsin primary, which is scheduled in the line-up for tonight. "It just doesn't move no matter what we do." The
film editor enters at that moment somewhat hassled. She
says, "I just can't make the story move. All the parts
are in place but nothing happens. Maybe I'm too close to
it, but I can put it together and why don't you decide?"
The EP asks what the alternatives are, and AP_2 suggests a

---

*Two of the three networks have special arrangements
with their affiliates and syndication that prohibit a
film story from being used by another part of the network
without an explicit release from the program originating
the film story. The network evening news has first option on all stories its staff gathers. If, for example,
a film story is to be used on the network news, it cannot be used by an affiliate or by syndication until after
it is broadcast or released by the EP. This creates a
virtually unbreachable obstacle for the local station,
since its broadcast usually appears just before the network newscast.

tax piece that discusses what has become the major issue
of the primary campaign. The EP decides to screen both,
and he wants to see them within the hour. AP_2 leaves
with the film editor, and the EP puts through a call to
his correspondent in Wisconsin and inquires about the importance of the tax issue. Atlanta calls with a potential interview with a major witness in a recent scandal
in government. The bureau chief wants to know if he
should assign a correspondent to the story. The EP gives
his consent and concludes the conversation, "See if we
can get her to bleed on camera. If he doesn't get any
more than the **Times** reported today, I'm not interested."
Washington calls, informing the EP that S__ has some exclusive material from a Vietnam briefing at the Pentagon
and is working on it now. The EP is interested. "If he
can do it in 45 seconds we will go for it."

It is now 3:30. The EP is in Viewing Room 4 screening the candidate profile and tax issue stories. Stopwatch in hand, he views the film with great intensity.
Both are completed, and there is silence. As he makes
his way to the exit door the EP says, "We'll go with the
tax issue tonight. Work on the candidate piece for tomorrow. You're right. It doesn't move. Try cutting the
interview and try for some more crowd scenes." The EP
returns to his desk. The written transcripts of the
three stories out of Hong Kong are waiting for him. The
stories are due for satellite feed at 5 p.m., New York
time. AP_1 is sitting in the office, where he has been
for the past two hours, continuously reading the latest
wire stories. While the EP was in the screening room
Washington called: the S__ story is 45 seconds, and the
Atlanta story did not work out.

There is a call from Los Angeles. The bureau chief
and the correspondent want to know why a story out of
their bureau yesterday was not included in last night's
newscast. The EP takes five minutes out to talk with
them and to explain, in great detail, why the story was
not included. It was too long; somehow it just did not
work out the way they had expected; we were going to carry
it but the other network did the same story the day before
and theirs appeared to be the better piece (said an EP,
"That may not have been a valid reason for rejecting it,
but whether the competition does it is a factor that goes
into the equation. It won't run if we can't do it better."); there was a squeeze on the news. We dropped it
at the last moment but gave it to the morning show and
syndication. After the conversation the EP comments,

"Morale is a very important factor in this job. I have to explain constantly why we don't air a piece. Sometimes I will put on a story that is not very current if it is from a correspondent whose regular beat has been light in news lately, just to keep up the morale. I listen to their ideas just so they feel that they are an important input into the program."

A transcript sent from London on a proposed satellite story is brought in. The EP reads the story. The decision: "I pass on this one." Why? "Vietnam is the big story of the day, and a lot is happening in Washington. It's a heavy day and that story wasn't vital. The foreign stories also tend to run long."

It is now 4 p.m. The leisurely pace that earlier pervaded the newsroom is gone. The writers are busily beating out stories. Young aides are coming in and out with the latest editions of the afternoon newspapers. Telephones are ringing wildly. The enormous wastepaper baskets in the EP's office have now been emptied at least twice of discarded wire sheets and morning newspapers. The pace is fast, each person quickly and diligently working at his or her job without any orders being given out. It is a well-tuned and coordinated team at work. At 4:30 the first feed is coming in. The APs are with the EP in his office. A writer who will write the lead for this story is brought in, as well as a secretary with a stopwatch. It is a film story out of Ottawa on the Chinese ping-pong players. AP_2 and the EP also have their stopwatches in motion. It is a feature describing the preparatory activities of the players as they await their more important journey to the United States. The story is 1 minute 10 seconds. "Nothing happens. No. Pass." AP_2 goes back to his production area, and the writer and secretary return to their desks. It is 4:45. There is a call from the Washington bureau. "The White House correspondent is in with the President and they don't know yet if there is a story." There might also be a possible additional story from Washington of unknown length, also on American reaction to the North Vietnamese offensive. The go-ahead is given on all three stories.

The EP decides to play the 45-second Pentagon story back-to-back with the potential White House story and the possible third Washington story with one or the other "bank" stories. If the first option runs short, he will use the Ottawa story to fill in the extra time. He puts in a call to AP_2 in the editing room, telling him that he wants to screen the Ottawa story again and a shorter

bank story. Another correspondent enters to lobby for a
film story he is working on that will be ready for tomorrow's broadcast. The graphics man comes in, and he and
the EP quickly discuss the pictorial illustrations to be
superimposed behind the anchorman for his talked stories.
Some stories will have an individual's portrait. The
talked part of the Vietnam story will have maps with
planes and aerial illustrations, artillery photos, and
arrows to indicate respective points of conflict and
troop movements. "Be sure you get them on the right
places this time" shouts the EP to his graphics man, who
is hurriedly exiting.

It is 5 p.m. Without being called, two writers and
a secretary join the EP and his two associates as the
three film pieces are being fed in from Vietnam. One film
is about the troop movements and contains a particularly
bloody scene of a wounded South Vietnamese soldier. As it
is transmitted the EP tells AP_2 to edit that sequence out.
"It can be edited out without hurting the film story."
("Common sense and good taste," he explains, "are the
verbal guide lines for this kind of thing--never violence
for the sake of violence.") The second story focuses on
the problems of getting food to the refugees and the mad
and uncontrolled scramble of the people to get the food.
It contains a particularly graphic scene of a supply truck
dropping the food supplies onto the road, with a sequence
of a man on crutches agonizingly hurrying to trap a food
parcel beneath his crutch-supported leg, the point at
which his foot had once been, only to have a parcel grabbed
from under him by a quicker young boy. The reaction in the
office is emotional. The tension of the scene and the
anguish created by this sequence is impossible to escape.
The third story was photographed from an American B-52 on
a raid over South Vietnam. The three stories are clocked
at 6 minutes 10 seconds. The writers hurry back to their
desks to write the introduction to the films, which will
be read by the anchorman. The anchorman has been at the
news desk now for half an hour, going over the materials
prepared for him, adjusting a phrase or two to accommodate
his speech pattern, asking a question here and requesting
an addition there.

Word comes to the EP that the exclusive interview
with Chaplin is first-rate but will not be broadcast until
6:45, which is 15 minutes into the first broadcast of the
network news and 15 minutes before the second broadcast
begins. The producer cannot, however, see the film until
it is actually broadcast on the local news, since it will
not be processed and edited before actual air time.

A call comes from Washington. There is a good 1 minute 20 second story from the White House and some good material out of the State Department. The EP tells the Washington producer to prepare all three and to get the exact times on each. AP_2 comes in with the exact time on the tax issue film. The EP has still not made up his mind whether to go with the Washington story or the "bank" piece. He quickly goes into Screening Room 3 with AP_2 and screens the Ottawa piece again as well as a shorter, feature item of 1 minute 25 seconds. No decision is made yet. The EP returns to his office. One of the vice-presidents comes into the office. "How does it look tonight?" The EP gives him a quick rundown of the major stories. "The competitor has leased cable time from Chicago," he is informed by the vice-president. "What is the story there and why don't we have something?" The EP is immediately on the telephone with the Chicago bureau chief and finds that it is a trial story that they had planned to cover tomorrow when the judge's ruling was expected. The competitor is apparently planning a two-part series on the story, today's story leading up to tomorrow's verdict. The issue is dropped.

A call comes in from Washington. The three stories take 5 minutes 45 seconds. They are all talking heads. It is now 5:55. The first broadcast is at 6:30. The decision is made to go with the Washington stories. A new, stand-by line-up is drawn up. It will lead with the anchorman presenting a recital of the facts of the day's events in Vietnam, with graphics and an introduction to the film story on the refugees and the battle scenes. After the commercial the B-52 film story will begin the segment, to be followed by a direct feed from Washington of the three standuppers (the stories were prepared too late for transmission and recording in New York, so the direct feed is employed). Both bank pieces are dropped, and a third, the short feature, is scheduled to begin the second half.

Once again the EP is on the telephone to Washington to get the exact time for the commentary piece that will be included in the second half. It is 2 minutes long. The EP does not particularly like to include these commentaries in the line-up. They are talking heads, and he has the impression that they turn off many of the viewers. "You have to be careful how deep you get with your audience. His reports are about too-sophisticated topics. We generally broadcast the commentary whenever the commentator decides to write one. He is one of the most experienced and honored men in the field. We do it more out of respect than anything else." The new line-up, this time written on a different-colored paper, is quickly distributed.

The atmosphere is hectic. It is 20 minutes before air time. The graphics man comes in quickly to show the EP the final graphics for the program. The show is still 45 seconds too short. Two stories are chosen from the wires, and a writer is called in and told to write the stories, each 45 seconds long. Three additional stories, 40, 25, and 50 seconds each, are prepared as insurance, for insertion into the program should it run too long or too short. There is still no word on the Chaplin footage, and the decision is made to use the prepared story with the old film footage for the first broadcast and to keep the second half of the second broadcast open.

NBC and CBS broadcast their news programs twice daily, at 6:30 and 7:00 p.m. ABC has three broadcasts, the first at 6 p.m. If there is no late-breaking story or mechanical fault, graphics error, or the like, the recording of the first broadcast is simply played back for the second or third broadcast. If, however, there is a change, a section of the whole program will be run through again live for the later broadcast. On the West Coast the broadcast is recorded and re-broadcast two hours later. There is a separate but small staff, which will add or subtract sections of the broadcast, should there be any vitally important, fast-breaking news that develops between the time of recording and the actual broadcast.

The EP is in and out of his office conferring with his associates to be sure that they have all the parts of the new line-up, double-checking the lengths of the talk pieces with the writers, and telephoning to Washington to make sure they are ready with the feed. At 6:20 the two APs come into the office with three secretaries, each with a clipboard and stopwatch. In the control room the director is busily briefing the men at the control desk and double-checking that all the film pieces are set to go.

At 6:30 the anchorman looks up into the camera and says "Good evening, this is B__ with the news. . . ." And so it begins. The secretaries have the stand-by line-up in front of them, and each clocks every third piece and compares its actual running time with that listed in the line-up: "plus 5," "plus 10," "minus 8," "minus 4 going into the commercial." The broadcast is running smoothly. Fifteen minutes into the program a vice-president comes in and says, "good film out of Vietnam," and departs.

AP$_1$ is continually checking the latest wire reports as
they come in during the broadcast for any possible late-
breaking stories. The feed from Washington works fine.
The show will be 45 seconds short. During the second commercial the EP picks up his direct line to the anchorman
in the studio and tells him to add a specific 45-second
story. On a second monitor in the office, the local New
York affiliate news program is viewed as it is being
broadcast. Twenty minutes into the program (it is now
6:50) their Chaplin piece comes on. AP$_2$ takes notes on
the final shots and times the piece. The EP likes the
new footage and reaffirms his decision to keep the second
half of the second broadcast open for the new Chaplin
piece. AP$_2$ is quickly out the door, his aide running
across the hall to the local affiliate's production room
to pick up the Chaplin film as soon as they finish with
it. The local Chaplin piece was 4 minutes long; it will
have to be edited down to 2 minutes 10 seconds. There
will be less than 20 minutes to do it if it is to get on
the air.

The first broadcast is now over. The anchorman remains at his desk while the first part of the program is
replayed exactly as recorded. He will be on the air live
for the second half. Now the atmosphere is somewhat more
relaxed. Everything checked out and it worked. The
second broadcast will be routine, and only the Chaplin
piece is outstanding. If the film is not ready on time
they will go again with the first piece.

On the three consoles the news broadcast of each of
the networks appears simultaneously as they are being
broadcast in New York. Now the evaluations and compari-
sons begin. Each network has Vietnam as the lead-off
story. The judgment is that this network had the better
film story: better, more dramatic shots, closer to the
news story line. The commercial breaks of all three networks come on the screen within seconds of each other,
and the EP puts a call through to AP$_2$ to check on the
Chaplin piece. AP$_2$ thinks it will be ready but can't be
sure.

So far each network's content is very similar. The
back-to-back Washington story is now on the air. A competitor has its Pentagon correspondent standing in front
of a wall map of Vietnam explaining the same story for
about the same period of time as the three correspondents
reporting the story on this network. The consensus is
that the competitor was roundly defeated. "Wasn't their
report awful! It just didn't move." They are into the

last quarter when a telephone call from AP$_2$ informs the
EP that the Chaplin piece is ready to go. The other networks have already aired their Chaplin stories, which
contained no new film footage. The new Chaplin piece is
on, and there is great satisfaction among the staff for
the "scoop" on the other networks. "It was worth the effort." A competitor has a story on Biafra: "Where'd
they get that story from?" is the general reaction. But
now the broadcast is over, and the consensus is that that
evening's broadcast competition was won. It was smoother.
It had better film stories. The actuality footage of
Chaplin was unbeatable. The vice-president comes into the
office again and says, "Fine show. We have given them as
big a beating as they have ever gotten. Fine show!" The
anchorman now enters the office and offers his positive
opinion. He asks about the other network's story on
Biafra and why they had missed the story. The story had
not come to the attention of any of the producers. A
call is made to the foreign news editor. It turns out
that it was a film taken by the BBC and the network had
had first option on it two days ago and decided to pass
it up. General agreement in the office is that the decision to pass was a mistake and made a good scoop for the
competition.

The broadcast is over, but the day is not yet complete. A call is put through to Washington, and the EP
congratulates them on their contribution and asks what
stories are planned for tomorrow. AP$_1$ tells the EP what
stories are anticipated from Vietnam, and AP$_2$ confirms
that the campaign footage will be ready for tomorrow's
broadcast as well. EP talks with the White House correspondent and congratulates him on his story. It is
agreed among his associates that the weekend staff will
be put to work on the other unedited film stories on the
election to be made ready for the following week. A general assignment correspondent enters with a plea for the
broadcast of his story in the bank. The EP assures him
that he will try but that the correspondent should see
if he can edit out a minute of it. The newsroom is just
about empty; the anchorman has gone home, and only the
EP and his APs remain sitting in the office discussing
tomorrow's stories and the film that will be available.
By 8 o'clock they too have gone home. It will start all
over again tomorrow at 9:30 a.m.

Time is the crucial, pervading factor throughout the
entire process: the deadline time of broadcast, the time
of actual broadcast allotment, the time of each story and

how it fits into the whole, time as an impression of movement and pace, the time of communication with correspondents out in the field, the time of transmission of stories to the New York center, the actual time of day of the broadcast, and the time in an audience's attention span. Producers live and breathe in minutes and seconds. Little time is left for reflection. Little time is available for depth.

IV

IMPACT AND POLITICAL CONSEQUENCES OF TELEVISION NEWS

8

THE IMPORTANCE
OF TELEVISION

HYPOTHESES AND THE RESEARCH FINDINGS

This study began with the usual research assumption
that in order to understand this new political phenomenon
in more than just the common-sense, impressionistic manner that is characteristic of most of the literature on
the subject, the general and recurrent aspects of this
phenomenon should be explored to discover if what appears
on the surface is indeed evidenced through systematic research. While this is only an exploratory study, the
general hypothesis that the television medium has both
mechanical and structural characteristics that have
caused the television press, in the area of foreign affairs coverage, to define and perform its role in a manner that is distinctive to this medium, has by and large
been substantiated.

One crucial qualification has been observed, reflected in a defense of the medium by the vice-president
and director of news operations at CBS News: "We are
innocent in this business. It hasn't been invented yet.
It's being invented every day." (Myer, 1968, p. 34.)
Television is a new medium that has changed considerably
over the last 30 years. However, its importance to our
society and political system has already become manifest,
and its potential consequences can no longer be ignored.
We are justified, therefore, in asking the larger question: Can television provide adequate information to enable the American citizenry to make sound judgments about
foreign affairs?

What constitutes adequate information? How can we
respond to Gabriel Almond's question, "Is the psychologi-
cal potential of the American people equal to the demands

that will be placed upon it?" (1960, p. xxi.) These are
questions that social scientists will continue to struggle
with for years to come. This study, however, is intended
to help the social scientist answer part of that question
and add to conceptual understanding of the constraints
imposed on the political system by the newest and most
pervasive communications system, television.

The first hypothesis, that the mechanical characteristics of television news coverage have a perceptible effect on the behavior of the electronic journalist in his
determination of what news to cover, how to report that
news, and how to transmit that news through the television
channel, has been confirmed. Specifically, it was found
that the medium's concern with time and picture affects
what stories will be covered and reported. Certain advantages accrue to a particular kind of story, but these
concerns exclude or make difficult the coverage of other
stories. Severe problems are imposed on the television
correspondent because his medium is visual, evanescent,
and costly. The tendency in this medium is to stress
technique at the expense of news content. This is not,
however, inherent to the medium. It is a perceptual criterion and not an inherent mechanical constraint.

Not all news is photographable. On the contrary,
the real issues behind what appears on the scene, whether
photographed by a camera or only witnessed through the
eyes of the correspondent, are taking place behind closed
doors and in the minds of men and women. The mechanics
of the medium limit the correspondent's ability to visualize these processes. It does not, however, restrain the
correspondent from reporting the story. The operational
objectives of the television news producer, however, determine that a good television newscast is one that visualizes the basic elements of a controversy. The correspondent makes his selections accordingly.

Foreign affairs news suffers especially in this case.
Too often the African or Asian story becomes a pictorial
guide to the natural wonders of the area rather than a
discourse on the ideas of nation-building, emerging nationalism, socialism, and modernization that are the
forces actually affecting these continents. The European
story often becomes one of human interest, the visual
stereotype of our prejudices. Soviet news becomes a
Presidential visit or parades of tanks and ICBMs, with
little or no discussion of Marxism-Leninism or Communism
versus Capitalism. For the military story, 3 million
tons of TNT dropped on Vietnam is illustrated as so many

216

railroad boxcars, but the effect of tons of TNT is not
the effect of so many boxcars. They are not the same.
The balance of payments is far more complex than the simple mechanism of a balance scale or the transference of
paper representations of silver dollars. It should be
stressed that while the medium permits certain stories to
be visualized it does not prohibit other stories from being told. However, these policy perceptions distort the
"map of the world" of the individual viewer and skew his
information.

If consideration for pictures has been shown to be
a constraining factor, so too is the concern for the limitations of time. The correspondent's story is generally
no longer than a paragraph or two, and much of the information comes from the wire services. The absence of adequate research facilities to background a story and the
limitations on time constrain him from considering more
than just the surface facts. Furthermore, the policy of
providing the front-page stories of the New York _Times_
in less than 30 minutes and the concurrent necessity to
"keep the show moving along" remove the incentive for the
correspondent to initiate his own research or to search
out his own story not yet in the headlines. The production criteria lean toward conciseness and simplicity, not
depth and completeness.

The news format, as it has developed in its appor-
tioning of time, encourages the presentation of many
stories of severely limited duration. The result is a
"hard news" emphasis on the recital of facts, often without accompanying background materials, requiring the correspondent to focus only on the surface of events. This
is a constraint, not limiting his ability to dig beneath
the surface of an event, but denying him an opportunity
to do so or the assurance that his findings will get air
time.

The cost factor poses an additional constraint on
foreign affairs news. Satellites, crews, and correspondent assignments make the television news story significantly more expensive than the newspaper story, which is
gathered by a newspaperman with a pad and pencil, using
a telephone line to transmit his story. This inhibits
the television correspondent, pressuring him to focus
only on the most prominent events in the news or on stories in which the visual component will be deemed to warrant the increased expense. Cost considerations reinforce the constraints of time and picture.

The competition among the three networks multiplies the effect of the cost factor. The coverage of an important event, or even a major news story on a given day, will find three correspondents and three crews with three different complements of the same equipment covering one event. Emphasis is too often placed on capturing the visual component of an event as a criterion of competition, rather than on the reportorial content of the story. Attention should be given to Fred Friendly's recommendation that the networks arrange pooled coverage of some events, such as press conferences and visiting dignitaries (Barrett, 1970-71, p. 85). This would greatly reduce costs and would release the correspondent from the mechanics of the story without the present extra expense of a larger crew for accomplishing the same thing, enabling him to concentrate on the verbal substance of that story. At the moment, competition promotes duplication at the expense of enterprise.

These constraints, however, are the result of the policy interpretations of the mechanical capabilities of the medium as part of the overall intent of its product, and are not constraints imposed by the inherent mechanical characteristics of the medium. There were found to be important differences in attitude between the producer and the correspondent. The correspondent in television is both happy and dissatisfied. He or she is pleased with the capabilities of his medium and happy with the national prominence he gains through its exposure, but more often than not he is more intelligent and more able, reflective, and knowledgeable than his medium demands. He is professionally dissatisfied because there is not enough time for his important, but page two stories. He is unhappy that he often has a story that is important but lacks the visual complement that would promote its broadcast. Because he can balance his professional dismay against the advantages of this medium, he remains both a competent and active television correspondent; however, television still has not found a fully satisfying role for the correspondent. Too often he laments that he has had to submit an article that the television audience should have received to a news magazine or trade paper because he knew it would not receive air time.

Producers do not share the reportorial experience or the frustration of the correspondent in search of a story's visual component. At the same time, they do not share his national reputation or his sense of direct communication. Their sense is one of total product, measured

in pictures, pacings, and audience ratings. It is here
that the nonjournalistic criteria have their greatest effect, spilling over to the correspondent and requiring
conformity to achieve personal as well as professional
objectives.

The balance between journalistic criteria and the
perceptual mechanical demands of the producer is established first at the production level, conditioning the
staff, the reportorial crew, and the new recruit to become obsessed by picture values, with only the most pressing nonvisual stories permitted air time. The producer
regrets this phenomenon; the correspondent laments it.
Actual broadcast of a news story is a decision that is
made by the producer.

Policy reflects the positive capabilities of the
medium, but it does not therefore follow that the mechanics prohibit the medium from being employed otherwise.
This is important for stories about foreign affairs. A
view of the bombings in Belfast does not tell the viewer
why the Protestants and Catholics are fighting one another.
The juxtaposition of a horse-drawn plow with a mechanized
tractor system does not adequately explain the politics or
the long-term implications of British entry into the Common Market. Who greets the President as he descends from
his plane in Moscow gives little knowledge about the ideological differences that separate these two nations; nor
does it give more than a superficial, often misinformed,
impression of the intricacies of international diplomacy.
Developing nationalism and modernization in Africa or
Asia can show Americans contrasts and similarities, but
does not provide the modern, technological American viewer
with a conceptualization of the significance for America
and for the foreign land of these developments, beyond the
limited tools of analysis the viewer brings with him to
the picture. Most foreign affairs occur out of reach of
the camera lens, either in the minds of men or behind
closed doors, and the event often represents only the out-
ward tip of the iceberg of diplomacy and relations among
governments.

The second major hypothesis, that certain structural
characteristics, including the national audience, the competition among networks and among correspondents, and the
corporate and nonjournalistic hierarchical structure of
television, play an important role in the journalists' behavior and role conception that affects the news, has received only partial confirmation.

Television's audience is national. This provides television with an important structural advantage for maintaining an informed public. Most local newspapers do very poorly in their reportage of foreign affairs news, often relegating these stories to the back pages. They are almost totally dependent on the wire services for their information. Wire service reports are not necessarily bad, but it is rare indeed to find any newspaper with as much as 25 percent of its total content devoted to foreign affairs news.

Television news, instead of being criticized for its inability to broadcast as much information as is contained on the front pages of newspapers like the New York Times, should receive high praise for its adoption of a frame of reference that includes the New York Times. Every day the network news producers and Washington bureau chiefs check the front page of the Times to see whether it contains a story that was not included in the previous evening's broadcast. There is always a great feeling of satisfaction among the producers when their professional news judgment is reflected in the New York Times. There is a greater pride when it is discovered that they included an important story in their broadcast that the Times omitted. In short, the national television audience, by and large not made up of readers of the New York Times or other equally sophisticated news journals, is receiving a daily outline of the day's events, reflective of that received by the more attentive public through the print media, although the print media give the news in greater depth.

It does not follow, however, that the television viewer is necessarily better informed or understands more clearly the complexities of foreign affairs, although the framework, the outline of the day's events may be more sophisticated than previously, for this particular audience. However, concern with the maintenance of the national audience contains a potential constraint mitigating the quality of news the viewer receives through the manner in which it is presented. Concomitant with this, and indeed a more explicit criterion for news selection than the frame of reference of the New York Times, is the producer's concern for providing his audience with what it wants and will readily understand, to hold the audience and maintain its interest. The audience, the producers argue, has a limited interest in foreign affairs news, cannot be selective, and is provided with the easy alternatives of two other news programs. Therefore, they conclude, the foreign affairs news story must conform to the mechanical attributes of the medium and have an "interesting" content. These criteria are made clear to the correspondent as he gathers his story. He must communicate to an audience that is in the "middle," of which the attention span is limited, and which does not always have the necessary background to comprehend the whole story. The story must be written simply. It should deal with only one major idea. It should be visual. It should conform to subjects and ideas that the viewers can readily comprehend, given their existing frames of reference. "You play to their stereotypes."

Producers "feel" that these criteria reflect the demands of the national structure of the medium, although they are unable to cite any proofs to substantiate this perception. Therefore television provides the viewing public with more information on foreign affairs, although the foreign affairs story that is broadcast does not guarantee that viewers will be better informed.

Two hypotheses did not receive confirmation in this study. Government regulation of the medium did not appear to have an important inhibiting effect on the electronic journalist or the production staff, nor was the corporate structure an inhibiting factor on the content of the news, although it is a prime limiter of the amount of time allocated to news broadcasts. Autonomy from government as well as corporate and commercial pressures in the television medium encourages the free flow of information among political structures such as the Executive, the Congress, and governmental agencies and from these structures to the populace and is an important feedback mechanism for the actors in these structures. The attitudes expressed by electronic journalists denying these inhibiting influences are encouraging advantages promoting a free and independent press.

There is, however, a perceptual pressure that affects television journalists. Television journalists are concerned with "balance" in a news story and in the news program: if one side is presented, the other side is sought. The prominence of this role conception tends to encourage the correspondent to gather filmed responses from actual protagonists and antagonists, withdrawing himself personally from the report and giving the impression that this representation is an "objective" account. That two sides of an issue are represented is not, however, a sufficient criterion to judge objectivity or truth of representation. Too often it is a misrepresentation to give equal weight to unequal parts.

The value of balance in reportage instead of partisanship or blatant bias is obvious and needs no further elaboration. The potential biases of balance, centrism, and fairness, however, are not the same and require exposure and discussion among media personnel and viewers alike. Contrast of opinions without the active participation of the selector, that is, the correspondent, to introduce, explain, and put into perspective the selected comments of others, places the viewer in a situation in which he is unaware of the editorial judgments and attitudes of the correspondent in composing his report.

TELEVISION NEWS AND AN INFORMED PUBLIC

According to democratic theory, television offers both advantages and disadvantages for maintaining and promoting an informed public and a responsive political system. Television, for example, employing its mechanical advantages with a working frame of reference of the more sophisticated print journals, provides its national audience with more news on more subjects concerning foreign affairs than is presently available in the average local newspaper.

Television correspondents are very conscious of their neutral role, and the political advantages of this role are fulfilled in television and indeed augmented. They do not seek the lowest common denominator when they write their stories; they aim for the middle, between the uninformed and often nonreading and the more sophisticated and predominantly print-oriented audiences. As a result it is reasonable to suggest that the average level of disseminated information has been raised.

Television also offers certain advantages as a result of its structure. It is a national medium with a national audience and a national responsibility. This is often translated by the policy-maker into a power conception, requiring him to be more responsive to the journalistic demands of the television correspondent.

The national character of the medium has its effect on the community level as well, offering the public an additional source of information independent of the local press, which is often tied to the special interests and prejudices of a community. Questions that might be ignored on the local level because of special pressures often receive air time on the "national press." Television's role in the civil rights movement is representative.

There are, however, some disadvantages created by television that potentially challenge the democratic theory upon which the system claims to stand and therefore affect the political process. Television's message is fragmented, capsulized, superficial, and evanescent, and the viewer is prevented from going beyond the surface of the story presented. Whoever desires additional detail must resort to another medium or another format within this medium (documentaries), which may or may not be concerned with a subject of interest to the viewer and which will appear at another and often inconvenient time.

It seems reasonable to assume that an informed citizenry requires not only the knowledge of an event but a degree of comprehension or perspective of that event. Television's present emphasis on "hard news," coupled with the strictures of time, prevents background information from being provided on a continual basis as an accompaniment to each story. Television producers operate under the assumption that if a story has been in the news for a period of time the viewer knows the background information. This assumption is not valid, however. A viewer tuned in to a broadcast may have missed yesterday's background story on today's continuing event. The viewer may not have the analytical tools to connect today's event with the stream of events occurring over the past four weeks. His "map of the world" becomes fragmented, with today's event potentially being viewed in isolation from its context.

The electronic journalist encourages this fragmentation through his newsgathering process. He searches for what is happening "today," often neglecting the effects of yesterday's events or the long-term implications for tomorrow. For television, once a story's currency has faded it is dropped instantly from the line-up, without any follow-through report on effect or implications. Ordinarily in a newspaper some follow-through on the story would appear on page ten or fifteen, but television has only a page one.

Because the broadcast format promotes simplicity, capsulation, and stereotyping, the individual's map lacks certain facets of the overall picture. Stories on complex ideas, long-term trends, and economics do not often receive air time. As a result the individual is not thinking about these stories because they are not broadcast.

The economics story is particularly ignored by this medium. The economic problems of balance of payments, special-drawing rights, international inflation, and

development aid are too difficult to visualize for the
electronic journalist. Once these become political stories, however, they are more likely to be broadcast.
When they lead to conflict between American political interests and the need to prevent Communism in the developing nations, or when devaluation of the dollar demands
are countered in Geneva by a particularly colorful Secretary of the Treasury, the story finds broadcast time. If
the problem can be translated into human-interest terms,
such as German, French, and American housewives contend-
ing with inflation in their respective local supermarkets,
then it too may be broadcast. However, representations
of this type leave the viewers ill-prepared to comprehend
the greater complexities and implications of these issues,
should they be motivated to respond to these events.

This becomes especially significant when one reflects
upon how many political events in our modern era revolve
around essentially economic issues. Can one ignore the
Common Market in Europe, the balance of trade of the
United States, or the terms of trade in the developing
nations? Can the viewer understand these issues only in
a "political" context broadcast sporadically as "events"
occur? Obviously it is not possible, although broadcast
news still has not learned how to deal adequately with
these subjects on their own economic terms.

Television began its own era of importance in a political age that had begun to distinguish itself by two
superpowers, fundamentally divided and opposed to one another on ideological principles. Indeed, since the conclusion of the second world war, international politics
has witnessed many new, complex, and conflicting, but
fundamentally important world ideas: socialism, affluent
societies, Maoism, emerging nationalisms, the knowledge
revolution, international corporations and conglomerates,
violence on an international level, the Cold War, national
liberation, Communism, meritocracy, transnationalism,
supranationalism, the generation gap, crises of confi-
dence, and so on. How do you explain emerging nationalism as one simple, comprehensible idea in 1 minute 30
seconds? You can't. But how can you comprehend the war
in Vietnam without explaining emerging nationalism? You
can't. Television finds these concepts, these fundamental ideas that govern our international system, too difficult and complex to handle in its present format. The
Vietnam war; the Palestinian acts of violence at the
Munich Olympics; Nixon's visits to Peking and Moscow;
the Nigerian conflict; students rioting at Columbia

University, at the University of Tokyo, at the Sorbonne, and at the Free University in Berlin, are all treated as "events," what occurred today. The underlying issues, the common characteristics, backgrounds, perspectives, and implications are left to the viewer to discover for himself, or so it is assumed.

Television, therefore, leaves the viewer inadequately informed on economic and conceptual matters. Television also tends to promote stereotypic views of the world. For example, when de Gaulle was an important news story the correspondent searched for that "one central sentence" that the viewer would readily comprehend and asked: "What is de Gaulle really like?" He found that the American government was somewhat annoyed with de Gaulle's policies, that he was a challenge to American policy, that he did not always cooperate with his allies, and that he made overtures to the Soviet Union. What was that simple, comprehensible idea? De Gaulle is anti-American. As a simplistic, superficial stereotype, he was. However, the story was far more complex than that. De Gaulle was the French president concerned with French interests, and his actions must also be understood in a French context. However, American correspondents were concerned only with American interests; from that vantage point, with encouragement from American political officials, television did encourage the stereotyped view of de Gaulle's anti-Americanism. Once the frame of reference was established, producers in New York accepted stories that reinforced this stereotype. It corresponded to their own impressions and the perceived needs of their audience and conformed to the demands of the medium. Thus television may create or reinforce a political stereotype detrimental to the individual's need to understand the international scene. To change these conceptual frames of reference, to approach the American audience with an idea that it will not readily accept, to deal with the complexities and nuances of French policy as contrasted with American international interests requires time, a very scarce resource in network television news. It is easier to deal with the stereotype, and once it is established, still easier to reinforce it and appeal to it.

In short, the demand for simplicity and conciseness and the need for the visually interesting story results not only in the potential danger of presentational bias and stereotyping, but in the words of a news magazine's advertisement, in creating a public that is "overnewsed and underinformed." However, confirmation of the

hypothesis needs qualification. These mechanical constraints are imposed on the process through the employment of policy that determines how the mechanics of the
medium will be used. They are not the result of any real
or inherent mechanical inabilities. It is not a question
of the adequacy of the medium itself, but rather of the
present governing policies of the medium.

These mechanical constraints also have their effect
on the behavior of the electronic journalist. Most correspondents recognize that limitations of time and the
need to have a picture tend to cede the information initiative to the policy-maker. An especially astute politician or administration attuned to the compositional demands of network news can easily restrict the flow of information or, conversely, flood the medium with especially
good television material that is substantively valueless
to an informed public. For example, a conscientious effort not to provide visually interesting opportunities to
the correspondent, especially in Washington, would dampen
the possibility of that information finding broadcast
time, whereas a flashy spokesman in a visual locale ob-
fuscating an issue might stand a good chance of obtaining
a spot in the broadcast. Television journalists are conscious of these dangers, but the pressures of the medium,
as presently established, and the possibility of an especially effective policy-maker, potentially work against
them.

Other factors were found to inhibit television's information function. For example, television's concern
about maintaining a national audience by following the
producers' prescription of giving the audience what it
wants and will easily understand is also a constraint on
an informed public. To the layman, not all foreign affairs stories are inherently of interest. For example,
the selling of wheat to the Soviet Union may not be a
seemingly interesting or visual story for the viewer,
but in 1973 it was a crucial step in the relations between the United States and the Soviet Union. The subtleties of the eight-point plan and the ten-point plan
of the NLF may not have been as interesting or colorful
as a speech by former Vice President Agnew denouncing
war critics, but they are probably more important to the
actual issues dividing the two parties or to an understanding of the causes for this dissent. Land redistri-
bution is not as visual as an earthquake in Peru, but for
the future of Peru the first has greater import than the
second. Along the same lines, the French have a wine

harvest each year, with a broadcast television film story
as regular as the season because it is very visual, stereotypic, and interesting; however, the emergence of a French
counterculture is far more important. The fact that the
Germans drink beer and the English frequent pubs does not
warrant the same importance in an American's concept of
European affairs as German-British relations in an expanded Common Market. In each case, the more trivial
stories received extensive air time and the important
ones little, if any. Even if television were to receive
more broadcast time, the criteria that are presently employed to attract a wide audience, which assume that it
is achieved not through content but through mechanical
manipulations, are a limiting factor.

These are perceptually imposed constraints. It is
not that the mechanics of the television medium prevent
the reporting of nonvisual, slow-moving, or analytically
complicated stories. Rather, because television's distinctive mechanical characteristics enable the correspondent and the producer to visualize some events and permit
them to transfer some experiences, they are inclined to
feel that, structurally, with a national audience and
sharp competition, they cannot often afford the inclusion
of a lengthy, less visual, or more complex story. Because they can so often provide a mechanically "good"
story, a compromise is often made at the expense of the
journalistically defined "good" story, which will suffer,
if not exclusion, at least by a diminution of time allotment or a dislocation of the hierarchical presentation.

Competition among the networks also tends to limit
the amount of information that the public can receive.
Three national network news programs compete for virtually the same audience and employ the same criteria in producing their own news programs. It appears that the producers' conception of the competition is an important,
explicit, and influential factor in the allocation of
time and news assignments. Duplication, beating the competition, and fear of being caught short by the competitor are often more frequent and explicit concerns for the
makers of news programs than are their democratic responsibilities or the larger question of what the public needs
to know. There is usually very little difference between
individual television broadcasts.

The networks pride themselves on the competitive relationship among them, citing the spirit of a free and
healthy press. This is not quite accurate. While there
are three news programs, the television viewer has only

the choice of viewing one, since they are broadcast simultaneously. These programs compete on the level of actual content of the story only on a day-to-day basis; for long-term maintenance of viewership they compete according to the images of their program, facilitated by the mechanics of their medium. This perception usually means that they are concerned with representing an event, a person in the news, or what was said, rather than with providing a running perspective on the news or an explanation of what an event portends for tomorrow's plans.

Television can raise the information level of a significant proportion of its viewers, especially the non-readers. Its message does not require literacy and is more interesting than a printed page. Therefore its news programs seek a middle plateau. This does, however, have a potentially negative effect, since the picture does not tell the whole story. Viewers who do not understand television's limitations and are inclined to support their opinions with "but I saw it on television," mistaking the selected impression for the whole event, cannot help but have inadequate bases for their opinions. Correspondents are very aware of these limitations, many advocating that the words should "fight the picture." However, disclaimers do not regularly appear on the network news broadcast, and although producers will quickly admit these limitations it does not inhibit them from introducing the film story as "an on-the-spot report of what happened" or one network anchorman from using the identifying closing phrase, "That's the way it is. . . ." Competition, especially in evaluating and promoting the visual story, tends to promote an exaggeration of the capabilities of this mechanical component, which both the electronic journalism staff and the television viewer must learn to identify and be very critical of.

An evaluative judgment seems in order. If we accept the underlying assumption that the press function is to provide information to the public that will, should it choose, assist it in making sound judgments, then we must be aware that as a result of the news departments' perception of the mechanical and structural characteristics of the medium this is often achieved only by luck, or secondarily through intention. To create an interest in the news is a worthy and legitimate activity that fulfills the democratic requisite of a responsible press. However, to base news judgments on the preexisting interests of the audience through the employment of the medium's positive facilitators, is to dislocate its primary role as a conscientious and steadfast contributor to a well-informed public. If the public wants amusement and triviality, picture and movement, and receives only what it wants, the implications for our democratic assumptions are obvious and foreboding, though they may not yet be manifest in actual fact.

Television succeeds in its efforts more often than the other media despite these constraints. My point is that there exist operating criteria within the news departments that potentially mitigate against sound, journalistic selection and composition. They substitute, or potentially supersede, these journalistic criteria with mechanical and structural considerations that may or may not contain the requisites promoting responsible fulfillment of our democratic assumptions. Only a thorough and sophisticated content analysis of television's news product could measure the frequency of success of the television news programs in actually fulfilling these theoretical tenets.

TELEVISION NEWS AND POLITICAL CALCULATION AND ACTION

Past experience with communication artifacts shows that some aspects of the political process will be fundamentally altered and new roles will be assumed. As information is transmitted in visual form at faster rates to a mass national audience, there must be some perceptible effect on political participation and action. Some suggestions about what this effect is have emerged from this study.

One can envision, and probably expect, an increase in the frequency of social movements. The availability of a national communications medium diminishes the influence of physical proximity as an inhibiting factor in the formation of social movements. Theodore Lowi addressed himself to this question in a futuristic sense when discussing information technology:

> U.S. history shows ample evidence for the
> notion that a change of information tech-
> nology will help spawn new social move-
> ments. The Populist movement of the late
> nineteenth century would have been impossi-
> ble without the mass newspapers of the time.
> And what the press did for geographically

dispersed social classes then, television
seems to be doing for (or to) races and
classes in concentrated areas today, as a
producer of images that strengthen weak
identifications and create aspirations
where there were none before. (1971,
p. 20.)

There are many studies that substantiate this notion
that television, as a mass medium, contributes to the
creation of rising aspirations. Also, for example, a
number of countries have invested significant portions of
their national development budgets in television, to
strengthen weak national identifications in order to promote statehood and economic development. There are examples of television's effect on the American political
system as well. The Kerner Commission, investigating the
riots in black communities in 1967, called to the public's attention the linkage function performed by this
national medium between the initial actions in Watts and
the promotion of imitative responses in Chicago, Detroit,
Newark, and elsewhere.

In 1970, during a student demonstration opposing the
American military excursion into Cambodia, four students
were killed on the campus of Kent State University. Almost
simultaneously, seemingly spontaneously, universities
across the nation were forced by students and faculty to
cease regular classes, set up workshops on Southeast Asia,
and hold memorial services for the slain students, while
thousands of students from all over the country converged
on the nation's capital to lobby their political representatives against the war. How or from whom did dissi-
dent groups at Harvard University, the University of
California at Berkeley, Texas State Teachers College, and
the University of Wisconsin learn the proper response to
take, what other groups across the nation were doing, and
how they might contribute to these efforts? This is not
to suggest that television was the only communications
link among these dispersed factions, but rather that the
speed with which this imitative behavior occurred, with
the concomitant impression of spontaneity, points to a
central role played by the most rapid and widely dispersed communications link, television.*

----

*A content analysis of the network's broadcasts dur-
ing this time will confirm their focus on these activities
and the large amount of time devoted to these actions,
which were, incidentally, "good television" material.

Civil rights leaders repeatedly point to television's role in arousing the aspirations of their followers. It served them as a channel they could employ to communicate with them and the policy makers. Television further assisted the civil rights movement through its visual message, permitting information dissemination to groups that were not necessarily reached by the more traditional print media.

Television can link dispersed groups and facilitate a movement response. At the same time it seems reasonable to suggest that while this national medium can promote an increase in the number and size of social movements, the opposite is also possible. The small, distinguishable group, not large enough to make itself heard on a national level and/or not linked to similar but dispersed groups throughout the country, yet constantly exposed to the overgeneralized message, may find television's message not applicable to its own concerns. Once it is realized that the generalization is not an employable resource and that no respite is found on the local level and no outlet to the national one, one might expect an increase in frustration, isolation, and discontent. The possible political action resulting from this condition might vary from one extreme of individual acts of violence to another of dropping out of the political system. More research is needed in this area to discover what are the actual, tangible effects of this generalized national message on smaller groups located on the local periphery of the social and political system.

The television camera is not automatically available, and certain things must be done in order to attract its attention. Knowing some of the behavioral characteristics of the medium helps us to understand some of these demands. The national audience is a prime consideration. A scatter-site housing dispute in New York will receive daily coverage on the local television news broadcast, but not until this issue receives wider interest, in similar and concurrent disputes in Chicago, Detroit, and Los Angeles, for example, will it receive air time on a national news broadcast. It is not simply that the story must have more than local significance as an issue, but more important, given the perceptions that determine the requirements for audience retention, it must be an issue or problem familiar to or experienced by more than one local community. In the foreign affairs area this is translated in terms of "having to be important to Americans." The power struggle between Brazil and Argentina

is not news for an American audience until it directly relates to an American concern from an American perspective.
That American perspective, for purposes of transmission,
demands some simplification (of values and interests) of
the message in order to appeal to this large and varied
audience.

This is important for that political actor who by
virtue of his position does not have ready access to the
informal channels of communication, as distinguished from
a President, department secretary, congressman, or labor
leader, who does. For example, the political actor on
the local community level who wants to communicate his
message to a wider but dispersed constituency, or who
seeks to communicate his demands via this medium to the
national political leadership, is forced to generalize,
simplify, and nationalize his ideas for television transmission. This is not simply because his message must be
comprehensible and identifiable to the wider audience he
seeks to reach, but also because the selection preferences
that now determine broadcast content are themselves pro-
grammed to produce messages that are generalized, simplified, and nationalized. This creates constraints on es-
tablishing the character of the national political debate,
particularly as it affects the educative function of the
political process.

For the aspiring political leader who wants to explain the complexities of his policy for rapprochement
with the People's Republic of China, the possibility of
his gaining a national audience by way of television is
slight unless he can capsulize his ideas, become identified with one issue, such as the candidate against trade
with the Soviet Union unless they open up their immigra-
tion policy, or represent a particular style of presentation that indicates a generalized approach to the issue.
For example, the "give the government hell" candidate who
is boisterous, not afraid to stand up for the little man
on issues of taxation, school busing, or the intellec-
tuals, derives an advantage, not so much from his stand
on the issues and the particulars of debate that gain him
access, but rather from the style and tone of his "generalized" approach.

An interesting subject for a follow-up study would
be the effect of television news on the emergence of
George McGovern as the 1972 Democratic Presidential candidate. Mechanically, television does not permit the
audience to select out certain stories. The viewer not
interested in Vietnam could not turn to the next page;

irrespective of the individual's reaction to the issues, it was the one story that appeared on the screen each and every day for seven years. What effect did this repetition have on George McGovern's introduction to the national public? What effect did the national structure of the medium and the concomitant idea of balance (of providing opposing viewpoints on the air) have on the national exposure for this aspiring candidate, the major spokesman against government policy on this issue?

Furthermore, we might ask whether, if he had not been given network exposure to address his national, but dispersed constituency, he would have been able to emerge as one of the two national party candidates. Would he have been ignored by this same medium if the cameras had focused on the issue of the Presidential campaign itself? Would the gatekeepers have looked to the more generalized frontrunner candidates for comment if stress had been on a different "issue"? A major concern like the issue of Vietnam focuses television's attention on the leading spokesmen of national stature on the particular issue.

Television and the behavioral patterns of the electronic journalist do not pose major problems in the educative role of the President or a national leader. This was found to be the case, not only because the President has access to this impersonal channel by virtue of his position, but also because he relates specifically to the demands of the medium. The correspondent's role is made easier, as this study shows, if he or she is able to focus on a single figure who is familiar and nationally well known. The President corresponds perfectly to these demands. If the President should so choose, television would not hinder him from using this medium to disseminate his ideas, explain the complexities of his programs, and justify his policies. However, this does not prevent the President or a national political leader from employing superficial arguments or from over-generalizing, sloganeering, or otherwise obscuring the issues. This is relatively easy to achieve in this medium; in fact, the operational pressures lean in this direction. What is important to note, however, is that this study clearly shows that the medium itself and the general operational behavior of the electronic journalist do not prevent the responsible political leader from gaining access to this medium on the national level and disseminating a more reasoned and educative message.

The national character of the medium has another potential effect on the political system: it makes the old political practice of addressing disparate groups in different regions of the country and promising one thing to this group and almost the opposite to another, more difficult. A statement on policy on inflation to an audience of businessmen in Texas is simultaneously communicated to college towns and urban and rural areas throughout the country. A reasoned debate on the issues on this national medium could potentially clarify the lines of division across the country, forcing the policy-maker to specify his statements and promote a national response, although an oversimplification and a generalization of the issues are also possible if the policy-makers homogenize their values so as not to offend major but disparate political groups.

CONCLUSIONS

Throughout, I have been concerned with the existing patterns of television news coverage of foreign affairs. It seems clear that the television medium is such an important information-dispensing institution that any pattern of news coverage would have an important effect on our society and on the fulfillment of the underlying assumptions of our political system. Focus has been placed on the most modern communications artifact created by man. In order to understand its operation I have had to place my greatest emphasis on the individual, the indispensable link in the process, as the producer and manipulator of symbols.

The television correspondent is a serious, highly competent, professional journalist who is compromised by production criteria that limit his ability to fulfill all his professional and personal objectives. The major problem is that television's production considerations have artificially relegated the correspondent's function to a secondary level, with mechanical and structural considerations gaining primacy. This placement is perceptually imposed, not inherent to the medium. Just as Benjamin Day chose in the 1830s to "sensationalize" his newspaper in order to attract more readers to his journal, so too has television determined to "visualize" and "transfer experience" in order to attract a national audience in a highly competitive arena. In the process, network news must be credited for doing fairly well. For a medium that could profitably choose to be sensational, it has conscientiously transferred to its medium the very

highest journalistic values and has chosen as its frame
of reference one of the most sophisticated of the country's newspapers. As a result, the framework or outline
of the day's events that is broadcast is as good as can
be found in any popular print medium.

It is not the conceptual journalistic framework that
constrains the electronic journalist, but rather the artificial policy impositions of time and structure. Policy
has determined that the broadcast will be 30 minutes long
and that the program will provide news items. This framework causes the mechanical characteristics to constrain
the activities of the electronic journalist to redefine
"news" through the manner in which he approaches his story
and the impositions of its compositional form, in which
pictures predominate in a thematic presentation. On the
production level, audience maintenance and attraction are
perceptual demands that create selection criteria for determining inclusion and exclusion of stories according to
mechanically facilitating criteria that further impose
constraints on the correspondent level.

Therefore it is the policy impositions placed upon
the medium that cause its mechanical and structural characteristics to affect newsgathering and broadcast activities, resulting in potentially superficial reflections of
world events. The initiative is in the hands of the maker
of policy, not the newsgatherer. Whether cause-to-effect
or effect-to-cause, the result is that the neutral role
conception becomes accentuated, apparently at the expense
of the participant role. Often the neutral television
correspondent is engaged in description instead of insight, surface instead of meaning, impression instead of
comprehension, simplicity instead of perspective, which
results in his "overnewsing" his audience instead of informing it. Too often the prevailing emphasis is on how
many reporters were involved, how many rolls of film were
shot, how many camera crews were deployed, how the information was transmitted, or how much money was spent.
This is frequently at the expense of consideration about
what information was transmitted or whether the people
"know" more as a result.

James Reston wrote of the journalism profession as
a whole:

> Our profession, which prides itself on be-
> ing up to date and is always shouting at
> governments to "keep up," is itself lagging
> behind the times. . . . Ideas are news:

see what John Maynard Keynes has done
to our society with his ideas, what the
conservatives backing Barry Goldwater
did to the Republican Party and the balance of political power in America with
their conservative revolt, what the Com-
munists are doing to China with their
savage ideology. . . .
    We are not covering the news of the
mind as we should. Here is where rebel-
lion, revolution, and war start, but we
minimize the conflict of ideas and emphasize the conflict in the street, without
relating the second to the first. (1966,
p. 84.)

The public is not necessarily wrongly informed through
television's news broadcast; it is only, at least potentially, inadequately informed.
    Television has made it increasingly possible to re-
port the physical event. The problem is that this concept of news is not serving the public adequately. Urgent
problems contain two other ingredients in addition to the
physical event: possible causes of the problem and potential directions available for action. The network news
broadcast has not dealt adequately with these two components, for reasons already discussed. However, these
are not impossible demands to place on the television
news staffs.
    Television can and has produced comprehensive and
enlightening news programs that were both visually interesting and well paced. During a newspaper strike in San
Francisco, local public television station KQED developed
its news program, Newsroom. Hiring journalists from the
struck newspapers, it covered the day's stories and
placed them on the air in a comprehensive form with considerable depth, including as few as ten stories in one
hour. Mel Wax wrote:

        Newsroom is now the most popular program
    on Channel 9, and it's the liveliest and,
    perhaps, the most controversial program
    in the San Francisco Bay area. . . .
    Film and still pictures were used, but
    sparingly. . . . The local commercial
    stations, by their own admission, were
    blanked. We beat them consistently with

news. We attracted an enormous audience--
so heavy that restaurants complained that
nobody came to eat between 7 and 8 p.m.
(1970, pp. 434-35.)

Newsroom concentrated on interpretive reporting of the
day's "hard news." The reporters talked and discussed
the news among themselves. They made news as well as
gathered news: "What also tickles me," wrote Max, "is
that, for the first time in San Francisco, both the Exam-
iner and Chronicle are monitoring our news programs. They
lift three to five news stories a week from us--rather
than the other way around." (Ibid., p. 345.) Concentration was on content, complemented by the mechanical capabilities of the medium.

John Chancellor, anchorman for NBC Nightly News, has
a card on his office wall that reads: "Form without content casts no shadow." It would be interesting to ob-
serve the effect a network news department would have if
it made the same commitment to interpretation and background stories so successfully employed by KQED, with a
concerted effort made to attract and maintain an audience
by the content of its news stories, rather than by its
mechanical format.

The network has the infrastructure and the talent
necessary to produce this product. Television correspondents are underemployed at the moment. To attribute the
medium's shortcomings to the absence of professional
standards is to beg the question and to misrepresent its
correspondents. Television correspondents are highly
competent, well trained, and among the best in any journalism medium. Longer reports, more talk pieces, and
perhaps a half-hour of hard news followed by a second
half-hour of the stories behind the headlines, would enable the correspondent to demonstrate his or her real
professional talents and provide a more informative, reflective journalistic composition. This format would not
eliminate conflict with the political system and would
probably increase debate about and criticism of the
medium, but it would also lead to the recognition that
world events are not fragmented bursts of conflict or
picture postcards, that our problems are complex, demanding, and long-term, but also approachable. This would
increase the participant role of the electronic journalist; assisted by the new policy of his medium, he could
more adequately fulfill his democratic responsibilities.
The importance of television as a source of news for the

237

majority of the population prohibits the medium from justifying its shortcomings with the passing phrase, "You can't depend on television as your sole source of information about the world." Too many people already do.

This study has isolated the communication function of the television news broadcast and empirically and systematically investigated it in terms of the role conceptions and attitudes of the actors within that system toward the newsgathering and composing processes of their medium. Many questions remain unanswered. We have observed and analyzed the electronic journalist in terms of what his objectives are, of how he goes about his work, and of the potential consequences of his behavior. A content analysis of the product that would analyze all the characteristics of this medium would be an important follow-up study to confirm or modify the perceptual conclusions posited here.

The perceptions of television's national audience, the mechanical capabilities of the medium, the behavior of the production staff, and their influence on the total television news process have been discussed. It is especially important that the perceptions of the television news audience and the consequent production demands be investigated. Follow-up studies should not simply ask what the audience wants, but rather what alternatives might be equally acceptable.

Networks might explore the possibility of competing for equally large but less homogeneous audiences, rather than locking themselves into the competitively restrictive limitations of the same middle audience. They might also try to educate and condition their audiences to different formats and approaches to the news, rather than competing to conform to their audience's more limited perceptions of the news. After all, the audience is not the news expert. It is rather its delegate, the qualified electronic journalist, who is. It would be an abdication of the correspondent's delegated responsibility not to use his expertise to provide his constituency with information that his specific training tells him is important and to present it to the audience in a way that it can understand and employ without making a compromise in its content.

At any given moment the public may not be psychologically prepared for the demands imposed upon it by the democratic system. The journalist's concern, however, is that when or if the citizen is prepared, that adequate information for sound judgment be available as a safeguard for coping with present and unforeseen problems in the social and political system. As stated in the NBC Policy Book, "the single greatest aid we have in overcoming those problems is the unifying tradition of a free press in America--a tradition that is mainly oral and passed along in work habits." (P. 5.) Television news is now in its third decade of operation, and it faces crucial challenges to its future as a free and competent journalistic force. It will assume its proper place in the political system the moment its actors and citizens realize its full idealistic traditions within the democratic role conception of a free press. It is here that the full promise of its mechanical and structural additions lies and where it must be found.

APPENDIX A:
TELEVISION JOURNALISM:
INTERVIEW SCHEDULE

1. What are the characteristics of the electronic journalist who specializes in foreign affairs news?
   - (1.1) What are his or her reasons for entering
     television news? foreign affairs news?
   - (1.2) What are the group properties of electronic
     journalism in foreign affairs reporting?
   - (1.3) What are the "goal" (personal) orientations
     of the electronic journalist?
   - (1.4) How are hierarchies delineated within the
     networks?

2. How does the electronic journalist conceive the function of the television press in the democratic process?
   - (2.1) How does the electronic journalist view the
     potential impact of what he reports?
   - (2.2) What democratic or political roles does the
     electronic journalist perceive himself as
     fulfilling as he gathers and reports the
     foreign affairs story?
     - (2.2a) To what extent is the electronic
       journalist concerned with the role
       of neutral reporter: informant?
       interpreter? instrument of govern-
       ment?
     - (2.2b) To what extent is the electronic
       journalist concerned with participant
       roles: representative of the people?
       critic of government? advocate of
       policy? policy maker?
     - (2.2c) Are there roles distinctive to the
       television medium?
   - (2.3) What skills do the electronic journalists
     think are required to fulfill these various
     roles?
   - (2.4) What are the goal orientations of these
     various roles?
   - (2.5) What are the electronic journalist's atti-
     tudes toward objectivity in news reporting?
3. How do electronic journalists define what is "news"?
   - (3.1) What do they believe to be the requirements
     of a "good news story"?
   - (3.2) What do they believe to be the requirements
     of a "good television news story"?

4. Where in practice do congruent judgments about foreign affairs news come from?
    (4.1) How conscious are the electronic journalists of the output of the other broadcast networks?
        (4.1a) What criteria are used to describe the forms of competition with the television and newspaper press?
    (4.2) To what extent is the electronic journalist affected by the frames of reference of the print media, the wire services, or the electronic media?
    (4.3) What other sources are available for determining what is news?
    (4.4) What are the links with reporters in the other networks?
    (4.5) How autonomous is the electronic journalist in covering a story?
    (4.6) What is the importance of personal contacts and friendships between television newsmen and public officials and policy-makers?
    (4.7) To what degree is television especially dependent on the cooperation of public officials for gathering and reporting the news story?

5. What are the important mechanical considerations of the medium for gathering and reporting the foreign affairs story?
    (5.1) To what extent does the visual value of the subject determine coverage?
    (5.2) What are the advantages (disadvantages) of the camera in reporting foreign affairs news?
    (5.3) Are time requirements important in the determination of subject matter?
    (5.4) How does the news format affect news selection and coverage?
    (5.5) What effect does the cost of production and recording have on news gathering and reporting?
    (5.6) How does the team approach of the medium affect foreign affairs reporting?

6. What are the important structural considerations of the medium for gathering and reporting the foreign affairs story?

(6.1) Does the electronic journalist have a concept of a particular audience when he gathers and writes his television news report?

(6.2) What effect does the "national audience" of television have on the selection and reporting of news on foreign affairs?

(6.3) Is there any attempt to "popularize," promote, develop, maintain, and/or not discourage an audience for foreign affairs news?

(6.4) What are the attitudes toward the broadcasting hierarchy?

(6.5) What effect does the legal obligation of the medium to act in the "public interest, convenience and necessity" have on the gathering and reporting of foreign affairs news?

(6.6) To what extent do commercial values (advertising) affect the newsgathering and reporting processes?

7. How do television correspondents perceive the flow of events?

(7.1) What are the electronic journalists' interests and disinterests in different parts of the world?

(7.2) What are the pressures of professionalism?

(7.3) What forms of incentive peculiar to the electronic medium are offered that affect the gathering and reporting of news? With what effect?

8. Are there certain subjects that are particularly suited for this electronic medium? Are there certain subjects that are too "complicated" or that cause special difficulties for this medium?

(8.1) What alternatives are or should be considered to adjust to these peculiarities?

(8.2) What advantages does this medium have over other news media? What are the disadvantages?

(8.3) What role does investigative reporting play in electronic journalism?

(8.4) Do commentaries have an important function in the news format?

Name:_____
Title: (at present):
      past:_____
     Date: a) of employment
            b) of interview

1) Education:
High School: _____
College: _____
  name: _____
  years: _____
  degree: _____
Graduate study: _____ yes _____ no
  name: _____
  degree(s): _____
Miscellaneous: _____
How important is your education to your present role?
_____
_____

2) Professional Experience:
              a) television
years: _____
area: _____
titles: _____
_____
_____
              b) print media
years: _____
area: _____
titles: _____
_____
_____
              c) other (e.g., radio)
years: _____
area: _____
titles: _____
_____
_____

3) Special Responsibilities:

APPENDIX C:
SAMPLE ABC EVENING
NEWS LINEUP

	Seconds of Time	Cumulative Time
Open	1:05	
BB & Announce	:10	1:15
HR - Situation	1:00	2:15
NYVT - Miller - Quang Tri	2:45	5:00
HR	:10	5:10
NYVT - Pearson - Dong Ha	1:45	6:55
HKS - Censorship in V. Nam, Peace Talk Demand	:40	7:35
Wash. - Koppel - What Hanoi Said	1:10	8:45
HKS	:05	8:50
Logo & Announce	:05	8:55
Commercial #1	1:05	10:00
HKS	:15	10:15
Sw/Chi - Reynolds - Wisconsin	1:25	11:40
HKS - Dita Beard Out	:10	11:50
Logo & Announce	:05	11:55
Commercial #2	1:05	13:00
HR - Salt, Bengla Desh Recognition, Ireland	:45	13:45
NY Film - Rolfson - IRA Funeral		
or Tuckner - Bengla Desh	1:40	15:25
HR - Cuba Blast	:25	15:50
Commercial #3 & #4	2:05	17:55
HKS - JCS - Abrams	:30	18:25
Wash. - Peterson - Army Recruiting	2:30	20:55
HKS	:05	21:00
Commercial #5	1:05	22:05
HR - PPT - Harrisburg 7	:25	22:30
HR Intro	:20	22:50
NY Film - Snell - Baseball Issues	2:30	25:20
HR	:05	25:25
Commercial #6	1:05	26:30
HKS Comment	1:45	28:15
HR GN	:05	28:20
Close	:09	28:29

Note: HKS is the initials of Howard K. Smith, the Washington anchorman, HR of Harry Reasoner, the New York anchorman. Underlined names are those of the correspondents, followed by the titles of their stories. NYVT means New York Video Tape. Sw/Chi means to switch to Chicago for a direct feed of the story. JCS means Joint Chiefs of Staff. BB means Billboard.

Agee, Warren K., ed. 1969. Mass Media in a Free Society. Kansas: The University of Kansas.

Almaney, Adnan. 1970. "International and Foreign Affairs on Network Television News." Journal of Broadcasting 14: 499-509.

Almond, Gabriel. 1960. The American People and Foreign Policy. New York: Frederick A. Praeger.

_____. 1960. "Introduction: A Functional Approach to Comparative Politics." In The Politics of the Developing Areas, edited by Gabriel Almond and James S. Coleman, pp. 3-64. Princeton, N.J.: Princeton University Press.

_____ and Powell, G. Bingham, Jr. 1966. Comparative Politics: A Developmental Approach. Boston: Little, Brown and Co.

Arlen, Michael. 1969. Living-Room War. New York: The Viking Press.

_____. 1972. "You'll Laugh! You'll Cry! You'll Watch Them Die! It's Today's News Spectacular." In Playboy, May 1972, p. 100.

Aronson, James. 1971. Packaging the News. New York: International Publishers.

Bailey, Robert Lee. 1968. "Network Television Prime-Time Special Political Programs." Journal of Broadcasting 12: 207-208.

Baker, Russell. 1972. "No Harry? No Walter? No John? No . . .? New York Times, 10 February, p. 34.

Balk, Alfred. 1969-70. "Beyond Agnewism." Columbia Journalism Review, Winter, pp. 14-21.

Barrett, Marvin, ed. 1969. Survey of Broadcast Journalism: 1968-1969. New York: Grosset and Dunlap.

_____. 1970. _Survey of Broadcast Journalism: 1969-1970_. New York: Grosset and Dunlap.

_____. 1971. _Survey of Broadcast Journalism: 1970-1971_. New York: Grosset and Dunlap.

Bass, Abraham Z. 1969. "Refining the 'Gatekeeper' Concept: A U.N. Radio Case Study." _Journalism Quarterly_ 46: 69-72.

Beville, Hugh M., Jr. 1962. "On Ratings." Testimony Before the Federal Communications Commission, January, a CBS in-house document.

Bliss, Edward, Jr., and Patterson, John M. 1971. _Writing News for Broadcast_. New York: Columbia University Press.

Bluem, A. William, and Manvell, Roger. 1967. _Television: The Creative Experience_. New York: Hastings House.

Bogart, Leo. 1969. "Violence in the Mass Media." _Television Quarterly_ 8: 36-47.

Boorstin, Daniel. 1961. _The Image_. New York: Harper and Row.

Breed, Warren. 1955. "Social Control in the Newsroom: A Functional Analysis." _Social Forces_ 33: 326-35.

"Brinkley Asserts that Newsmen Are Unintimidated." 1971. New York _Times_, October 20, p. 95.

Buckalew, James K. 1969-70. "News Elements and Selection by Television News Editors." _Journalism of Broadcasting_ 14: 47-54.

Budd, Richard; MacLean, Malcolm S., Jr.; and Barnes, Arthur M. 1966. "Regularities in the Diffusion of Two Major News Events." _Journalism Quarterly_ 43: 221-30.

Cater, Douglass. 1959. _The Fourth Branch of Government_. Boston: Houghton Mifflin Co.

_____. 1964. _Power in Washington_. New York: Random House.

Cathcart, William L. 1969-70. "Viewer Needs and Desires in Television Newscasters." Journal of Broadcasting 14: 69.

CBS News. 1958. Television News Reporting. New York: McGraw-Hill Book Co.

Chester, Edward W. 1969. Radio, Television and American Politics. New York: Sheed and Ward.

Cogley, John. 1961. "The Troubles of the News Services." In The New Republic, April 24, pp. 37-39.

Cohen, Bernard. 1963. The Press and Foreign Policy. Princeton, N.J.: Princeton University Press.

Cornwell, Elmer E., Jr. 1966. "The Johnson Press Relations Style." Journalism Quarterly 43: 3-9.

Cronkite, Walter. 1966. "WCBS Radio Looks at Television." WCBS Radio Program Information Department Letter, 3 February.

_____. 1967. "The Journalist at Thermopole: A Time for Change." Frank Kent Lecture, February 9, at Johns Hopkins University.

_____. 1967. Remarks at the Management/Programming Seminar of TV Stations, Hilton Hotel, New York, 29 September, CBS News archives.

_____. 1969. William Allen White Lecture at the University of Kansas, March 24.

_____. 1970. "Why Johnny Can't Understand the News Reports." In Signature, May.

_____. 1970. "What It's Like to Broadcast News." In Saturday Review, December 12, pp. 53-55.

_____. 1971. Remarks to the International Radio and Television Society, Waldorf Astoria Hotel, New York, May 18, CBS News archives.

_____. 1971. The Challenges of Change. Washington, D.C.: Public Affairs Press.

_____. 1972. "A Conversation with Cronkite." In _TV Guide_, March 4, pp. 18-20.

DeFleur, Melvin L. 1970. _Theories of Mass Communication_. 2nd ed. New York: David McKay Co.

de Sola Pool, Ithiel. 1970. "How Influential is TV News." _Columbia Journalism Review_, p. 20.

Diamond, Edwin. 1969-70. "Multiplying Media Voices." _Columbia Journalism Review_, Winter, pp. 22-27.

Dizard, Wilson. 1966. _Television, A World View_. Syracuse, N.Y.: Syracuse University Press.

Dunn, Delmer D. 1969. _Public Officials and the Press_. Reading, Mass.: Addison-Wesley Publishing Co.

Dworkin, Ronald M. 1971. "A Deliberate Censorship." New York _Times_, February 13, p. 11.

Eck, Robert. 1967. "The Real Masters of Television." In _Harper's_, March, pp. 45-52.

Efron, Edith. 1971. _The News Twisters_. Los Angeles, Calif.: Nash Publishing.

Fagen, Richard. 1966. _Politics and Communication_. New York: Little, Brown and Co.

Fang, I. E. 1968. _Television News_. New York: Hastings House.

Farrar, Ronald T., and Stevens, John, eds. 1971. _Mass Media and the National Experience_. New York: Harper and Row.

Ferretti, Fred. 1969. "CBS Memo Sets TV Reporting Rules." New York _Times_, 31 October, p. 62.

Frank, Reuven. 1969. "The Ugly Mirror." _Television Quarterly_ 8: 82-96.

_____. 1970. "An Anatomy of Television News." _Television Quarterly_ 9: (Winter): 11-23.

_____. 1970. "An Artificial Innocence Is the Essence of
Traditional American Journalism at Its Best." State-
ment to the Student Officers, Yale Political Union,
February 18.

_____. 1971. "Our Hands Are Cleaner Than Theirs." NBC
in-house reprint of speech.

Friendly, Fred W. 1967. Due to Circumstances beyond Our
Control . . . New York: Random House.

Gattegno, Caleb. 1969. Towards a Visual Culture. New
York: Avon Books.

Gieber, Walter. 1964. "News Is What Newspapermen Make It."
In People, Society, and Mass Communications. Edited
by Lewis A. Dexter and David M. White. New York:
Free Press, pp. 173-80.

Guback, Thomas. 1968. "Political Broadcasting and Public
Policy." Journal of Broadcasting 12: 191-211.

Hazard, William R. 1962-63. "On the Impact of Television's Pictured News." Journal of Broadcasting 7:
43-52.

_____, ed. 1966. TV As Art. Champaign, Ill.: National
Council of Teachers of English.

Hohenberg, John. 1971. Free Press/Free People. New
York: Columbia University Press.

International Broadcast Institute. 1970. "How Influential Is TV News?" Columbia Journalism Review,
Summer, pp. 19-29.

Johnson, Nicholas. 1970. How to Talk Back to Your Television Set. Boston: Little, Brown and Co.

Katz, Elihu, and Lazarsfeld, Paul F. 1955. Personal Influence. Glencoe, Ill.: Free Press of Glencoe.

Keeley, Joseph. 1971. The Left-Leaning Antenna: Political Bias in Television. New Rochelle, N.Y.: Arling-
ton House.

Kendrick, Alexander. 1969. *Prime Time: The Life of Edward R. Murrow*. New York: Avon Books.

Key, V. O. 1965. *Public Opinion and American Democracy*. New York: Alfred A. Knopf.

Kinkel, Jack. 1966. "When the Tail Wags the Dog." In *Saturday Review*, March 12, p. 140.

Kintner, Robert E. 1965. "Broadcasting and the News." In *Harper's*, April, pp. 49-55.

Klapper, Joseph T. 1950. *The Effects of Mass Media*. New York: Bureau of Applied Social Research.

Lang, Kurt, and Lang, Gladys Engel. 1968. *Politics and Television*. Chicago: Quadrangle Books.

Lee, Robert W., ed. 1970. *Politics and the Press*. Washington, D.C.: Acropolis Books.

Lippmann, Walter. 1922. *Public Opinion*. New York: Harcourt, Brace, and Co.

Lowi, Theodore. 1971. "Government and Politics: Blurring of Sector Lines. Rise of New Elites - From One Vantage Point." *Information Technology*. New York: The Conference Board. pp. a/pol - 43/pol.

Lyle, Jack, and Wilcox, Walter. 1963. "Television News-- An Interim Report." *Journal of Broadcasting* 7: 157-66.

Lyons, Louis M., ed. 1965. *Reporting Television News: Selections from the Nieman Reports*. Cambridge, Mass.: Harvard University Press.

MacNeil, Robert. 1968. *The People Machine*. New York: Harper and Row.

_____. 1968. "The News on TV and How It Is Unmade." In *Harper's*, October, pp. 72-80.

Maeroff, Gene I. 1972. "New Dude in Town." *New York*, May 1, pp. 40-42.

McAndrews, William R. 1965. "NBC News: Television Places Viewer at Center of Events and Challenges

Him to Take Stand on Issues." Statement in Accepting USC Distinguished Achievement Award, November 10, NBC New York archives.

Merton, Robert K. 1949. Social Theory and Social Structure. Glencoe, Ill.: Free Press of Glencoe.

Millikan, Max F. 1968. "Emerging Nations--What the Public Should Know." Television Quarterly 7: 76-83.

Minor, Dale. 1970. The Information War. New York: Hawthorn Books.

Monroe, Bill. 1972. Statement before the U.S. Senate Subcommittee on Congressional Rights, February 8, NBC Washington archives.

Myer, Caroline. 1968. "News Shows in Transition: Longer Forms, Different Hours, a Search for Individuality." Television 25: 34.

NBC News. 1971. "How NBC News Does Its Job." Press Circular Release, p. 12.

NBC Policy Book, 1972.

Newcomb, Theodore; Tanner, Ralph H.; and Converse, Philip E. 1965. Social Psychology. New York: Holt, Rinehart and Winston, Inc.

Nimmo, Dan. 1964. Newsgathering in Washington. New York: Atherton Press.

O'Connor, John J. 1971. "TV: Informal Chancellor Keynotes NBC News." New York Times, October 28, p. 83.

_____. 1971. "TV: With Smith-Reasoner Combination, ABC's News Operation Finds Itself back in the Ballgame." New York Times, November 12, p. 84.

_____. 1972. "TV: Debates about Broadcast Journalism Fill Air." New York Times, April 28, p. 83.

_____. 1972. "TV: Diverse Ventures in News and Public Affairs." New York Times, May 25, p. 91.

Paley, William. 1954. "The Road to Responsibility." Address before the National Association of Radio and Television Broadcasters, Chicago, May 25.

Pennybacker, John H., and Braden, Waldon W., eds. 1969. _Broadcasting and the Public Interest_. New York: Random House.

"Penthouse Interview: John Chancellor." 1972. In _Penthouse_, April, pp. 36ff.

Powers, Ron, and Oppenheim, Jerrold. 1972. "Is TV Too Profitable?" _Columbia Journalism Review_, May-June, pp. 7-13.

Quaal, Ward L., and Martin, Leo A. 1968. _Broadcast Management_. New York: Hastings House.

Rasky, Harry. 1971. "Television." In _The Nation_, 15 February, p. 37.

Reston, James. 1966. _The Artillery of the Press_. New York: Harper and Row.

Rivers, William L., and Schramm, Wilbur. 1969. _Responsibility in Mass Communication_. Rev. ed. New York: Harper and Row.

Robinson, James P., and Swinehart, James W. 1968. "World Affairs and the TV Audience." _Television Quarterly_ 7: 24-32.

Robinson, Michael, and Burgess, Philip M. 1970. "The Edward M. Kennedy Speech: The Impact of a Prime-Time Television Appeal." _Television Quarterly_ 9: 29-39.

Rosenau, James. 1961. _Public Opinion and Foreign Policy_. New York: Random House.

Rubin, Bernard. 1967. _Political Television_. Belmont, Calif.: Wadsworth Publishing Co.

Rugabel, Walter. 1971. "Cronkite and Professor Differ on Press Freedom." New York _Times_, October 1, p. 24.

Sargent, Leslie W. 1965. "Communicator Image and News Reception." _Journalism Quarterly_ 42: 35.

Schuneman, R. Smith. 1966. "Visual Aspects of Television News: Communicator, Message, Equipment." _Journalism Quarterly_ 43: 281-86.

Sevareid, Eric. 1953. "The Big Truth." Seventh Annual
Memorial Lecture, American NP Guild, Twin Cities
Local, CIO and School of Journalism, at the Univer-
sity of Minnesota, October 23.

_____. 1967. "Politics and the Press." Address before
a joint session of the Massachusetts Legislature,
24 January.

Shibutani, Tamotsu. 1966. Improvised News: A Sociologi-
cal Study of Rumor. New York: Bobbs-Merrill Co.,
Inc.

Siller, Bob; White, Tom; and Terkel, Hal. 1960. Television and Radio News. New York: Macmillan Co.

Skornia, Harry J. 1968. Television and the News: A
Critical Appraisal. Palo Alto, Calif.: Pacific
Books.

Small, William. 1970. To Kill a Messenger. New York:
Hastings House.

Smith, Desmond. 1968. "The Seven O'Clock Superman." In
The Nation, March 18, pp. 375-79.

Stanton, Frank. 1958. "The Critical Necessity for an
Informed Public." Journal of Broadcasting 2: 7-14.

Stone, Vernon A. 1969-70. "Sources of Most News: Evidence and Inference." Journal of Broadcasting 14:
1-4.

Swallow, Norman. 1966. Factual Television. New York:
Hastings House.

Tetlow, Karin. 1972. "How Much Can a Person Make for a
Job Like That?" In New York, May 2, pp. 28-35.

Tobin, Richard L. 1966. "Communications: The Star System and TV News." In Saturday Review, April 9, p. 59.

Tunstall, Jeremy. 1970. The Westminster Lobby Correspondent. London: Routledge and Kegan Paul.

Warner, Malcolm. 1968. "TV Coverage of International
Affairs." Television Quarterly 12: 60-76.

Wax, Mel. 1970. "TV News: Wrong Mix." In The Nation, April 13, pp. 433-35.

Weaver, Paul H. 1972. "Is Television News Biased?" Public Interest 26: 57-74.

Weisberger, Bernard. 1961. The American Newspaperman. Chicago: University of Chicago Press.

Westin, Av. 1972. (unpublished chapter of a proposed book, ABC News).

Whale, John. 1969. The Half-Shut Eye. New York: St. Martin's Press, Inc.

White, David Manning. 1950. "The 'Gate Keeper': A Case Study in the Selection of News." Journalism Quarterly 27: 383-90.

White, Paul W. 1953. "Spot News Is Better on Radio." Broadcasting - Telecasting, February 9, p. 84.

White, Theodore H. 1969-70. "America's Two Cultures." Columbia Journalism Review, Winter, pp. 8-13.

Whiteside, Thomas. 1968-69. "Corridor of Mirrors." Columbia Journalism Review, Winter, pp. 35-54.

Wood, William A. 1967. Electronic Journalism. New York: Columbia University Press.

Zeidenberg, Leonard. 1968. "The 21-Inch View of Vietnam: Big Enough Picture?" Television 25: 288.

ROBERT M. BATSCHA is Associate Professor and Director of the Communication Fellows Program at Queens College of the City University of New York. He also serves as a senior consultant to the Development Center of the Organization for Economic Cooperation and Development in Paris.

Professor Batscha lived in Paris from 1972 to 1974 as a resident senior consultant to the OECD, during which time he directed a project on "The Dissemination of Economic and Social Science Development Research." He is at present coordinator and consultant for a series of related case studies he initiated, now being carried out in selected developing countries. He has published articles in the International Social Science Journal and Public Opinion Quarterly; a book on his investigations on dissemination will appear in 1975.

Dr. Batscha received his Ph.D. in International Affairs from Columbia University; he has also studied at the University of Vienna.

MASS COMMUNICATION AND CONFLICT RESOLUTIONS:
The Role of the Information Media in the
Advancement of International Understanding
                              W. Phillips Davison

MASS COMMUNICATION RESEARCH:
Major Issues and Future Directions
                              edited by W. Phillips Davison
                              and Frederick T.C. Yu

PUBLIC OPINION AND COMMUNICATIONS: A Classic
Collection from Thirty-Five Years of the POQ
                              Robert O. Carlson